A journalist and author of several fict[...]
Malcolm MacPherson grew up in Ca[...] and [...]y
graduated from Trinity College, served in the Marine Corps,
and worked as a staff journalist for *Time* and *Newsweek*
magazines, the latter for twelve years as a correspondent in Los
Angeles, Nairobi, Paris, and London, covering quotidian events,
sectarian war in Ireland, and conflicts in Africa and the Middle
East. Most recently, he reported from Iraq on assignment with
Time. He has published an acclaimed history of the Holocaust,
narrative histories, and novels, including thrillers and a coming-
of-age story set in Disneyland. He lives in Virginia with his
family.

nonfiction

The Blood of His Servants
Black Box
Time Bomb
Black Box II
The Cowboy & His Elephant
On a Wing and a Prayer

fiction

Protégé
Lucifer Key
In Cahoots
Deadlock

ROBERTS RIDGE

MALCOLM MacPHERSON

CORGI BOOKS

ROBERTS RIDGE
A CORGI BOOK: 0552151394
9780552151399

Originally published in Great Britain by Bantam Press,
a division of Transworld Publishers

PRINTING HISTORY
Bantam Press edition published 2005
Corgi edition published 2006

1 3 5 7 9 10 8 6 4 2

Copyright © Malcolm MacPherson 2005
Maps by Dave Stephenson

The right of Malcolm MacPherson to be identified as the author of
this work has been asserted in accordance with sections 77
and 78 of the Copyright Designs and Patents Act 1988.

Set in 11/14.5pt Minion by
Falcon Oast Graphic Art Ltd.

Corgi Books are published by Transworld Publishers,
61–63 Uxbridge Road, London W5 5SA,
a division of The Random House Group Ltd,
in Australia by Random House Australia (Pty) Ltd,
20 Alfred Street, Milsons Point, Sydney, NSW 2061, Australia,
in New Zealand by Random House New Zealand Ltd,
18 Poland Road, Glenfield, Auckland 10, New Zealand
and in South Africa by Random House (Pty) Ltd,
Isle of Houghton, Corner of Boundary Road & Carse O'Gowrie,
Houghton 2198, South Africa.

Printed and bound in Great Britain by
Cox & Wyman Ltd, Reading, Berkshire.

Papers used by Transworld Publishers are natural, recyclable products made from
wood grown in sustainable forests. The manufacturing processes conform to the
environmental regulations of the country of origin.

I wouldnt leave you and you wouldnt leave me. That aint no argument.

—Cormac McCarthy, *All the Pretty Horses*

I'm not trying to be a hero. If you think I like this, you're crazy.

—Will Kane (Gary Cooper) in *High Noon*

A NOTE TO THE READER

The following story is true. It takes place over 17 hours.

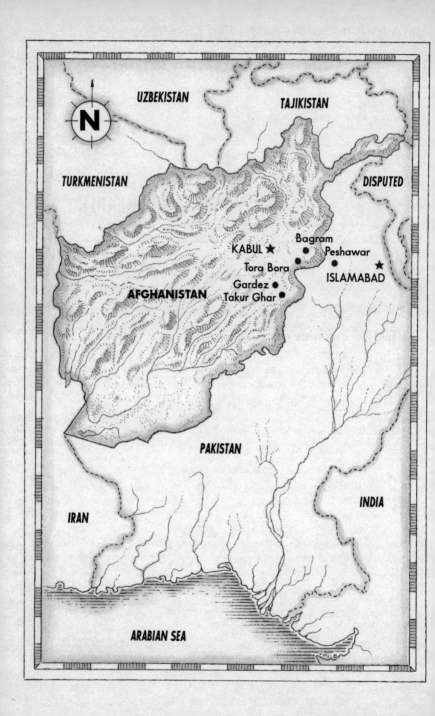

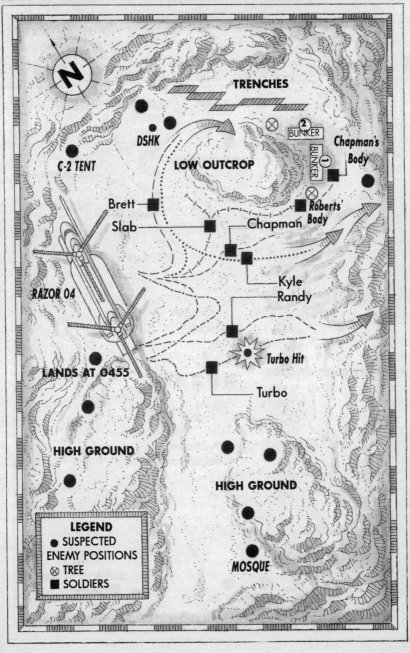

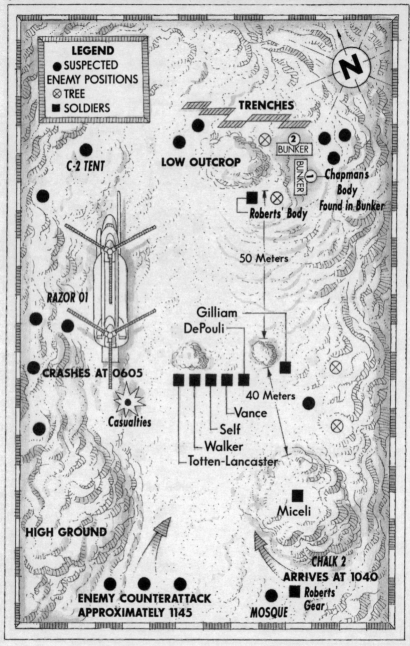

QRF CHALKS 1&2 RESCUE ATTEMPT 4 MARCH 2002 APPROXIMATELY 0530

ROBERTS RIDGE

PROLOGUE

UNDER A SINGLE LIGHT THAT HUNG ON A CORD from a low ceiling of cedar beams and hardened mud, the U.S. Navy SEAL whom everyone called just "Slab" was leaning on his arms over maps spread out on a table. A good-looking, slim, blond-haired thirty-three-year-old whom strangers often mistook for the hockey legend Wayne Gretzky, Slab was planning how best his sniper reconnaissance team could help regular Army troops who were taking a shellacking from a large al-Qaeda and Taliban force.

The sound of a gas generator blew through a window. It was cold enough for Slab to see his breath in this room of a dilapidated mud fort near the Afghan provincial capital of

Gardez. Slab and his team had shuttled down from Bagram Air Base that morning by helicopter to see how they could salvage the largest offensive yet in the war on terrorism—one that had collapsed only ten minutes after it began. Making the debacle doubly painful, Army commanders had initiated Operation Anaconda, as it was called, presumably to recoup the opportunities that were squandered earlier at Tora Bora, where hundreds of al-Qaeda fighters, including Osama bin Laden and possibly his chief lieutenant, Ayman al-Zawahiri, had all but waltzed across the border of Afghanistan into the sanctuaries of Pakistan's tribal areas. Many Chechens and Uzbeks among these hardened terrorists later had made their way south to this valley, called the Shah-i-Kot.

The original plan for Anaconda had called for the use of American and friendly Afghan troops to hammer Taliban and al-Qaeda forces, known to have regrouped in the valley in force for the winter, into a steep wall of high mountains. American troops would serve as the blocking anvil against which the routed enemy would be crushed, in theory. But the hammer never swung; it fled from the battlefield under lethal friendly fire from a U.S. gunship, from a shocked reaction to a "softening-up" bombardment that fizzled, and by ferocious mortar attacks by an enemy that was not going to be easily routed anywhere, much to nearly everyone's surprise.

The enemy fighters weren't as much in the valley, as imagined, as they were in the mountains looking down on the Americans through the sights of heavy machine guns and mortars. Making this already bad situation even worse, the highest American commanders had failed to equip elements from the 10th Mountain and 101st Airborne divisions with artillery with which to defend themselves. Bombers and strike aircraft assumed that role, which in turn required hastily placed special "operators"—some, like Slab, on loan from the secret "black" world of the Joint Special Operations Command—to provide aircraft with targets and coordinates.

At the moment, with Slab studying maps, the fight was ragged and tentative, and the Army troops might not be able to hold out. As a sign of the crisis, commanders were even debating whether to pull back and call off the operation altogether.

Slab and his team were only seven men—six SEALs and an Air Force combat controller. It might have seemed preposterous to believe that they alone could change the course of an entire battle involving 1,400 American troops. They couldn't, not alone, but at their fingertips they commanded an endless supply of 2,000-pound high-explosive bombs, guided by tiny navigation systems that could slam targets from on high within yards of where they were intended. All the SEALs required for the job was a radio, a good high site with a view of the valley, and a snug place to hide.

The highest mountain overlooking the valley on the maps was called Takur Ghar, which translated as "Tall Mountain" from Pushto. Takur Ghar was chosen for Slab as an observation post, as one of his commanders told him, "because of its superbly strategic position." Intelligence reports that he had read informed him that the enemy was being resupplied with munitions and reinforcements down "ratlines" through "the biggest hole in the area of Takur Ghar."

It dawned on Slab that if Takur Ghar would be advantageous to the Americans, why wouldn't it also be appealing to the enemy fighters? After all, the local Taliban hardly needed satellites and computers to realize the advantages of mountains that they already knew as well as the faces of their children. Slab studied satellite imagery that by now was three days old. No snow showed on the peak in these pictures. He saw an old trench on the mountain peak that he assumed local fighters had occupied at one time, probably long ago. He did not plan to drop right down on the peak, in the unlikely event that an enemy force already occupied it. He'd land on an offset below the summit and then patrol up the steep mountainside. He was aiming that night literally to scope out the peak, which the team would take over once they were reassured of its vacancy through quiet observation. His job was not to make contact with the enemy; it was to stay out of reach and drop massive amounts of ordnance.

All the same, he expected to encounter enemy soldiers crisscrossing a pass under the peak. Slab knew these fighters might be carrying heavy weapons—but not necessarily on Takur Ghar. He figured his chances of running into an enemy were probably "100 percent." But they would be in "onesies or twosies or a small patrol of four guys." He weighed the risks, and they seemed reasonable. Besides, he thought at the time, *This is not how we work, reducing risk to zero—otherwise, send accountants up there.*

He called his team into the light of the fort. He told them, "Look, this is what we're lookin' at doing." He offered ideas, as usual leading by consensus rather than dictate. They bounced suggestions off one another for twenty minutes, and when they were done, they had a plan. It was standard stuff that they'd practiced a hundred times. Slab had lived with these men for years. He could tell what they were thinking by looking in their faces. They were excited to be getting a piece of the action, expectant and alert, aggressive and ready to knock heads. He trusted them with his life. When they finished, he told them, "OK. We got a timeline to go in. We got aircraft scheduled, so get to your final gear preparation."

Now Slab's team—called MAKO 30—was waiting for nightfall before it could begin killing in the hope that by their actions the tide of a battle gone seriously wrong would turn.

I
"Slicker'n Snot"

1

CHIEF WARRANT OFFICER AL MACK SAT BEHIND the left controls of a Chinook helicopter, heading southeast along a crest through a brilliant moonrise. As he flew through the night, the terrain reminded him of Mordor and Mt. Doom in the *Lord of the Rings* movies. He told people, "Imagine landing on *that* at night without a light. And if a landing zone isn't big enough, what you do is set the aircraft's aft gear down, hover, and several thousand feet below you is the bottom, with no visual reference. Put the ramp down. Guys get out."

Take away some of the bluster and that was what Mack was about to do on the 10,240-foot peak of Takur Ghar.

He was happy to be moving again after frustrations that aggrieved even a sixteen-year Army veteran. Earlier, he had ferried his Chinook, code-named Razor 03, down from Bagram Air Base near Kabul to a temporary special operations airfield. He was working Operation Anaconda, the largest military offensive thus far in America's fight against al-Qaeda terrorists in Afghanistan, which had kicked off, depending on who was doing the counting, either the previous day or two days before. He'd been dropping off special operations teams in the mountains on both sides of the Shah-i-Kot valley, often relying for guidance on outdated maps and imagery.

Since before midnight, he had been trying to deliver MAKO 30, his "customers," to a landing zone at the base of Takur Ghar, the highest mountain in the area. On his first try, only six minutes away from the LZ, he had asked a nearby Spectre gunship circling over the valley to take a look with its sensors at the landing zone to see if it was clear of hostile forces.

"I can't look at your LZ," the Spectre's fire control officer told him. "There's a B-52 strike coming in," and the gunship, with a wide, looping orbit, had to push off until it was safe to return, probably in less than an hour.

"OK," Mack had replied, with no real good choice but to suck it up and return to where they had picked up the SEALs. He was aware of the importance of delivering his customers to their offset LZ in a timely manner, and what it could mean for the revised plan for Operation Anaconda. In mission preparation, he'd been vested in the ground/air tactical plan and knew exactly what his customers—and his higher com-manders—needed from him. That was why his frustration peaked when a glance told him that he was running low on gas. He always planned his missions with precision, calculating a gas supply sufficient to get him through a task with fifteen minutes to spare for emergencies, and nothing more.

Over all the hours Mack had flown Chinooks, he had achieved a nearly perfect spiritual fusion of man with machine. It came as no surprise that he admitted to a deep fondness for the bird. He saw charm and personality in its homely design. Veterans like him sometimes compared the helo to a "Winnebago with rotors," and indeed it was little more than a rectangular box with big fans in front and back, about 50 feet long and weighing in at around 40,000 pounds. To anyone else's eye, it was not sleek and it was not pretty. It had bumps and a weak chin, spindly legs, and a hay stalk sticking out the corner of its "mouth." Mack's version of the Chinook was a model (the MH-47E) made by Boeing and specifically con-figured at a significant cost for special operations missions. Several enhancements helped the twenty-four copies ever made to fly where and when other helos could not.

Instead of circling and wasting fuel until the B-52 pointed for home, Mack flew 22 miles back to the grubby and nearly abandoned airstrip where they had started, outside Gardez. He sat on the ground and waited in the dark, keeping the rotors at flat pitch to burn less fuel, like idling the engine of a car. Finally, the bomber pulled off and the Chinook took off, but it had not gained more than a thousand feet when Mack was told, "Razor 03, there's an air assault coming in. You need to abort and go back to Gardez and wait."

Saving on gas, this time Mack shut down the aircraft with the expectation that they would be on the ground for a while. Slab put out security around the aircraft. He understood the urgency to "put a cork stopper in that valley," but reaching the peak from an offset location, as planned, increasingly looked like it was going to require more time than prudence allowed, given these delays. Even in the best of circumstances, without the holds, they were starting to cut the time short. They probably would have been able to crest the peak, after an extremely long early morning climb, as the sun was coming up. To do it in stealth, they would have been on the margin of daylight in any case. Time was eating at Slab. The last thing he wanted was to get stuck out in the open on low ground in the middle of the day.

Two of his teammates were sitting back to back outside by the aircraft in the dark. One, named Turbo, a biker fanatic who had decorated his body from neck to ankles and wrists with a riot of tattoos, was listening through earbuds to a portable CD player, rocking to the sounds. The other teammates were talking quietly. Slab told them to tweak their gear, and with his combat controller, he used the delay to go over the list one last time to see that they had everything they might need.

Ninety minutes passed before Mack told Slab they had clearance to go. The SEALs got back onto the helo, and as usual, they did not bother to snap in their safety harnesses. Slab plugged in the inter-crew communication system (ICS). He heard a voice say, "You are cleared to go."

Up front, Mack hit the switches. The number-two engine spooled up and ran away, like a car accelerator that was stuck on the floor. The engine spike damaged a computer. Flames like the thrust of a rocket shot out of the engine and lit up the night, catching the wary attention of the SEALs in the cabin. The turbine blades would have disintegrated if Mack did not shut down the aircraft. He had no choice but to declare the machine non-mission-operable.

It was that kind of a night.

"Team leader," Mack alerted Slab, who was plugged into the ICS on the right side of the helo by the ramp hinge, "I can't take you in this helicopter." A spare would take two hours to arrive from Bagram, what with preparation and the hour flight south. That would push them up against daylight. The occupants of Mack's helicopter dreaded being out in the light of day.

Eavesdropping on Mack's radio net, the other pilots of his Razor cohort, flying in the area with their deliveries and pick-ups of special operations teams to and from the mountains of the Hindu Kush, proposed an easy solution to the broken helicopter and the onward rush of daylight: a front-end swap in which the pilots, who were briefed on the operation, and their passengers would switch to a healthy aircraft. The crews would stay behind. Mack talked to Slab, who was designated the mission commander.

"Here's the deal," Mack told him. "Best case, I can get you to the LZ by 2200 Zulu."

The original timeline had called for Mack to drop off the

team three and a half hours earlier at the base of Takur Ghar. From there, the team needed at least four hours to climb 2,000 feet to an upper ridge and find a defensible position in which to hide and observe the peak before taking it over. With the delays—the B-52 sortie, the engine failure—they would be climbing up the mountain against a light sky. The timing did not mesh, and Slab did not like what he was hearing. It wasn't that he and his team couldn't ascend the mountain with the agility of young goats, night or day. As members of SEAL Team 6 and the Air Force's 24th Special Tactics Squadron, MAKO 30 was trained to operate in any environment on earth. Making them even more specialized, the operators of Team 6, who were fewer in number than 150, did not answer to the Navy's regular chain of command. They, a handful of Air Force combat controllers like MAKO 30's Tech Sergeant John "Chappy" Chapman, and the Army's fabled DELTA force took orders from a shadowy military organization known by its initials, JSOC—Joint Special Operations Command, based at Pope AFB adjacent to Ft. Bragg, in Fayetteville, North Carolina. These "black" commandos did not officially exist on the Pentagon's roster. In Afghanistan they had been assigned to Task Force 11 to hunt down and kill or capture "high-value targets" like bin Laden and his top lieutenants. Trained to a fine point, they were described as "Tier 1 operators" for their single-minded dedication and their ability to make hard choices in dynamic, dangerous settings and scenarios. They often operated independent of higher command to accomplish quietly what nobody else in the United States military was able—or, frankly, wanted—to do.

Slab conferred in the dark of the cabin with his point man, Randy,* and his combat controller, Chapman, the oldest team member, who both offered analyses that Slab knew to trust. Slab and Chapman, despite their age difference, were similar, both taciturn and deeply emotional. Slab could enter and leave a room as softly as a cat. Looking at his clean, open face, any suggestion that he was a commando of the highest order could provoke incredulity. Indeed, the same could be said of Chapman, a gentle family man and proud dad who carried his daughters' hair ties in his pocket as mementos.

Slab was further trained as a medic. He had served in the Navy for sixteen years, eight of them with JSOC, and as a reconnaissance team member and leader for six years. He'd been a SEAL since graduating from Navy boot camp, enlisting not long after graduating from high school. He had tried college for a short time, but with relationships at home deteriorating, he felt that he had to get away. Slab's father had spent four years as a SEAL when the organization was still called Underwater Demolition Teams (UDT). He had gone through Class 13 in 1953, and his influence was always present. He took Slab to the reunions and talked about his exploits. He had regretted getting out when he did, and that dissatisfaction often turned to sourness that had served to push Slab to get

---

*I honored the request of USSOCOM, for security reasons, that I refrain from using the surnames of the operators in MAKO 30, relying instead on their correct given names or nicknames.

away and finish for him. As a teenager Slab wanted to do something hard. He was mad at the world. He wanted to just go out and *do* something.

Slab had already distinguished himself in Afghanistan. Two weeks earlier, he had been sitting aboard a Chinook flying in the Kush, and the KC-130 refueling tanker from which they had just filled up with gas suddenly plowed into the side of a snow-covered mountain. Slab's helo dropped down and landed beside the tanker. Slab and two SEALs slogged through waist-deep snow to help pull out the survivors. One crewman was trapped in the wreckage. Slab went inside the broken fuselage and crawled amid CO_2 hoses and spilled fuel, expecting the aircraft to blow up any second. The trapped man was facedown in snow, with a foot wedged under a structural beam. Slab strapped a Maglite on his SIG Sauer pistol. He aimed the light at the crewman, who thought he was going to take care of the problem by shooting him.

"Don't shoot! Don't shoot me!" he screamed.

Slab, in his own inimical way, tried to calm him down. "Dude, I gotta cut your foot off to get you out of here," he told him—sardonically, he thought—and the crewman started screaming again. "I'm just kidding," Slab reassured him, thinking, *Hey, we could all be dead in a minute, so what else is there to do but put some humor in it?* Finally, after trying other approaches, he poured hydraulic fluid on the crewman's foot and ripped it out, tearing up muscles, but the crewman kept his foot. Slab was awarded the Navy/Marine Corps Lifesaving Medal for his effort.

That was nothing like this now. That had been simple; this was complex, and far more was at stake.

His first option was to push for a twenty-four-hour delay. He knew the urgency; he knew what his commanders expected of him. He felt under increasing pressure to ignore the rules, which would put him and his team in danger. He finally decided that the risks of going now were greater than the rewards, no matter what the tide of battle in the valley. He called back to Bagram to his highest commander, Air Force General Gregory Trebon, who was deputy commander of JSOC and the commander of Task Force 11. Chance alone put Trebon at Bagram that evening, instead of at JSOC's staging base on Masirah Island, off Oman in the Hormuz Straits.

Slab said, "Hey, I really—we're not going to be able to get up there by the time the sun comes up. I want a twenty-four-hour push. Let's do this tomorrow night."

By way of reply, Trebon never told Slab yes, and he never told him no. He said, "We need you to rethink that. We really need to get you in there tonight." Trebon was giving Slab latitude to decide for himself while letting him know his strong feelings in favor of continuing despite the onset of daylight. He did not think to tell Slab that another special operations team had tried to reach Takur Ghar the day before, but the presence of al-Qaeda fighters in the southern draw had turned them back. After that delay, a further twenty-four hours seemed somewhat inappropriate, especially considering that JSOC had "chopped" Slab's elite team to Operation Anaconda, arguing that it was underused in Task Force 11. Trebon knew that Takur

Ghar was going to be occupied as an observation post sooner or later, and later meant further casualties inflicted on Army troops in the valley. He reasoned that Takur Ghar was simply too valuable not to occupy right now. And if for some unforeseen reason the team encountered resistance, it would happen regardless of whether they went to Takur Ghar that night or the next night.

No matter what words Trebon chose to use with him, Slab was hearing him say, "You got to go."

He walked up to the cockpit to talk with Mack. He knew that what he was preparing to ask the pilot was born of necessity, and he rationalized it with each step up the cabin floor toward the cockpit. *Our offset LZ is only 4 kilometers away from the peak, and if there are enemy there, they will hear us anyway up top. The pressure is on us to get bombs on targets by sunup. Only one way that can happen.* He looked at Mack and asked, "Can you take me to the top?"

Slab knew what he was asking: in principle, reconnaissance teams should never land on their intended observation points. Helicopters instead inserted them a distance away, and they walked in (or up or down), hiding themselves and their ultimate destination from the enemy. Now, forced to choose between the pressures to help the beleaguered 10th Mountain Division troops in the valley and competing pressures to safeguard his team, Slab was placed in an unenviable, if not impossible, position. He did not see any need to inform Trebon of this. He knew the risks, but he understood the urgency. JSOC had empowered him with significant, short of ultimate, authority for just these moments.

Mack had no problem with Slab's request. He checked the Chinook's performance levels to see if the helo would be able to land at that altitude with the weight that it would be carrying. In and around this valley, soldiers, special operations teams, and pilots alike already were operating on the highest battlefield in U.S. history and at the peak elevation, nearly 2,000 feet higher than the valley, the helo and MAKO 30 would be testing wholly new combat ground. Many of the effects of altitude and temperature on men and machines were simply untested.

"I can do it," he finally told Slab. "But I can't guarantee I can land up there. I have not seen the imagery." Mack issued Slab a not-too-gentle reminder. "If I take you up there and hover around without landing and don't let you out, I'll have compromised your position. The enemy will know we are interested in that terrain. Is that OK with you?"

"I've seen the imagery," Slab replied. "There's room up there for you to land." He went back to the cabin to tell his teammates. "Here's the deal. I asked for a twenty-four-hour push and it was denied. We're going to the top." He could see in their faces that it was not a good idea. But he also knew they would follow him.

By now low on fuel, the Spectre gunship that had peeled off to make room for the B-52 had handed off its duties to a replacement gunship with the call sign NAIL-22. The origins of these signs—NAIL, MAKO, RAZOR, and so on—seem as obscure as the origins of the operations' names, like Anaconda and Enduring Freedom, except that one Pentagon requirement seems to be punchy consumer product-like names, the easier to say and to remember.

Knowing well the potential implications of the plan, Mack asked NAIL-22 to sweep the mountaintop with its array of sensors to hedge the risk. He passed along to the gunship the grid coordinates for the peak of Takur Ghar. Special optical heat sensors aboard the gunship could identify human-sized signatures from nearly 20,000 feet up in the air.

In no time NAIL-22 replied, "Nobody is there. You are cleared in."

Something about that response bothered Slab. NAIL-22 had swept the landing zone. But in all the confusion and delay and changed plans, he worried that the gunship might have cleared the wrong one. In his training with them, gunship crews had a hit-or-miss record of finding heat signatures quickly. And Slab knew that their sensors could be defeated. The time between Mack's request for a sweep and NAIL-22's reply seemed too quick. He wondered how the gunship could have flown to the mountain, entered the airspace over the peak, trained its sensors, and scanned for the presence of heat, all in a matter of minutes.

But he placed his trust in the technology. In Afghanistan, he had used the C-130 gunships often as another form of reference. They gave him a comfort factor—he knew he could "hit the ditch" if he got into trouble and the gunships would bail him out. SEALs on his level of excellence trained and fought with state-of-the-art weaponry, radios, body armor, night vision aids, targeting devices, and other equipment, plus other technologies like special operations helicopters, Spectre gunships, and submarines that were refitted for their exclusive use. Combined, these technologies were transforming war.

If he had delved into the theory of war, he might have known that he was about to become ensnared in a dangerous paradoxical logic centered on technology, which states, "Nothing fails like success."

More worrisome, NAIL-22 radioed Mack that it was peeling off to assist "troops in contact," and so could not cover them with guns and sensors as they approached the LZ on the peak.

Mack gave him a roger. He felt OK with that. "You are cleared in," he'd been told.

Slab had reached a point of denial. Go in without gunship coverage? It wasn't done. It broke the rules. But he heard Trebon telling him, *We need you to rethink that.* Events were building to the point where he knew he should say no, but in the back of his mind, voices whispered, *We really need you to get in there.* Should he ask one more time for a delay? Should he tell Trebon, "I don't feel comfortable with this"? He could imagine Trebon's response: "I said it once. You're a smart guy. We need you to rethink that."

In the helicopter, Slab told Mack, "Well, I guess that means we're going."

2

MACK AND SLAB, WITH MAKO 30, WERE FLYING along a military crest to the peak of Takur Ghar.

The summit—now covered in snow from a blizzard the day before—glistened in the light of a rising moon. The time was just before three in the morning, Monday, March 4, 2002. With luck, Mack could return to Bagram, take a hot shower, and, after a quick breakfast, be in his bunk before sunrise. He alerted his crew of the time out to the landing zone—three minutes. He looked through his night vision goggles (NVGs) at the peak over the helo's nose. He looked closer. From less than a mile out, he saw a dark scar in the snow that cut across a saddle just down from the peak. As they flew over the southern draw, the scar turned out to be narrow ruts in the snow. Afghan goatherds lived in these mountains, he reminded himself, even up to heights of 14,000 feet. He had seen them before, and these ruts in the snow, too.

The SEALs in the utterly dark cabin were staring out the windows at the ground through NVGs, which hung from brackets on their helmets and flipped down over their eyes, giving them an otherworldly look. For once they had not punched out the helo's windows in deference to the cold, and looked through the Plexiglas instead. One SEAL in the left door with the mini gunner saw the tracks in the snow, but before he could call them out, Mack was already up on the ICS. "Team leader, footprints in the LZ. Do you want to continue?" It was Slab's call as mission commander whether to abort.

"Do you see anybody?" asked Slab.

"No," Mack replied.

"Continue," Slab said.

As the Chinook flared to land, snow billowed up around the aircraft like a gauzy white curtain, momentarily obscuring the cockpit view. Through the blizzard of ice and snow, 150 feet off to the left of the chin bubble, Mack thought he saw what looked like a DShK, a Russian-made machine gun with the power to punch holes in a half-inch-thick plate of armor at 500 yards. It was a monster intended primarily to knock helicopters out of the sky. Mack blanched but continued to settle the huge helicopter down on the ground. The DShK was pointing away, as if it had once, long ago, been employed to defend the peak, perhaps against the Russians in the late 1980s. This kind of military salvage was found throughout Afghanistan, and it had not functioned in years. But Mack could not take his eyes off the DShK or the 2-foot-high circular sandbag and rock wall around its base.

He reported to Slab, "We got an unmanned DShK at our one o'clock position."

"Roger," Slab replied, thinking, *What's that doing here? Why didn't the gunship see it?*

In the back of the Chinook, the MAKO 30 team was ready to leave. The first out would be the point, Randy, followed by Slab and the SAW (squad automatic weapon) gunner, Neil Roberts, and the other three SEALs. Chapman, the combat controller, would be the last to leave with the radio. When it came, the infiltration would be a blur of muscles and motion—twenty seconds max, with the SEALs moving out in opposite directions off the ramp.

The SAW gunner, Neil, edged toward the ramp hinge. The adrenaline was pumping; not a word was spoken in the dark. The team had performed this maneuver hundreds of times. What they were about to do now was routine, except for the terrain and the altitude, but it was never taken for granted; a landing zone was always "hot" until facts proved otherwise.

Mack set the Chinook down with its nose on a 30-degree slick upslope on the edge of a natural saddle, rotors spinning. He clasped the controls, one in his left hand and one in his right, while snow swirled up around the windows and ramp. The helo's crew chiefs, looking out through NVGs from four different positions on both sides and at the rear, reported to Mack.

"Got a donkey at three o'clock in the tree line," the rear right ramp gunner and crew chief, Sergeant Dan Madden, announced through the ICS.

Hearing that, Slab thought, *What the fuck's going on?*

Randy, on the right side of the helo, yelled, "I got goats hanging in a tree." Decapitated goat carcasses hung by their legs from branches.

The left ramp gunner and crew chief, Jeremy Curran, said, "Guy just popped his head up."

"What's *he* doing?" Mack asked him, his voice crisp.

"He put his head back down."

"Can you see him anymore?"

"No."

Slab was thinking, *Why hasn't that guy been cut in half by now?*

"Weapons hold," Mack reminded his gunners. He was telling them to fire only if fired on.

"Roger, weapons hold," came their response.

Slab thought, *Why didn't I brief Mack to have his guys shoot anything they saw?* He knew that Mack had to flip a switch in the cockpit to send electrical power to the mini guns before they could be fired.

The guy out in the snow could be anybody, Mack was thinking. Friendly Afghans roamed these mountains, some of them allies of the coalition forces. Christ, they *lived* here; this was their patch. Neither Mack nor anybody else knew at any given time exactly where to expect them to appear. And whether they were enemy or friendly, they all looked the same.

Slab was processing the information, trying to reach a decision. *OK, we got a donkey, goats in a tree, one dude over there. Is he armed? Guy said he didn't know. Engines turning, sitting there way too long, tracks up here. We'd seen that before. One dude. For now. Gunship swept it and said nothing. DShK up there off the nose. OK, we're going.* He blurted out to his team, "OK, we're taking the LZ." He stripped off his headset and stepped toward the ramp to get off, but the crewman on the right side, Madden, threw out his arm to stop him. Slab moved back and put his headset on.

In the cockpit, Mack looked up through the windshield. The man he'd seen seconds ago popped up again from behind a snowy berm about twenty-five yards away. He was launching a rocket-propelled grenade (RPG). *It's a doggone lava lamp with sparks and it's coming right at me.* Through his NVGs, the rocket's glare blinded him. The Kevlar armor plate on his chest had made him feel brave, but when something like this RPG happened, the armor shrank to the size of a postage stamp. He stared out his front window. The enemy at eleven o'clock was loading to shoot again. Machine-gun fire was raking the back right side of the aircraft.

The SEAL, Kyle, standing in the left side gunner's door shouted, "RPG!" as he turned around and shoved the SEALs within his reach to the floor.

The RPG punched through the aircraft's electrical pod a couple of feet below and in back of Mack and only inches away from the long, bulbous gas tank. The RPG, almost certain to be a shaped charge with the penetrating power of an artillery shell, went clear through the left mini gun ammo can before exploding in the interior of the aircraft. The blast stunned Mike Nutall, the right door mini gunner, and Jeremy Curran, on the left door, was knocked down. Flames shot up in the soundproofing on the inner wall. Before the crew could recover, another RPG hit the right-side radar pod.

In an instant, the helo lost AC electrical power. The mini guns, which the system powered, now were out of action. In the cockpit, the cathode ray screens spooled down and faded to black: the Chinook had lost use of its multifunction displays that supplied the pilots with engine data. Also out were the navigation systems with GPS, the critical automatic flight control systems, radios, and nearly every other operating component; without these, only a few good pilots can even taxi a Chinook. Mack's NVGs, powered by AA batteries, and the ICS, which ran on DC power, still functioned, but that was all.

A third RPG exploded in the snow by the right front and peppered the aircraft with shrapnel. Two large explosions rocked the helo. A fourth RPG, Mack thought, hit the right-side turbine on the tail.

Two RPGs had hit "like golden BBs" at the exact angles required to take out the Chinook's three generators, which were designed into the architecture of the helo to avoid total battle damage. Worst, machine-gun bullets were slicing through exposed bundles of live electric wires about 30 feet back from the generators. Burning hot, slick liquids from burst rotor transmission and hydraulic lines sprayed the cabin interior.

Mack asked himself, *How can I lose all these systems? It can't be happening, but it is.*

Automatic weapons fire from the front, the front right, and the left raked the aircraft, which sat out in the open like a house trailer in the desert. The sound was like a hundred sledgehammers on sheets of steel. The bullet-blasted soundproofing filled the pitch-black interior like confetti. The angle at which Mack had set down the Chinook somewhat screened its occupants from the bullets that pounded through the fuselage above where the men crouched. Mack did not know if Slab's team had yet run out of the aircraft. His crew chiefs were not talking to him.

"What's going on back there?" he shouted into the ICS. "We're just sitting here!"

Madden came up on the headset. He said, "Fire in the cabin. Go! Go! Go!"

The SEALs were standing up. The SAW gunner, Neil, was a step or two ahead of Slab, on the hinge, ready to go. Rounds were coming in, and smoke filled the cabin. The SEALs hit the deck again. Slab was lying sideways, NVGs on, looking out the ramp.

Forty-five seconds had elapsed since Razor 03 had touched down.

Mack snatched the controls and tried to save their lives.

3

DAN MADDEN HAD FELT A MOST UNCOMMON foreboding for most of the day. He ascribed it to an earthquake that morning, measuring 7.2 on the Richter scale. The quake had shaken his crew's shabby quarters at Bagram and rattled him on his canvas-bottomed cot. But nobody else took the quake as a sign of anything, good or bad, or even talked about it. He'd sought comfort watching his friend Phil Svitak, a door gunner and crew chief, slurp up most of a gallon can of butterscotch pudding for breakfast.

Madden, the helo's right rear crew chief, was a maverick and self-described "loudmouth pain in the ass" who busted people's chops and didn't care what they thought about him.

He refused to play according to the Army's rules, like regulation haircuts and looking sharp. He did not hang out with the guys he flew with, and thought most of them did not like him. He relied on his professionalism—he was arguably the best ramp crewman in the service and had earned a Distinguished Flying Cross as proof.

His job, as he described it, was to take care of the customers in the back of his helicopter, monitor certain mechanical systems in flight, act as a spotter, call out altitudes on landing, work the ramp up and down during infils and exfils, and man an M-60 machine gun. Madden's counterpart on the helo's left side—that night it was roly-poly Alexander Pedrossa, "Prod" or "PD" to friends—controlled an M-60 plugged into a socket on the ramp. Called a "stinger," the gun swiveled 90 degrees between Prod's legs, which he dangled over the ramp. In transit to cold landing zones, the M-60 was lashed down with bungee cords.

Madden enjoyed nearly everything about his job except the cold. The frigid winter air whipped back through the open front door gunners' windows and through the wide opening over the ramp where he stood. Nothing he wore made a difference. That day he had left his cold-weather gear behind, including his Belleville boots with the snowshoe tread pattern on the soles, expecting to fly only at lower altitudes in and around the valley. He wore regular Army boots, and his toes were numb with cold. At least it didn't matter that the soles of those boots were smoother than his Bellevilles. The Chinook's ramp was unforgiving with a slick metal surface and shiny steel ridges of raised pallet skids. No matter how he was shod, unless he was wearing his safety harness, an expandable tether that hooked to his waist in front on a belt, he would drop off the aircraft—there wasn't a single doubt in his mind. This night, Madden had anticipated "a quick down-and-dirty—put these guys in and go home." Then crack a can of butterscotch pudding.

As a matter of routine, his customers came and went, and if he knew them by sight, he said hi and bye. He dealt with only the Tier 1 JSOC special operators like Slab and his team. He had his opinions about them, as did everybody else who worked with them on a regular basis. The SEALs were thought of as standoffish, tightly focused, good men beside you in a tight place but very different in their views. They just did things differently—like smashing out the windows on the Chinooks to see better, until there were no replacement windows left in Afghanistan, and refusing to snap in their safety harnesses like other troops were made to do. An opinion was shared of them as prima donnas, leading those who weren't SEALs to wonder if they had earned their vaunted reputation through actual exploits or if their glamour was not partly derived from the fictions of movies starring Chuck Norris, Charlie Sheen, and Demi Moore. The SEALs dismissed such talk as penis envy.

This night the SEALs were packing hefty rucksacks that weighed 80-plus pounds, with the food and water and warm gear they would need to live and work while remaining hidden on Takur Ghar for several days. Madden respected their endurance, but some of the other stuff about them went over the top, like what they wore and looked like. In Afghanistan they sported beards to fit in with the locals, wore shaggy hair, and looked studiedly raffish. Tonight, they dressed in Rhodesian-type vests with pouches for extra magazines and pockets for gear, and Army tricolored camo pants; some wore Pro-Tec skateboarding helmets. On the shoulders of their dun-colored shirts they wrote their blood types in black marker.

Like them or not, they were his customers, and right now Madden had other things to think about as he peered over the ramp while the helo came in on short final. He saw trenches he thought were like an ant farm, like people had walked back and forth along the same paths. He called it out to the cockpit.

"Roger," Al Mack said.

Madden looked to the right. He saw chickens and a donkey that was tied to a tree. He fixed the location of the donkey in his mind. Another crew chief called out another machine gun. Madden saw "little bitty stuff" that made him wonder why the pilots were not hauling ass out of there. The earth came up at him, fifteen feet, ten feet, and the Chinook touched down, aft wheels first, blowing snow and ice that burned his face and clouded his NVGs. Now stationary, he worked a static reconnaissance, looking around. Impatient and nervous, he called Mack. "We've been on the ground fifteen seconds already. Am I ramp-clear down?"

"Yeah, ramp's clear," Mack confirmed.

Madden pulled the lever.

The left front mini gunner, Jeremy Curran, called up. "I see somebody," he reported.

Madden stretched on his tiptoes to his full 6-foot-2-inch height. He turned around and saw Slab throw off his ICS headset. Madden did not know why, but with his authority to decide if his passengers got off, he threw out his arm and stopped him. And in the same instant, the world seemed to dissolve. Slab went down on the floor. A ball of orange flame mushroomed in the forward cabin. Madden smelled burning cordite. The helicopter rocked. A flare went off in the cabin. Smoke and fire burned along the walls. The helo shuttered. Madden heard a boom over his head. The engines were screaming with the effort of lifting off. Bullets pierced the metal skin with the sound of hammers. He was slammed to the floor by what he thought was the concussion of an RPG exploding against the right engine. He had actually taken two AK-47 rounds to his head. One bullet skimmed along the side of his crew helmet and knocked off his visor mounts. His NVG goggles stayed attached. The other bullet came in over his right ear, followed the path of the Styrofoam in his helmet over the top, and went out the other side. His helmet was not ballistic, not bulletproof. After a few seconds, he jumped to his feet. The burning oil and fluids spraying out of the aft transmission, the bearings, and the hydraulic lines blurred his vision. In the dark, he was looking with NVGs through what seemed to him a goldfish bowl. The ramp floor, covered with oil and hydraulic fluid, was "slicker'n snot."

Madden clutched his M-60; his machine gun worked

(Prod's gun was lashed to the ramp and useless), but its field of fire was limited to the right side and behind the aircraft. He keyed the mike. "We're hit, we're taking fire. Pick it up. Go! Go! Go!"

Al Mack was already pulling power. The Chinook rocked sideways, back and forth, with the turbulence of its effort to become airborne. Madden reached over and yanked the ramp lever to the up position. But the ramp did not move. It could not operate without hydraulic pressure. Madden laid into his M-60, searching for targets. He shot at and missed the donkey. He heard two more explosions. The helicopter was shaking violently. Small arms fire was peppering the length of the fuselage. Madden glanced to his right. Someone—one of the customers—was falling down the ramp past the hinge in the dark. Or, he wondered, had the SEAL mistaken whom he thought Madden was telling to go? Prod was chasing him, trying to tackle him, desperately attempting to stop him. Madden glanced left. *Ramp's down. He's going to fall out!*

Madden lunged at the SEAL. Prod grabbed the SEAL by his ruck handle. The guy was carrying an M-249 machine gun that weighed 27 pounds and an 80-pound pack, and with this burden, he weighed 300 pounds or more. Stopping him was like holding back a bulldozer in a mudslide. The helicopter jerked. The SEAL was thrown further off balance and was almost running backward, trying to backpedal to stop himself from flying over the edge. Prod and the SEAL both twisted in an agony of desperation. They clutched at each other for stability. The SEAL snatched at the ramp combing. His foot flew in the air. Madden grabbed his boot and held on. The SEAL was halfway out of the bird. Neither Madden nor Prod could stop him now. Madden's restraining harness snapped tight. He held the SEAL's boot for three seconds. The three men edged a couple of feet from the lip. Mack pulled power, sucking the guts out of the Chinook, and the engines did not have the juice to respond. The floor angle was level. Mack pulled so much power that the engines could not keep up the RPMs, and the bird came back down and went up again. It jerked harder. The violence of the motion snatched the SEAL out of Madden's grip, and both Prod and the SEAL went out the back over the ramp. Gone in the night. That quick.

The SEAL landed on his back, falling about 10 feet straight down through the dark onto a waist-deep cushion of snow.

One of the pilots shouted in the ICS, "We lost an engine."

Madden keyed his mike. "Both engines are *humming*. Power! Power!" He was scared, panicked, freaking out. "We lost one," he shouted in the ICS. "We got a man on the ground. Break right! We got to go back in."

Immediately, the bird pitched right. Madden went to the edge of the ramp to haul in Prod, who was dangling by a thread over a 2,000-foot void. Madden grabbed his jacket and heaved. Prod climbed up the M-60, but his weight ripped the gun out of its socket. He fell back in the open air and bobbed on his tether, the machine gun in his arms. Madden reached down for the weapon, threw it back in the cabin, then braced and reeled in Prod, who pulled up with his arms and hands on the ramp.

Now, with Prod in the aircraft, Madden moved forward.

The bird tipped wildly in a hard right turn. About six seconds had elapsed since the SEAL fell out. Madden got on the ICS—the pilots were talking about losing an engine and landing. Madden told them that both engines had power. He repeated, "We lost one. Man out. Guy on the ground. Break right. Get back in there."

Madden stepped to check the maintenance panel. The aircraft had lost electrical power. The mini guns were quiet, so Madden assumed that Curran and Mike Nutall were dead. He keyed the ICS. "Got a hydraulic leak," he reported. "Maintenance panel's dead. No fluid." The levels in the gauges worked off DC power. The fact that Madden was talking on the ICS, which also operated off DC, meant that the levels were accurate, locked on zero.

Mack ordered the crew to test-fire the guns.

Madden said, "No, the mini guns are down."

Mack asked, "Can we get one anyway?"

"The mini guns are down. I got a 60. That's *all* we got."

4

WITH NO ELECTRICITY TO POWER UP THE AUTO-matic flight control system, the Chinook was barely flyable, but it *was* flying. Mack started pulling power, and there was no rotor droop. He banked hard right to the southwest and dove down.

Mack had been too preoccupied before this instant to realize what Madden had told him—"There's a guy on the LZ"—and he nearly shouted in the ICS, "What? What did you say?"

"There's a *guy* on the LZ," Madden repeated. "One of the team guys is on the LZ."

"You better be right," Mack told him.

"I saw him go out."

Mack said, "All right, guys, we're going back." He reviewed his options. He had none. He could not leave a man behind, he thought. If he did, he couldn't live with himself.

Jeremy Curran got up on the ICS. "What the hell's going on, sir?" he asked, wondering where they were heading.

Mack told him, "We're going back. There's a guy on the LZ."

"But the guns don't work."

"Test-fire 'em."

Curran and Nutall did, and they did not work.

Mack said, "All right, we're going in anyway. Any complaints?"

"No, sir, let's get him," came from several points on the ICS.

The bird started to make a sharp teardrop turn in a bank to the right that strained the rivets. Mack gained altitude and leveled off from the first turn, and the cyclic stick in his left hand started pulling away. Then it failed to move. Mack now had a Chinook with no hydraulics, which he compared to driving a car without a key to the ignition.

"I can't move the controls," he shouted. Everybody knew what that meant. Suddenly, the ICS went quiet.

"Status on the hydraulics?" he asked Madden.

In the back, Madden checked the panel. "Fluid pressure zero, fluid level zero."

They were flying 2,000 feet over the ground. Mack thought, *We're dead. So, this is how it goes?*

In the back, Madden stabbed a beer can opener on the end of a string into the top of a quart can of hydraulic fluid that he'd stored just in case in the skeleton of the fuselage, below the maintenance panel. He poured the viscous liquid into an emergency port at his station, and cranked a small handle up and down to feed the fluid into the lines.

Suddenly, the controls sputtered. Mack could move them. He banked to the right, looking through the right side panel window at landmarks below, including the 2-mile-long geological oddity in the middle of the valley that the Americans called "the whale" because of its elongated bulbous shape. He thought, *OK, there's the Whale and there's HLZ 15. So the guy who fell out must be over there.* He made another turn, completing a circle. They were approaching the peak from the same direction as before. A couple of seconds passed. The controls started pulling again. Mack realized that even if he got the controls back, he could not risk a landing. He had to put the bird down *now* in a safe place or they would crash. He told the crew, "I can't move controls again. Guys, we're going to abort the rescue."

As the helicopter was about to skim the ridge and plummet in a controlled crash 2,000 feet to the valley below, Madden looked out, straining his eyes for a sight of the SEAL who'd fallen out. The helo started taking fire again. The enemy was peppering the night sky with tracers. Rounds came in the back of the helo at an upward angle, piercing the ceiling. The helicopter was shaking like it was breaking up. Madden heard the pilot say, "Lost flight control."

Madden uttered, "Huh?"

Then he saw him. He was running up the saddle in the snow, toward the peak. The muzzle flash on his machine gun was unmistakable. The sight horrified Madden. *He was my passenger. He was on my ramp and on my helicopter. And he fell out. A passenger should not fall out of my aircraft. It should never happen. There was nothing I could do. I made the right decisions. It should not have happened.*

He envisioned the SEAL watching the helo circle back—the hope at hearing the engines. He had charged up the saddle pushing hard against the knee-deep snow, his lungs burning in the thin cold air, straining to get back on board. In an instant, the helicopter disappeared over the crest, stranding him. The enemy circled him in the dark. He was alone. Madden could feel his despair.

5

THE LOST MAN WAS PETTY OFFICER FIRST CLASS
Neil Christopher Roberts, a twelve-year SEAL veteran
whom his teammates since BUD/S Class 184, the
rigorous course that candidates must pass to become SEALs,
called "Fifi."

The ridiculous contrast of this name made them smile,
and with his sturdy self-confidence, Roberts was beyond caring
what name they used. His hair was red and tightly curled, but
otherwise nothing compared him to a pampered French
poodle named Fifi. As hard as he was—and teammates said he
was "harder than a woodpecker's lips"—Roberts was
unabashedly sentimental, and when out on operations in

Afghanistan, he carried a tiny blue unicorn on a key chain as a talisman to remind him of home, his wife, Patricia, and the family they had started with the birth of their son, Nathan, in Virginia Beach, Virginia. And for good luck, he attached another tiny figure on a chain to his ruck, this one of the red-bearded cartoon character Yukon Cornelius from the old animated TV show *Rudolph the Red-Nosed Reindeer*. Yukon, he thought, looked just like him.

For a man of his complexity, the SEALs might have seemed a strange occupation, which he had reached by a circuitous route that delineated a growing, though delayed, maturity. His father had served in the U.S. Navy's submarine service, and Neil and his nine siblings in Woodland, California, outside of Sacramento, grew up with their father often away from home. Neil idolized him and chose to follow him into the Navy after Woodland High School, the home of the "Wolves," where he had graduated in the top third of his class. He was liked and popular, smart and ambitious, but he was known as a class cutup who did not see much point in school. And so he enlisted in the Navy in '87 and trained as an aviation mechanic, stationed in Guam, where he sought adventure to stir a restless soul by off-hours scuba diving, mountain biking, sky diving, and surfing. He was happy-go-lucky, but the point of the Navy eluded him. He fought the Gulf War from the balcony of a luxury hotel in Kuwait City, fixing broken airplanes during his shifts. He had heard about the SEALs—the Navy's matinee idols, its poster boys, its stars. The SEALs were seen as adventurers, optimists, and romanticists; they were tough and embraced danger, silly as that sounded to actual SEALs. It made sense to Roberts, on the outside looking in. Maybe that was how he might fit in the Navy. All SEALs were a little nutty, and everyone said he was too. After his discharge, returning home to Woodland, he made a decision to try. It posed a risk. If he failed to make the grade, he would pay by spending another boring four years in the Navy as a mechanic. To prepare for the extreme physical qualifications, he jogged up and down the hills near his house with a heavy sea bag on his shoulders.

He earned his Trident "Budweiser" SEAL badge in '92, and in the course of time was assigned to Team 2 in Little Creek, Virginia, where he impressed officers with his quiet, watchful manner. Team leaders noticed the new men who showed up with their mouths shut and ears open. Neil was motivated and willing to please. He wanted to learn. Only after he settled in and was accepted did he loosen up, and the joker came out. He especially loved the sea part of being a sea-air-land specialist. In, on, or under the water, he felt at home and happiest. One winter when a team was swimming in 40-degree seas off Virginia, wearing wet and dry suits to prevent hypothermia, the team's commander spied Roberts on the shore dressed only in swimming shorts. He called for him to take a boat to bring out an item of gear. Instead Roberts plowed into the waves, swimming out 300 yards, and swimming back. His CO said, "The word *can't* isn't in his psyche. Some guys, when you ask them to do something, say they can't. Neil you have to *tell* he can't."

He was an important few years older than his teammates, and maturity was the first quality that SEAL Team 6 sought, all others being equal. Roberts was level-headed, confident, and aggressive. He was not big, but he was solid. He had reached a point of excellence at shooting, swimming, and endurance, showing no signs of arrogance or belligerence. And a sense of humor made him a pleasure to be around. Once during this time, preparing for an ongoing SEAL mission in northern Europe, he was assigned to Bridgestone's Winter Driving School's two-week course in Steamboat Springs, Colorado. The point of the training was to see how fast drivers could run cars around a nine-turn, one-mile track on ice and snow. The civilian instructors had never taught a SEAL, and when they told the civilian students not to worry about the cars, Roberts took their advice. He smashed his car regularly into the snow banks. The instructors reacted to this daring with utter annoyance. "What's wrong?" Neil wanted to know. He *knew* what was wrong. "Did you ask me to go as fast as I can and make it to the end? You did? What you really meant was to go as fast as I can *without hitting anything* and make it to the end." The instructors debated kicking him out. Called before them, Neil explained his rationale. "Look, how can I know what the limit is unless I exceed it, and rein it in a little bit from there? Anybody can go 3 miles an hour on this stuff."

Now in SEAL Team 6 and often deployed around the world, he guarded his privacy like a dog with a bone when he was home. He had two families, and the SEALs were the jealous and needy one. At thirty-two, he wanted just to be with his wife and son. And most days off in the warmer months would find him on his driveway under the engine of a sixties Chevy pickup truck he was bringing back to life. He was not long for the active life of a SEAL anymore, and he knew it. But he was never one to worry about the future.

In Afghanistan in the days leading up to Operation Anaconda, Roberts posed for a photograph that provided a revealing glimpse into his character. With the six other men of MAKO 30, he was standing on the delta wing of a MiG-21 "Fishbed," one of the attack jets that the Russians had scrapped at Bagram Air Base. The jet looked quaint with its puny nose shock cone, peeling dun paint, and 20-foot wingspan. The snow-capped peaks of the Kush rose against the horizon. Roberts' leg was cocked, and he slouched, with sand goggles strapped to his forehead. He sported a raffish red beard and moustache and was dressed in BDUs (Battle Dress Uniforms) with a thick woolen scarf coiled around his neck against the bitter cold. His SAW machine gun hung down from a sling across his chest. Caught in that moment, his posture and the glint in his eyes showed a clear exhilaration, like a gunslinger before a fight, with a sense of being in the center of the universe, satisfied, proud, and even happy.

His confidence stemmed from his life's experience, filtered through an inner, mysterious core. Surely one pillar, known to each man in special operations, propped up everything else: the knowledge that he would never be left behind in a fight, no matter what. The belief was ancient as the New Testament: "What man of you, having an hundred sheep, if he lose one of them, doth not leave the ninety and nine in the wilderness, and go after that which is lost, until he find it? And when he hath found it, he layeth it on his shoulders, rejoicing" (Luke 15:4–7). The parable embodied compassion for the defenseless and frightened. It defined a real search, an uplifting and necessary deed of service initiated on the assumption of success through perseverance. At its most fundamental level, it was an expression of profound love and, at its successful conclusion, of great joy.

In times more recent than the biblical era, the "lost sheep" principle was integral to the male-bonding myths of America's Old West, initiated by a need in a savage and unforgiving natural world for reliance on a single steadfast companion, later to be copied onto the pages of penny dreadfuls, throughout Louis L'Amour's oeuvre, in the TV serials of Hopalong Cassidy and Tom Mix, and of course in the movies. In real war, the tradition was etched in the fifth paragraph of the Ranger Creed: "I will never leave a fallen comrade to fall into the hands of the enemy." The pledge set warriors apart from the rest of (civilian) mankind, the dog-eat-dog, fuck-you crowd who eschewed allegiance and even simple sharing of more-than-enough bounty. For special operators such as Roberts and those of the SEALs, SOAR, STS, DELTA, and Rangers, leaving a teammate in the lurch and not returning was far more serious than breaking any social vow, in a fundamental, even atavistic way, because it entailed death, and the dead man easily could be you. Returning for a lost brother required no thought, no decision. It was an ingrained reaction, not an idea.

6

AL MACK HAD THOUGHT HE WANTED THIS LEVEL of excitement. He loved to fly, and mere wings had thwarted the full expression of his desire. Helicopters going backward, left and right, and straight up and down, sitting in the air like a hummingbird—*that* was flying. Even as a youngster watching TV back home in Concord, New Hampshire, before he caught the excitement of girls, watching Huey slicks flare on Vietnam news footage gave him goose bumps. From then on, that was his passion. Now he was thirty-nine, a geezer by combat standards who had shaved off his beard because it was showing telltale gray. Just getting into a cockpit had taken him nine years schlepping tools as a helicopter mechanic in places like the Republic of Korea, but seven years ago, after proving himself as a superior pilot in the regular Army, he accepted a coveted invitation to join the Army's elite 160th Special Operations Air Regiment (SOAR), *the* who's-who-at-the-zoo of chopper pilots. For the risks and for the unscripted maneuvers they put themselves and aircraft through, they were thought of as candidates for psychotherapy. They did things that challenged belief. A former SEAL had joined SOAR for thrills, and if that didn't say enough already, in one of his first training sessions he was taking off a Chinook and was powering through 150 feet when his instructor in the next seat leaned over and shut down both engines. The SEAL's eyes widened and he screamed, *"What the fuck are you doing?"* The instructor folded his hands as the bird autorotated in its powerless descent, hard to earth.

Before this infil into Takur Ghar, Mack had felt almost wistful, with only days left before he was to leave for home. His first months in Afghanistan had been like living in a dream. His aircraft was shot at each night he went up. Sixteen surface-to-air missiles, countless RPGs, splattered airbursts, cannon fire, even stones came from behind his helo and not out in front, where he could see. He felt a little let down and had whined about it: "We don't get to see this stuff they shoot at us up in the front."

Right now he was in shock, with the Chinook off the peak in a controlled crash, slightly more crash than control. At a 35-degree nose-down angle, the 40,000-pound bird was partly autorotating, like a winged maple seed pair wheeling down to the ground from a tree. The up force of the descent spun the long, thick, flat twin rotor blades. The rate of descent was remarkable: it burst Mack's eardrum.

"Airspeed 90 knots. Rate of descent 700 feet a minute," his copilot in the right seat shouted.

"How do you *know* that?" Mack yelled back.

His copilot aimed the beam of a Maglite on the panel at a small LED backup altitude and airspeed indicator with an artificial horizon. "Right there," he replied, then replaced his hands on the cyclic and the stick between his legs, backing up Mack on the controls.

If Mack could keep the aircraft upright, they might survive the fall from 10,240 feet to 8,500 on the valley floor. However, given his lack of control, he was relieved that they were not slamming toward the ground at 2,000 feet a minute. A Chinook can land at 700 feet a minute, ripping the wheels off, killing some passengers, and the cockpit crew (who have automobile shock absorbers under their seats) coming out of it barely alive. Mack had been aiming for a known LZ, closest to the northern base of Takur Ghar. But he had to get on the ground sooner than that. He steered the helo toward a level patch to his left front just as the controls started going out again. He shouted to Madden to pump in another quart of hydraulic fluid. One can remained. The controls came back. Mack estimated about fifty seconds of control per can of fluid.

Ten feet off the ground, the aircraft was shaking and dangerously unsteady, and the noise was a loud, incessant clatter of metal parts at their limits of strain. The cyclic started to yank to the right against Mack's left hand. He wanted to land straight ahead, so he turned, and suddenly the aircraft was moving sideways. If the wheels touched the ground now with this lateral movement, the helo would hit and roll. The cyclic would not move. He repeated the mantra, *Never stop flying the aircraft*. He jammed the right rudder pedal on the nose, which kicked the aircraft around. He pushed down the thrust. Razor 03 slammed into the ground at 17 degrees nose high and 18 to 20 degrees roll to the left. Mack was certain they would flip over.

7

ON THE RAMP, MADDEN'S STOMACH FELT LIKE IT was in his nose. He had experienced precipitous loss of elevation before in wind shears, but that was not in combat. The tossing now disoriented him. Which direction was up? He stared at the pump in his fist and the fluid can in his hand. He was cranking the handle as fast as the pressure allowed.

A voice called, "Fifty feet. I got an LZ in sight." Madden stopped pouring a third can of fluid long enough to grab Slab, who was braced against his M-60.

"Get all your guys on the *floor*! We're goin' in hot!"

"Huh?"

He threw Slab to the floor; the team got down. Back at his station, Madden heard Mack say, "Controls are locking up again." He pumped harder.

"Twenty-five feet."

Madden thought, *I'm dead*. That was his last thought.

The Chinook ramp hit the ground first, taking the full brunt of the impact, with the right side high, on the verge of rolling over. The collision with the ground tossed Madden to the ceiling against the gearbox and driveshaft above his head. He flew back down and hit the floor and went back up again and hit the ceiling and came back down, like a ping-pong ball. The impact cracked his helmet. He suffered compression fractures of four vertebrae, two broken ribs, and disc and nerve injuries that, even after four surgeries, would never be fully repaired.

When he woke up, the MAKO 30 team had already run off the aircraft. Madden rose unsteadily on his feet and told Prod, on the left ramp clearing his head and coming down from the shock of hanging out over nearly 2,000 feet of open air, "Get your 60 and get out of the airplane." Madden grabbed his own M-60 and a 750-round ammo can. Leaving out the back was like running on Jell-O, and as a final insult, he slipped on the hydraulic fluid and fell off his own ramp.

8

U P FRONT, MACK HIT THE EMERGENCY SHUTDOWN switches and applied the rotor brake, and the Chinook's blades spooled down and stopped. Gentle, hilly terrain sloped off on both sides of the helo. It was not where Mack had wanted to ditch, but he was not complaining; indeed, he was reluctant to call the landing a crash. His only thought now was to get out. He pushed out of his seat and leaned into the companionway, which was blocked by a folding chair that had come off its latches. Shock confused him. His copilot had jettisoned his door and jumped out the side. He yelled back at Mack, "Al, don't go out that way. Come out my door."

Mack thought, *Door? Ah! Door!* And he popped his emergency hatch, dropping seven feet to the ground. He ran to the back of the aircraft and yelled, "Who's the team leader?"

Slab raised his hand.

It was dark, and Mack had left his NVGs in the cockpit; he could not see Slab's face. "Who *are* you?" he asked.

"Slab."

"Who?"

"The shithead, remember?" Slab replied.

A couple of weeks before, a flare-up of tempers had resulted in name-calling after Slab and his Task Force 11 team had snatched an important Taliban leader and were told there could be no helo to pick them up. Nearly three hundred angry villagers were up in arms and ready to attack at first light. The pickup was delayed by ground fog, through which Mack had flown nearly blind to reach the team at great risk. Slab had all but forgotten the details of that mission by now, except for the shithead part, and was making a subtle, self-effacing joke. He was thinking, *This is pretty serious, but I have to tone it down.* He was shaken up, sitting with his hand on his knee, reaching for nonchalance. The flight from the mountaintop, he'd thought, had gone straight down. The landing had thrown him forward and knocked the wind out of his lungs. Struggling to regain his breath, he'd yelled, "Drop your kit and get out." He'd been in the middle of the helo's floor, physically moving his team out. "Get out, get out!" They'd gone left, searching the high ground, and set up security.

Now Mack told him, "OK, I got you out of the shit then. It's your turn to get me out of it now."

"Deal," said Slab.

"Hey! I need a head count," Mack shouted. "How many guys fell out?"

"Nobody fell out," one of the SEALs replied.

"Yes, you guys lost a guy. There's a guy on the LZ."

"No, there isn't."

"Yes, there *is*," said Mack.

Slab knew about Fifi. He'd been lying on his side, facing the ramp. He'd seen him fall. He was deeply concerned about him, but right now he was responsible for the safety of his team and the helo crew. He had no idea where they had landed—possibly in the midst of the enemy, who roamed all over this side of the valley and were giving the 10th Mountain Division troops the fight of their life. His SEALs had established a 360-degree security perimeter around the Chinook with the help of the helo's crew. Looking around through NVGs, though, he did not want to have to fight on this terrain of rolling hills. A fight would delay his return for Fifi. The sight of a mountain looming just over his shoulder in the moonlight inspired the idea that his team could walk and climb back up the mountain.

He thought, *That's my mountain right there. OK, it's pretty big, we'll trim down and go with NODs [NVGs], two mags, radio, and nothing else, and haul ass up there. Get there as fast as we can. Get there at daylight.* He talked to Randy, his point man, and Kyle. He told them, "Look, I need a route. Get me to the LZ." He was pointing to the mountain. After a couple of minutes, Kyle came back. "That ain't it," he told him. "That's it over there." "Over there" was 7 miles away and 2,000 feet higher in elevation. "We ain't going to make it," Kyle declared. "We can only get there with wings."

Slab went over to his radio operator, Chapman, who was setting up a 13-pound multiband, multimission marriage of a computer with a radio. He extended a spiderweb antenna and got comms. Chapman said, "Any ground, any NAIL, this is MAKO 30." He waited a moment. Then he heard, "This is GRIM-32, what can we do for you?" By now, two Spectre gunships with the call sign GRIM had taken over for the NAILs, which were flying back to their base in Uzbekistan.

Chapman gave the gunship their grid coordinates and asked how long before they would reach them. He was told fifteen minutes. Chapman gave the gunship a status report to pass, if needed, to higher command. "All pax are on the ground. We have one pax that fell off the helo at the HLZ when an RPG went off." He had already tried to reach Roberts; the half-watt multiband interteam radio (MBITR) was well out of range. Chapman asked the gunship to sweep the area around them for the presence of enemy and, when that was done, to fly over the peak ASAP. He wanted the question resolved whether Roberts was dead or alive.

Chapman listened to the voices on the net with increasing concern. As word of the downed helo spread as far as Masirah off Oman, commanders in the rear wanted enough information to form a picture in their minds of what was going on. It seemed to Chapman like they only wanted to *talk* about what to do. He was demanding a rescue helo to come and pick them up.

"*Who the hell is that?* Who am I talking to?" demanded General Trebon, MAKO 30's senior commander that day, who seemed annoyed at Chapman's tone, as if to ask what right he had to order anybody to do anything.

As a special operator in a jam, Chapman only wanted action, with or without approval. "Tech Sergeant John Chapman, sir."

Trebon said, "I thought *I* was supposed to be the one making the calls on this."

"Yes, sir, you are," Chapman replied.

The thought of Roberts' dying kept going through Slab's mind. He thought, *He's probably doing one of two things. One, he's hauling ass, running downslope getting away, or two, he's hurt and he's hunkering down and waiting for us to come back. If he's hunkered down and he's turned on his strobe light—that being SOP [standard operating procedure]—he'll come up on his radio. He's going to protect himself. Either way, a gunship will see his strobe and move in close. We'll come get him, assess him, move him to another LZ, and get picked up. That's our best-case scenario.*

Twenty minutes went by on the ground; nobody was happy with waiting for a rescue helo to arrive. No simple plan worked to put the team back on the peak without risking lives. The SEALs, crew, and pilots of Razor 03 had survived a lethal ambush on the peak and had crashed in a valley populated by enemy. And the day was only beginning.

On the ground in the dark, someone set out an infrared

(IR) strobe, a beacon that would guide in a rescue helo. On the SATCOM radio, Chapman remained in touch with a gunship circling overhead. After they had been on the ground for nearly twenty-five minutes, the gunship, named GRIM-33, which had just received updated information from a roving Orion P-3 reconnaissance aircraft, warned him, "Hey, you have bad guys heading your way. *Get out of there now!*"

9

CHIEF WARRANT OFFICER JASON FRIEL, A SPECIAL operations Chinook pilot, worried about his tardy wingman. He and Mack had agreed to give each other fifteen minutes, and if one did not hear from the other in that time, he was to start a search. Fifteen minutes had passed more than fifteen minutes ago, with no word.

Friel was sitting on the ground at Gardez. He had delivered his special operations customers to the northwestern side of the valley, according to plan. Usually, attack helicopters like Cobras and Black Hawks protected the Chinooks on these infiltration missions, but in Operation Anaconda, the loss of four of these helos to enemy RPGs had stretched their resources thin. To compensate for the loss, pairs of Chinooks flew together for mutual protection. This night, for the sake of expedience, Friel and Mack had decided to fly their separate routes, delivering their teams unaccompanied. They had agreed that if one of them was not back at Gardez in the time they set, it meant trouble. Friel put out a call to the net. "Hey, I'm looking for my wingman, Razor 03."

"Yeah, he was shot down," the Spectre gunship, GRIM-32, which was heading toward Takur Ghar, informed him.

"Where is he? Is he alive?"

He was assured that Mack had survived. GRIM-32 passed him Mack's map coordinates, and Friel spun up the helo. Once in the air, he talked over options to get the SEAL team back to the peak. With its performance levels, Friel's Chinook could not take the weight of his crew, Mack's crew, and the MAKO 30 team up to the altitude of the peak. Somebody had to stay behind. "When you get here," Chapman radioed to Friel, with Mack sitting nearby and nodding in full agreement, "what I want to do is, this crew will stay here. We'll fly up to the mountain and get Roberts and come back and get the crew, and we'll all get out of here."

Mack had asked Slab to leave him a SEAL with a gun to help him defend the helicopter if they were attacked. Slab had agreed—reluctantly, because he wanted every member of MAKO 30 as shooters to go back for Roberts. Mack had insisted. Enemy soldiers were reported to be moving in their direction, and besides, a savage firefight a short distance away between the 10th Mountain Division elements and al-Qaeda near the village of Marzak threatened to spread in their direction.

Now, General Trebon told Chapman, "You can't stay. You have to get out of there now." He was also in receipt of the Orion P-3's warning that forty enemy soldiers were moving on foot toward the helo. The P-3 had eyes on the enemy; it was certain of its facts. Its electronic eavesdropping devices had verified the enemy soldiers by language and sight.

Trebon seemed to be telling them to go immediately, which meant back to Gardez. But when the rescue helo arrived, Chapman, Slab, and Mack wanted to exhaust every possible way to reach Roberts first. Going back to Gardez would only mean further delays. Chapman, after conferring with Slab and Mack, radioed a plan to Friel. When he reached them at the crash site, he would fly Mack and his crew to a friendly LZ only a couple of kilometers away. Friel then would come back to the crash site for Slab and the team, who would go up to Takur Ghar and get off. If all went well, they would fly together to Gardez with Roberts onboard.

"Naw, that's not going to happen," said Friel, who was now about five minutes away.

Slab was fed up arguing. He got on the radio and said, "Put me there. You can *do* this."

Friel said, "Not with that LZ under fire. And it is under fire. I'm taking all of you to Gardez and we'll sort it out there."

10

TO THE MEN WAITING ON THE GROUND, THE
clatter of the Chinook's rotors in the distance
sounded like a church choir. Leaving the engines
running, Friel settled the Chinook on the ground about 75 feet
from the broken bird. With the rotors at flat pitch, he handed
the controls to his copilot before exiting the aircraft. Running
up to Mack in the dark, the two men met with a hug. The crews
and the MAKO 30 team set to work transferring the crashed
helo's gear and weapons.

As they were about to leave, Mack thought it was proper
and fitting for him to be the last person to leave the crash site.
As he stood alone in the dark, however, images started running

through his mind that disabused him of any notion of heroism—*like in the movies,* he thought, *when right about now the last guy gets shot in the head and he slow-motions in a dying fall.*

Suddenly terrified, he started running with his gear and his M-4 rifle, ducking his head to protect his eyes from the dust and sand of the rotor wash. He imagined what he looked like. He had watched the movie *Black Hawk Down* and the video of the guy doing what Mack was supposed to do, running to a helicopter, with his commanders watching on Predator feeds. *I'd better do this right,* he was thinking. Ten feet from the helo, he tripped and went down, knocking the wind out of himself. He staggered to his feet and boarded the aircraft. He put on a headset in front by the companionway into the cockpit, and sat down on the floor.

Jason Friel waited. Mack yelled at him, "Go! Go! Go!"

Friel yelled back, "Two of my guys are still over there, and I don't have commo with them."

In a panic to get back in the air, Friel shot lasers and his cockpit crew aimed flashlight beams at the broken helo. The two crewmen were busy working to ensure that the helo was cleared of any gear that the enemy might carry away, and did not see the signals. Friel pulled power to reposition his Chinook closer. When the turbines roared, the two crewmen recognized the sound and ran off the ramp like their hair was on fire, screaming, "Don't leave us, don't leave us."

On the floor of the helo, Mack said to himself, "God, please, I won't do bad again—just get me out of this."

II
"We Are Not Going to Leave Him"

1

Aɪʀ Fᴏʀᴄᴇ Mᴀᴊᴏʀ Dᴀɴɪᴇʟ "D. J." Tᴜʀɴᴇʀ ʜᴀᴅ been pulling his Spectre gunship off a tanker with a full load of gas when he was informed by radio that a helicopter was down in the valley. As he flew away from the refueling boom, he headed southeast through a moonlit, cloudless night sky to see how he could assist. His Spectre, nicknamed "Iron Maiden" and decorated with the rakish image of a quarter moon and a wraith holding a 20 mm cannon, had a lot to offer a helo—or a single man—in distress.

With chain guns, 105 mm cannon, a 25 mm Gatling gun, and a Bofors 40 mm cannon, the Air Force special operations gunship was a brute. It could saturate a battlefield with more rounds per square foot than any other combat system in the world, and for that reason, the sound of its engines alone could strike fear into the enemy. Backing that up was the pinpoint accuracy of its weapons. After calibration and test firing, the 105 mm tank-gun projectile, targeted by computers and radar, could strike a cup on a putting green from 17,000 feet up.

The propeller-driven Spectre was a complicated, complex, and sophisticated piece of machinery with an airframe design that was fifty years old. Its computers and avionics, racked on the starboard side midfuselage, contained 609,000 lines of software code. Like owls, Spectres hunted at night, with no lights, their skin painted a light-absorbing matte gray, and infrared shields mounted underneath their four engines dispersed and hid heat that could attract antiaircraft missiles. As it orbited in a counterclockwise motion at around 17,000 feet, the fuselage yawed 45 degrees to point its weapons down. Several feet below and behind the left-side cockpit windows, a hinged door in the fuselage opened to a hatch not much larger than a kitchen dishwasher. The door was kept open during operations to provide a view of the ground to a suite of optics that made the AC-130 such an awesome threat: radar and high-resolution sensors (all-light-level television) allowed the crews to see in the dark, and infrared sensors had the power to detect body heat from three miles up. The IR sensors were said to be so sensitive, they could identify human tracks on the ground from residual heat left by footprints.

Now over the valley, Turner's Spectre—with the code name GRIM-32—identified the IR strobe that the crew had placed on the ground near the downed helo; IR glint tape—strips of tape worn on the shoulders of American troops that reflected brightly when seen by infrared sensors—also identified the presence of friendly troops on the ground around the helo.

"We are here for you," Turner radioed Chapman. "What can we do for you?"

Even before Chapman replied, the Spectre's crew was pushing its sensors a thousand yards out from the downed helicopter over the valley floor looking for enemies. General Trebon had not yet come up on the net with the warning of enemies. While the gunship searched, Turner asked whether the downed helo had wounded onboard. Was the helo broken, or had it merely set down for repairs?

Chapman told him, "It looks like we've got a problem. We just did a head count and we are missing one. We think we lost somebody on the LZ." In the next breath, he asked Turner to fly the Spectre over the peak to look for Roberts. Turner was willing to go, but he had no idea where until Chapman dug out the coordinates and passed them along. Turner contacted his sister gunship, GRIM-33, also flying to assist, asking it to take up his station over the downed helo and continue to monitor for enemy troops while he went in search of Roberts.

As Turner vectored "to look for somebody who fell out, to make radio contact, and protect him with the guns," right away he saw Takur Ghar off his nose. Even from a distance of 7 miles, the pulse of an IR strobe shone brightly on the peak; it had to belong to Roberts. Turner's fire control officer (FCO),

Ian Marr, seated behind him, thought, *This is our lucky day. We don't have to look for this guy. We got him.*

Night visibility was perfect in the moonlight. As the Spectre rolled in over Takur Ghar, Marr looked at his screen. A person on the peak was sitting down, leaning against a small tree, with the strobe on the ground at his feet. He thought, *It looks like he's propped himself up against the tree. That must be him. If I'd fallen out of a helicopter, I might want to lean against a tree, too. Seems pretty normal.*

Less than twenty-five minutes had gone by since Roberts fell out.

Turner got on the radio and reported to Chapman and Slab, waiting for Friel to pick them up at the crash site, "We may have what you're looking for."

Marr leaned on his elbows into the screen. He saw the footprints in the snow. He assumed they had been made by friendly troops with whom Roberts had linked up after falling out. Orbiting in a tight circle, the Spectre kept its electronic eyes focused on an area no more than 200 feet long by 50 feet wide. People, who showed on the screen as blurry heat signatures, appeared as if from nowhere. Marr told the navigator, sitting on his right, "Hey, I got a guy over here. There's another guy over here." The more he looked, the more people popped into view. That single person sitting against a tree had grown into a small gathering.

Marr called Chapman and Slab. "No kidding, we have people up here. We need to know if these are other friendly forces."

Slab replied, "There shouldn't be anybody else but Roberts."

Turner watched in his head-up display; one person holding the IR strobe soon became ten or more people passing the strobe around like a hot potato. The Spectre's crew could not identify whether they were friendly or enemy. Marr did not see IR glint tape on their uniforms. He told Turner, who reminded himself, *It is not uncommon for good guys on top of these peaks to have pretty good clothing on and stuff, so as far as IR tape on their uniforms, that probably isn't going to be visible anyway.*

As far as Turner knew, only one person had fallen off the helicopter. He and his crew were looking for only one person. But had other special operations teams linked up with Roberts? Turner had no idea how long the event had been unfolding. Amid the torrent of chatter on the radio, someone said, "We think a friendly team has got there." The story changed according to the moment: in rapid succession Turner heard that the search for Roberts was a combat search and rescue (CSAR) event, that Roberts was in evasion mode and descending the peak, that friendly forces had found him and he was in good hands, and that nobody had made contact with him or even knew where he was. Turner had no way to distinguish truth from rumors. He thought, *This is nightmarish.* A senior evaluator of Spectre pilots with the 16th Special Operations Wing, he had more flying experience in gunships than anybody else still on active duty, except for three or four AF special operations commanders at the wing's air base in Uzbekistan.

There shouldn't be any other friendly troops on the mountaintop but Roberts, Slab had reported.

The gunship's navigator said, "If that is the case, he's dead or rolled up."

Marr told the navigator, "If he's alive, he's been captured. Whatever happens, if that guy is still alive, I want him to know we are here. We are not going to leave him. If they start to move him, once we've lost sight of him, he's gone." Marr ordered the crew to paint the peak with a laser marker that Roberts should have been able to see through his NVGs.

2

S LAB TALKED WITH FRIEL ON THE FLIGHT BACK TO
Gardez.

"After we offload gear, you are going to take me
back on top."

Friel replied without hesitation, "OK."

Slab did not inform commanders at either Masirah or
Bagram about his plan to return. But Friel told them what they
had already assumed—that Slab was pressured by the clock,
knowing that further delays might give the enemy on the peak
time to capture and kill Roberts. He was not certain, anyway, that
he could execute any plans once he and his team took to the air
again. Whether or not he wanted to be, he was now on his own.

Their plan called for Friel to fly a couple of "racetrack" circles over the peak. The crew and the MAKO 30 team, peering intently out the windows and doors, would see Roberts, land, get off and rescue him, and be flying back to Gardez in thirty minutes or less.

Friel had one serious problem. He told Slab, "I don't have too much gas."

"Where do you need to go?" Slab asked.

He said either FARP Texaco, a forward area refueling point that was a 20-mile flight, or Bagram. Fuel was not available at Gardez.

Slab asked him to push it, to try with the fuel he had.

The margin of safety would be razor thin. Since its last fill-up, Friel's Chinook had flown to pick up Mack, MAKO 30, and the crews on the valley floor. The helo had sat on the ground with rotors spinning, burning fuel, for nearly thirty minutes. He had flown the overloaded helo back to Gardez, and now he was burning fuel while MAKO 30 unloaded their gear. Because his tanks were on reserve already and he would be fuel-critical once he approached the peak, Friel could not risk searching the flanks of the mountain for an offset LZ. He'd have to land on top. The risks might have been dismaying, but Friel was a "Night Stalker" who lived by the motto of the 160th SOAR, NSNQ—"Night Stalkers never quit." Calculated risk formed the core of their esprit. To deny their motto and quit now, even if he lived to fly another day, was unthinkable. NSNQ.

Confused and struggling to catch up, commanders at

Masirah insisted that Slab confirm the numbers in his team. Slab had to make his explanation graphic for them. He took out his notepad. He said, "I had this many when I left." He wrote down seven names—himself, Randy, Fifi, Kyle, Brett, Turbo, and Chappy. He turned the page. "Now I have this many—six." He wrote down the names of everyone but Roberts. Masirah came back asking twice more for a confirmation. Finally, Slab said, "Look, we lost a guy. I have everybody except for Fifi. You have to believe me on this."

The men in MAKO 30 threw off unneeded gear, including Claymore mines, Chapman's SATCOM radio, and the rucksacks with extra clothing, water, food, and batteries. Brett carried the M-60 machine gun. Chapman and Turbo had their M-4s. And Kyle, Slab, and Randy packed Stoner SR-25 .308 caliber sniper rifles fitted with grenade launchers. Slab's gun was named "Barney"—his six-year-old son's name for it; Slab had glued a tiny head of the pudgy purple dinosaur to the weapon's receiver. The guns came equipped with aiming devices that shot out beams of red laser and invisible light at targets. Each man also packed eight fragmentation grenades and wore standard SEAL SIG Sauer 9 mm automatic pistols strapped to their legs. They carried knives in scabbards. And with their NVGs, they still owned what remained of the night. Chapman wore his Rhodesian vest and black gaiters over his boots to keep out the snow.

Slab called the men around. He asked for a crewman to turn on the red light in the cabin so they could see without using NVGs. The men were on their feet with their backs to the door. He looked in their faces—Turbo, Kyle, Brett, Randy, and Chappy. "OK, here's what I know," he told them. "Reports have come across that the gunship saw a strobe up there. Four or six dudes are around Fifi. That was the last report I heard. The strobe is on. He is alive. Four to six dudes are with him. We can deal with that. We'll set up a strobe when we get there, identify ourselves, and anybody that is outside our circle, the gunship will light 'em up. And we'll search for Fifi, the best methodical search we can. We'll get a foothold up there. We'll find a place, clear it, and move on into it. We're going up there and the bird's going to land. We are getting off fast in pairs. Don't wait for the ramp to get all the way down. Get the hell off."

He was telling them that they were going back on top. They had just been ambushed with heavy armaments from a defended position, and now they were going back. They looked worried. Slab gave them a "fire-and-brimstone speech" that ended with, "Hey, we're going back up there and killing every last one of those motherfuckers." They were going to wreak havoc and bring Roberts home. Slab never thought for an instant that he wasn't. No one in his team did.

"We're goin'!" they roared in unison.

Slab pulled Chapman aside. "Your sole job is to get to cover and get guns on. Do nothing else but get to cover and get on the radio. We'll take care of everything else. We need you on that radio." Chapman carried his interteam MBITR with a line-of-sight range of under a mile. He was an expert shot with his M-4, and perhaps for the first time ever, his principal weapon would not be his SATCOM radio.

The rotors of Razor 04 spun up to takeoff speed. They had been on the ground at Gardez less than thirty minutes.

3

IT WAS NOT POSSIBLE TO PUT A FACE ON A PREDATOR. From a distance and without scale, the aerial vehicle resembled a model airplane a child would want to fly, with straight wings, an upside-down swallow tail, spindly extended legs that did not retract, and a front end that resembled the head of a sightless dolphin. And like a model, it carried neither pilots nor passengers.

That morning, to find its human face required opening the doors to an encampment of air-conditioned trailers a thousand miles to the west and north and a time zone away from Takur Ghar at the Prince Sultan Air Base in al-Kharj, Saudi Arabia. No one in the command and control net at

Masirah Island or at Bagram knew the name of the "pilot" who was "flying" this Predator over Takur Ghar at an altitude only a couple of thousand feet above the peak. He was paid by the CIA, which "owned" the Predators that were flying in Afghanistan.

But now, ninety minutes after Roberts had fallen off Mack's helo, a Predator was transmitting back to Saudi Arabia—and on near-simultaneous feeds retransmitting around the world—live images of Roberts and the enemy who wanted to kill him.

The drone's modest four-cylinder engine pushed the Predator through the skies at about 83 m.p.h. Two Hellfire antitank missiles hung under its wings. In its first wartime deployment in Afghanistan, the armed drone was being compared with the Wright brothers and Lindbergh for ushering in the newest era of aerial innovation. Indeed, over Takur Ghar that morning, Predator added a factor rarely, if ever, seen in the history of warfare. Its video feeds gave commanders in the rear a view of a live battle, delayed only by seconds, as they sat in the comfort of their operations centers at MacDill Air Force Base in Tampa (7,750 miles and eight and a half time zones away), at Masirah Island, Oman (1,000 miles and one time zone away), at Bagram, and in the Pentagon. The Predator concept and its execution gave commanders what they had only dreamed of, total situational awareness—making them like gods, omniscient and all-seeing.

And yet the promise was not quite realized. Predator's vision was no better than Mr. Magoo's, at an acuity of 20/200.

Watching the feeds, no matter how hard commanders stared and no matter what they wished for, they could not know for certain what they were seeing. The Predator circled over the mountain in a tight orbit. Its lenses, mounted under the aircraft's nose, looked down. At Masirah and in Tampa, commanders in front of plasma screens watched greenish gray blobs of fuzzy heat-read light from dizzying perspectives. The snowy peak of Takur Ghar offered few points of reference. Certainly nothing gave commanders enough information, second by second, to formulate decisions on which men relied for their lives. Without sound and with disembodied images flickering on screens, commanders were looking down "through a soda straw" at the peak. Actions that were taking place on the mountain at incredible speeds required viewers of the feeds to twist mental perspectives to maintain a consistent image. On several occasions, the Predator operator in Saudi Arabia shifted the orientation of the drone's lenses with no idea what commanders in the rear needed to see. Requested changes in lens orientation—shift there, look there—took valuable time, ten, fifteen, twenty minutes for each new view. Soon, with daylight, the clarity of the feeds would improve and perspectives would sharpen. But in the minutes after Roberts fell, a technology that could make day of night kept commanders very much in the dark of their own imaginations.

Despite the drawbacks, the Predator gave JSOC commanders at Masirah confidence. The feeds, however imperfect, empowered them in a new way. The effect of hovering over the action was transforming, and something else besides—something that could have been described as almost metaphysical. Another thing that no one would have anticipated was that the Predator's immediate, if imperfect sight collapsed the emotional distance that traditionally existed between commanders and their men in battle. Seeing their men shoot and run and die, seeing the enemy do the same, they gained another stake in the fight that showed in the strain of emotions. It was far too easy to portray commanders in the rear as insensitive and complacent. The Predator, as a new technology, gave and took away in equal measure.

General Trebon, who commanded Slab and his Task Force 11 team and therefore, overall, Roberts' rescue, occupied an area of the Bagram base where the Predator feeds were not easily available. The Predator feeds were available to Trebon a hundred yards or so down a frozen street in a building occupied by the Army's Joint Task Force Mountain, but the points of view in each building were light-years apart. That night every need was being weighed against every other need. The safety of Neil Roberts and MAKO 30 worried Trebon. Operation Anaconda overall, and its initial failings, equally concerned the commanders of Task Force Mountain, led by General Franklin L. "Buster" Hagenbeck, commander of the 10th Mountain Division. Conflicts arose, as they normally do. For instance, should Task Force Mountain's commanders delay or suspend bombing runs over the valley in support of the 10th Mountain and 101st Airborne divisions, at the risk of their soldiers' lives, to clear airspace to help JSOC rescue Roberts? Or should Trebon defer to Task Force Mountain's commanders and wait until the bombers completed their runs? Tempers flared and nerves frayed at the highest levels.

No one commander had been given the authority to issue orders to everybody else; Hagenbeck had no authority to dictate terms to Trebon, who in turn had no authority over Task Force Mountain. JSOC was fighting on its battlefield, and TF Mountain on its own. CENTCOM and its commander, General Tommy Franks, had not authorized Hagenbeck to command the special operations forces working in Operation Anaconda. Liaison officers sat in each other's tactical operations center tents, but the arrangement served a limited practical purpose. With no Predator feeds available to Trebon, he maintained command over the rescue, but the control authority for MAKO 30 went to JSOC's battle staff base on Masirah Island, linking itself to events in Afghanistan through a fuzzy Predator feed.

Everybody was working to save Roberts. The immeasurable anguish created among commanders by a soldier alone and in peril spread anxiety that bordered on panic up and down the chain of command. Watching blobs of green Predator light move across plasma screens, commanders felt a powerful, irresistible urge to act.

Whether Roberts was dead or was sending them a signal with the strobe that he was still alive, either way commanders still had to take Takur Ghar, or men would die on the valley floor.

4

AFTER THE FALL, ROBERTS HAD PICKED HIMSELF off the snow. He slogged forward with his heavy gear, firing uphill with his SAW. The snow tugged at his boots, and its crust and uneven depths made him stumble. The sound of his gun certainly drowned out the noise of the Razor 03's turbines returning for him. He was likely running up the slope to reach a point on the ridge where he presumed Mack would come back to pick him up on the fly. He was laying down suppressing fire to assist the helo's safe return. He probably tried to call the helo through his MBITR radio hooked in his ear, its small boom mike near the edge of his mouth, but he could not have known that Mack's radios did not work.

When the Chinook, feet over his head, had scraped off the northern ridge and disappeared into the valley below, Roberts was left alone, with his gun, grenades, and automatic pistol. He had nothing else now to rely on for his life but his own ingenuity and luck. He probably (but not certainly) triggered his IR strobe to lead his rescuers back to him, knowing they would come. He had reached a low rock outcrop on the peak near a dwarf pine tree when he was struck. He fell between the tree and a bunker, later identified as bunker #1, only feet to the east of a low outcrop. He was bleeding. Blood spewed into the receiver mechanism of his SAW, and this caused a bullet to jam in the chamber, rendering the machine gun useless. He lay in the dark in a narrow space between that low rock outcrop and bunker #1. He could not move and probably was dying from loss of blood, if he was not already dead.

Only minutes after Roberts was wounded, the al-Qaeda fighters emerged from bunker #1 and a second bunker, identified as bunker #2, about a dozen feet behind the first, guarding the mountain's northern and eastern approaches. They came out of hiding under tarps in a tented command and control compound fifty yards to the west on the edge of a sheer cliff, and from across the open saddle, anchored 100 yards to the southeast by a huge rock outcrop. In the dark, without NVGs, the enemy fighters could not have known if the helo had dropped off a number of Americans who might now be waiting to ambush them.

In a short time, they discovered Roberts. If he was still alive, he did not shoot his SIG Sauer. Indeed, his fully loaded pistol remained in its holster, indicating that his wounds were grievous, or that he was unconscious or already dead. If Roberts was still alive—and nobody except the enemy fighters on the peak was close enough to him to have known his condition—he could not have prepared himself for what was to come. A separation as mental as it was physical formed an enemy in soldiers' minds as an abstraction. That was how Roberts must have hoped they would remain. His enemies were targets at the far end of a laser on his SAW; adversaries were distant figures on a ridge that a 2,000-pound smart bomb, dropped from 40,000 feet, atomized in a flash of light and a blast of sound. Until now, his enemy was a charred hunk of flesh torn beyond recognition as anything human. Or he was a face as seen on the TV news. He appeared in nightmares. He was all of these images, but he was *not* another human being.

A Chechen approached him who seemed to be in charge. He pointed the muzzle of an AK-47 at Roberts' head. And if Roberts was still alive, the Chechen executed him with a single bullet. If he wasn't alive, then the shot was meant as a "security round" to guarantee that he was indeed dead. The local time was 0427.

Before leaving home for Afghanistan, Roberts had jotted down a few thoughts and sealed them in an envelope to be opened only if he did not return. "I consider myself blessed with the best things a man could ever hope for. My childhood is something I'll always treasure. My family is the reason I'm the person I am today. . . . My time in the Teams was special. For all the times I was cold, wet, tired, sore, scared, hungry and angry, I had a blast. . . . All the times spent in the company of my teammates was when I felt the closest to the men I had the privilege to work with. I loved being a SEAL. If I died doing something for the Teams, then I died doing what made me happy. Very few people have the luxury of that."

Now, the Chechen who had shot Roberts from close range bent down and straddled his body. He drew a blade and tried to decapitate him, cutting his throat to the bone. He bent over his body for two minutes, searching him. He found the strobe, which he handed to other fighters gathering around. Then he disappeared into bunker #2.

The other enemy fighters casually shook out Roberts' heavy ruck on the snow. They passed the strobe from hand to hand, perhaps without knowing its nature. One put on Roberts' black woolen watch cap. Another dressed in an extra pair of Gore-Tex BDUs. Another one, a Chechen as well, finally dragged the ruck and what contents remained, along with Roberts' helmet, across the snow nearly 100 yards down the saddle to a rock sleeping shelter lined with blankets, a few yards from a rustic mountain mosque that was nothing more than an arrow on a rock pointing to Mecca.

The other enemy fighters split up, with the excitement over for now. Some returned to the cliffside command and control shelters, others to the two bunkers beside the low rock outcrop, others to the DShK machine gun emplacement, and still others to an area to the immediate west of the bunkers under a pine tree, on which a decapitated goat carcass hung, where there was a camp kitchen with a gasoline stove and a shelter for the donkey. Some departed the peak altogether. Enough time elapsed for them to believe that the night was finished and the Americans would not return for their dead.

Watching the Predator feeds, what they imagined they saw horrified commanders at Bagram, Masirah, and Tampa, and set the wheels of imagination turning. Interpreting green blobs, they saw that Roberts was executed, as well he might have been. Their firsthand sight of the events excited emotions that would not subside for some time to come. Everyone wanted revenge. They wanted payback as much as they wanted to bring Roberts home. And they still needed to take control of Takur Ghar.

J OHN "CHAPPY" CHAPMAN WAS A THREE-PACK-A-DAY
man and beer-blubbery at 240 pounds on a 5-foot-9-inch
frame. An Air Force computer techie in Colorado
Springs, he was bored flying a desk under fluorescent lights in
a subbasement of a computer facility. He was single with no
steady girlfriend. He had already flunked out of university
halfway through his freshman year and had worked driving a
tow truck for Andy's Auto Repair while living at home with his
ma.

As a young man who should have been floating on a sea of
opportunity, he had chosen the Air Force—"three pushups and
you're in"—for no other reason than to get away from his

hometown of Windsor Locks, a middle-class town north of Hartford on the Connecticut River, where most people worked for Hamilton Standard making airplane propellers, for the Dexter Corporation producing paper for tea bags and diapers, or for Bradley Airport, where Chapman's dad, Gene, humped bags.

Now, after three years in the Air Force, he should have been on the upswing, but even the military had turned into a cul de sac.

One day, he heard about an Air Force job that hardly anybody knew about. Combat controllers (CCTs)—now *that* sounded fun to Chapman. He asked around. Fewer than a hundred CCTs were in the Air Force. The selection process was daunting. In the initial indoctrination course usually fewer than one in ten candidates made the first cut. The trials only started there. Once accepted, CCTs had to prove themselves worthy, because they were new in the special operations area. They had to find a way to fit in with Navy SEALs and Army DELTA. They were not shooters per se, and that was a strike against them in the special operations world, where shooting excellence was the sine qua non. A CCT's weapon was his radio, which he worked like an orchestra conductor with his musicians to call in weapons-laden aircraft from the sky. A 2,000-pound bomb could be far more useful in a fight than a 5.56 mm bullet.

In Chapman's imagination, CCTs represented glamour, excitement, challenge, and danger. And they held out the one thing he hungered for—hope.

When he mentioned his desire to try out, a friend laughed in his face. "Chappy, *look* at yourself!" he'd exclaimed.

Chappy did. Indeed, he looked deeper into himself than anyone would have imagined.

He had flunked out of the University of Connecticut because his heart wasn't in academics. His mom's heart was, and he loved her enough to try. Academics—book learning, reading, and writing—pained him. Bright and eager, he learned by doing in a world tailored otherwise; Chapman thought with his hands. All young men and women seek to prove themselves, but more often men need to overcome physical obstacles to make their mark, and Chapman grew up in an unfortunate society in which danger was associated with liability, leaving young men like him with unappealing choices. In high school and college, he dove. He had discovered himself to be a stoic who rose above pain. His high school coaches remarked on a persistence that bordered on mania when he was slicing through the air. The freedom of those weightless seconds made the ultimate punishment of hitting the water seem almost worthwhile. He forced his body into contortions and slammed against the surface, with his skin chafed to the color of a lobster. He would not stop until the coach turned out the lights. At the state championships, he and the team's ace diver, Michael Miller, dueled for first place, far ahead of the other competitors. On the tenth dive, Miller was fifty points ahead, and then he missed his eleventh dive. Now, Chapman went for the dive he had not hit all year, in order to win. He launched, and the motion was perfect—10 feet over the top of the board. Judges awarded him straight 9.5s and two 10s. He had won. But when he climbed out of the pool, he looked like he had lost. He said, "I feel bad for Mike."

He showed up in San Antonio at combat controllers' indoc training behind the wheel of a '75 Ford LTD painted gold over eruptions of rust. Duct tape held the bumper on. To Chapman, the car was an object of beauty. Still pudgy and down to an "occasional" cigarette, he looked at the other candidates—fat guys like him, skinny guys, short guys, tall guys, officers and enlisted. Nobody knew who would make the grade. Those who arrived in the best physical shape often failed the mental tests. Chapman was not the fastest runner, but he could run fast enough. Nothing was *too* difficult. He kept his cool under stress, where other candidates flashed with anger and were soon gone. At the end of indoc, Chapman went home looking changed. When his sister, Tammy, saw him, she said, "Damn! What happened to *you*?" He had slimmed down and was almost buff. The family could tell that he loved what he was doing. He said they were paying him to have fun with the best toys that Uncle Sam could buy. What a life. He had definitely found his niche.

After sweeping through tests and courses called the "pipeline"—air traffic controllers' and combat controllers' schools, jump school, survival school, scuba school, HALO (high altitude—low opening) parachute qualification, and such—he was awarded the coveted red beret of a fully fledged Air Force combat controller. At a graduation ceremony, he stood with seven men in his CCT school Class 8904.

Working with SEALs and Special Forces DELTA operators, his personality uniquely qualified him for success. He was balanced and skillful—he shot well, he dove well, he knew his job, and he had endurance. The teams watched him, assessing whether he might do something stupid to get them killed or slow them down. They did not have to accept him, nor did Chapman have to accept them. He enjoyed the SEALs. He thought of them as "cowboys with a wild hair" and with more ego than was healthy. They trained together. Soon, the team leaders with whom he worked deferred decisions until they talked them over with Chapman. They called him smart and focused.

He used his radio like a master chef in a kitchen. He always knew what ingredients he needed. As a CCT, he requested close air support (CAS) from aircraft overhead carrying varieties of munitions for use against people, tanks, buildings, and so on. An F-15 pilot would tell Chapman what he was carrying, and Chapman used words to draw pictures for pilots of where to hit. When nothing was preplanned, the tempo was faster than the speed of sound, and one consequence of failure was death.

Now Chapman was missing just one thing to balance his life.

He found her through a friend.

He had dated plenty. His wacky humor and his laid-back manner drew women to him. But he had not yet found the one. One evening he was feeling down and asked his sister, Tammy, who was happily married, "Am I ever going to find her? Will I ever have what you have?" Months later, at a party at the home of friends in Pennsylvania, Valerie appeared. She had a nervous laugh. She wore her blond hair long. She was about 5 feet 5 inches, petite, attractive, with a broad brow and a small nose. Her preferred outfit was sweats, a workout jacket, and sneakers.

On their first date, he explained what he did. It would be their choice together, or they would go their separate ways. She would be called on to make sacrifices. But he said, "This is my job."

The unusual, abnormal life of a special operations family became their baseline. With marriage, Chapman's life changed again. Slowly, daughters Brianna and Madison replaced his Harley and other toys. He made do with motorcycle magazines. The dream car was orphaned up against the garage. But he held on to his Pink Floyd CDs, his complete *Star Trek* collection, videos of *Planet of the Apes, Star Wars, Jurassic Park*, and *Meatballs*. When he was not deployed in places that he avoided talking about at home, he spent his time with Val and the girls. As a couple, they were open and close. They knew each other as well as two people can, and nothing was held back.

Less than a year after his marriage, Chapman was invited to join the elite of the elite, the 24th Special Tactics Squadron, assigned to JSOC at Ft. Bragg. He would call Val to say he was leaving on a mission but he could not tell her where. He said, "I'll call you when I get home." Val was curious about his job. Sometimes she could guess where he had gone by what she saw on the news. She understood most of his work. Killing was part of what he did. He told her that nobody normal wanted to kill another human. He was not in JSOC to kill. But he had no problems with it if that was how it had to be. The men in the teams seemed very normal to Val. She asked herself what made them special. They came from different backgrounds. Some were quiet, some were loud. But when it came to what they did, she guessed the special ingredient was a fierce will to succeed.

As for her Chappy, he was special to her as a husband and father who adored his children. He said, "I love being a dad. I love finding children's things everywhere. They're my treasures." He often put his hand in his pocket and pulled out a hair tie. "Little reminders of my little angels," he called them. He carried them on deployments. He played Barbie dolls with the girls at home, splashed with them in their backyard blow-up kiddie pool. As much as he loved to laugh, he was not afraid to cry. He wore his emotions on his sleeve: he hugged and kissed and touched and loved. He lived life large, never backing down from the expression of deep emotions. He told Val, "I'm a man, but I've got a *heart*."

When constructing a backyard deck, he just about drove Val insane. After he finished, the meticulous measurements, the precise saw cuts, the absolute levels, he stood back and told her, pushing his fingers through his thick brown hair, "This isn't right. It needs to be rebuilt."

She said to him, "Well, John, if we'd hired somebody to build it, would it have turned out as well as *your* deck?"

"No," he acknowledged.

"Well, there you go."

"It still isn't good enough."

Getting annoyed now, she said, "If it's standing, John, it's a deck. It's fine, hon."

And he replied, "Yeah, but . . . but . . ."

She had to walk away to avoid saying something she didn't mean.

They were living on an even, happy plane, looking forward to his retirement and to new worlds, when September 11, 2001, came along. Chapman was thirty-six and in the sweet spot of his life, and suddenly everything was different. That night he and Val talked about the attacks in New York and Washington. He was not surprised.

He told Val, "Everybody's packed. We don't know what's going to happen, you know?" as if to ask her if she understood. "I might not be home tomorrow. I know *you* know what's going on."

III
"He's in a Hurt Locker"

1

MAKO 30 WAS LIFTING OFF FROM GARDEZ, AND Slab was planning for what he needed in advance of landing on the peak. On the radio, he told the crew of GRIM-32, "I will need preassault fire. When we are a minute out, you are free to fire on anything you see on that LZ." He wanted to give Roberts a chance to break away if he was still alive.

As he orbited his gunship over Takur Ghar, working his end of affairs to coordinate the return to the mountain, what D. J. Turner had just heard appalled him. The risk of killing Roberts if he fired, Turner felt, tied his hands. What and when he would shoot was for him alone to decide, anyway. What if

Roberts was hiding behind a rock or had burrowed in the snow? Turner felt optimistic about Roberts' chances; indeed, he half expected to hear his voice come up on his radio. The Spectre would give him ample fire when they knew where he was, and not until. Turner did not want his search and rescue mission to turn ugly because he reacted too quickly. If Roberts came up on the radio and said, "Hey, I'm fifty meters away from those twelve or fifteen guys you are looking at," Turner would open fire. But not until then.

Ian Marr also had a say about the use of the gunship's weapons. He told the crew, "Listen, we don't know who's who down there. Most likely one of them is an American who may be captured or killed, but I am not going to kill him if he's alive." He recalled hearing talk about the SEAL team climbing the mountain for Roberts. Were the SEALs in the process of making the arduous climb? Could those men on the peak passing the IR strobe actually be the SEAL team, or might it be another special operations team that had come to the lost man's rescue? Marr told Slab that without a positive identification of the people on the peak, the Spectre would not fire its weapons.

Slab argued, "Well, whoever has the strobe when we approach the LZ, that's Roberts."

Marr told his crew, "I don't think the strobe is a litmus test anymore. Anybody could have it at this point."

Slab offered another idea: Turner's Spectre could fire on the peak as it approached the LZ, and whoever ran free of the other men would be Roberts.

Marr replied to this, "No, we're still not going to engage. If he fell out of a helicopter, there's a good chance that he's injured and can't run, and if he's captured, he may be restrained, and again not be able to run."

Slab knew a less nuanced reality. If Roberts was already dead, no amount of gunfire on the peak would change that. If he had been captured, the enemy would not have let him live for long; he'd be dead by now. And if he wasn't dead or captured and was hiding, anything that could be done to distract the enemy could help save his life.

The GRIM-32 crew was too acutely aware of the dangers of loose trigger fingers. There had been some of that already. Two days before, at dawn on Saturday, March 2, Operation Anaconda had begun with a planned aerial bombardment followed by the insertion of the "anvils." The bombardment fizzled, and when a local Afghani warlord named Zia Lodin and 380 of his Afghan troops, trained by the U.S. Army's 5th Special Operations Group, entered the field of battle as the "hammer," their transport of clearly marked "Jinga trucks" and pickups bogged down in freezing rain and snow. GRIM-31, with Turner piloting, lost and with a broken navigational computer, mistook the convoy for al-Qaeda and Taliban fighters. An Army Special Forces chief warrant officer named Stanley Harriman, riding with Lodin's troops, could hear the AC-130 describing what they saw. Harriman radioed in a panic, "You are describing us. You're describing us." A lethal barrage scattered Lodin's troops, terrified them, miraculously killing only two, including Harriman, and wounding fourteen.

With good reason to wonder whose side they were fighting on, Lodin's troops fled the battlefield and refused to return for nearly a week, until the battle was all but over. The incident chastened Turner—indeed, every gunship crew flying in Afghanistan—and they drew in their wings, becoming far more circumspect. Slab was faced with the consequences of that now, aboard Razor 04 and approaching the peak.

Turner told Slab, "OK, we do not know the status of the missing person on the ridge; we don't know if he's among those people or hidden nearby. There's going to be a danger of us striking him if we shoot. We just don't put rounds out of the plane willy-nilly. That's not going to happen. Are you sure higher is clearing us to shoot on that ridge?" He told his crew to keep the guns on safe.

Slab needed preassault fire. Roberts needed it, if he was alive. The gunships were meant to support the ground troops, and they were not supporting Slab in any useful way. "Motherfuckers," he blurted, thinking, *If their guns are so accurate, let them prove it now*. "Go around," he told Friel. "I want the fires."

"No, it isn't going to happen," Friel replied.

"Go around again," Slab told him, hoping that by going around they could induce GRIM-32 to cooperate.

There wasn't enough fuel to go around again.

Friel declared a fuel emergency.

Slab realized that the decision had been made for him. He now had no other choice but to land on the peak without preassault fire, which at the very least would have forced the enemy to dig into their bunkers and keep their heads down. He was about to do now exactly what he'd done before on Razor 03—plow into an ambush without the help of the gunships, which had failed him miserably once already and were failing him again, and would do so a further time before the morning light. There was no use in arguing with Turner and his crew. They had made their decision. Slab and Friel had made theirs.

Now that he'd denied Slab, Turner tried to help MAKO 30 in other ways. His crew identified an offset landing zone between 600 and 800 yards to the east and several hundred feet below the peak on a steep and snowy ledge where Friel might be able to get a wheel down and let the team off. However, Friel had already said there was no offset he'd approve of. He saw nothing even remotely workable as an LZ on the mountainside within an approachable distance of the peak. Besides, he was fuel-critical. Slab wanted nothing to do with the offset plan from the start. Climbing to the peak was even less of an option now than before. It was almost daylight. A climb from an offset would take MAKO 30 more than an hour, and in that time Roberts would surely be dead.

As GRIM-32 droned over the mountain, Turner studied the head-up display, an angled, semireflective screen against the cockpit window on his left shoulder that fused all the available sensor data in one place. Through heat signatures, he could see twenty-five people on the peak, who he now had to assume were al-Qaeda. Their numbers changed as more of them moved in and out of shelters, bunkers, crevasses in rocks, and from under tarps. Marr saw the same images in his screen.

He said to the crew, "We've been watching these guys for a while now. Two guys have been walking around that rock all night and I know they are bad. Why don't we shoot them?" He was asking because he had to ask. If one person in the crew objected to firing the guns, the trigger was not pulled. Now, upon Marr's request to fire, an officer in the cockpit raised an objection, and the gunship held fire.

Turner discussed with Masirah marking the offset LZ to ensure that Friel knew where to land. The back-of-the-envelope plan that he was developing called for Friel to radio him when he was five minutes out. At that time, Turner would mark the offset LZ with invisible laser light that Friel would be able to see through his NVGs. Once MAKO 30 had departed the helicopter, Friel would fly to the Texaco refueling point, if he felt the helo could make it that far, while Turner would remain on station overhead MAKO 30 to fire on the ground in advance of their climb up from the offset LZ.

After minutes went by with nothing from Friel, Turner called Bagram. "What's the status of that?" he asked. "What time can we expect that to happen?"

"They are now inside one minute out."

Turner could not reach Friel. The SATCOM radio on his gunship, he said later, inexplicably refused to function. He was forced to relay his communications through a line-of-sight system, and relays had a high potential for errors of interpretation and understanding. This kind of relay through multiple nodes was like the old parlor game of telephone, whispering a single sentence around the dinner table to see how garbled it came out at the end. Turner said that maybe the Air Force was jamming signals to prevent al-Qaeda and Taliban from communicating. Or maybe it was the mountains, or the moonlight, or gremlins in the systems. Or maybe it was what Turner knew from long experience to be a real possibility: that the radio itself had failed. SATCOM radios were unreliable at the best of times. They balked when overloaded with traffic, and Turner rarely had heard such rapid-fire communication on the satellite nets as he had since Roberts had fallen. Or maybe it was that Slab and Friel just weren't listening. They no longer gave a damn what the gunship said. The official explanation was that the radio jinx had spread to Friel's helo, and neither the gunship nor Razor 04 was communicating back and forth, relay or no relay. In fact, they were not hearing each other, like a squabbling married couple fails to hear what the other is saying, because no understanding of what was needed could be reached, the divisions being what they were.

Turner told his crew, "They're holding."

But they were not holding. Slab was telling Friel to go around again for further reconnaissance of the peak.

Turner relayed to Friel, "Look for the burn east." The gunship continued to mark the offset LZ. The infrared operator, seated in the enclosed booth in the body of the aircraft, suddenly shouted on the internal radio net, "Holy crap! The helicopter has gone back to the original LZ!" Turner shouted in his radio, as if shouting could help, "Don't bring that helo in there. It's a hot LZ. Hold position, hold position, hot LZ. Stand by for words! Hold off!"

Aboard Razor 04, Friel had already alerted his customers for final approach. The MAKO 30 team members stuck their faces in windows and the two doors, looking down through NVGs for a sign of Roberts and enemy on the peak. Slab peered through the bubble window. Nothing was going on that he could see.

Friel told him, "It ain't going to be good."

The time was 0458—thirty-one minutes after Roberts had died.

2

IT MIGHT HAVE BEEN COMFORTING TO THINK THAT the high ground was the enemy soldiers' only advantage. It might have been convenient to think of them as desperate, as having climbed to the peak in the dark of night, alerted by the clatter of attack helos and the crash of bombs initiating Operation Anaconda. But the enemy who had taken up this established position overlooking the valley, and who were there to stay, were Chechens, and they were superb mountain fighters.

The Chechens had come from afar—a thousand miles to the north and west of Takur Ghar—in many ways besides. Four months earlier, they had fled Jalalabad in northern Afghanistan for the mountain redoubts and caves at Tora Bora, near the Pakistani border. Surviving a relentless American aerial bombardment, about 1,600 young, zealous, and well-trained foreign terrorists, among them these Chechens, had slipped the noose to fight another day. In their desire to face the Americans in a fight, the Chechens had tried to stop Arab al-Qaeda fighters from fleeing Tora Bora and heading across the Pakistani border. And while most of the al-Qaeda at Tora Bora had done just that, an inspection of the Tora Bora caves by the U.S. Special Forces 5th Group after the bombings had harvested intelligence indicating that as many as 1,000 Arab Afghans, Chechens, Pakistanis, and Uzbeks had moved overland on foot and mule, by bicycle and cart, a hundred miles south to an ancient valley in Paktia province called Shah-i-Kot, the "Place of the King." They had not traveled to hide from American and coalition forces; they could have sought refuge on the tribal territories' side of the Pakistani border if that was their motive. They had come to the Shah-i-Kot for a showdown with the Americans in a place of their own choosing.

With a unique geography that was as suited for military defense as any medieval European keep, the Shah-i-Kot consisted of steep ridgelines overlooking a turbulent and hostile high-altitude terrain along a north-south axis that measured no more than 9 miles by 9 miles. As a battle space, it compared in size to the Civil War battlefield at Chancellorsville. The Shah-i-Kot was the Afghans' Masada, their final defensive place, and it had served them for more than two thousand years—against the forces of Alexander the

Great in 327 BC, against British colonial troops in the 1840s, and against the Soviet Union in the late 1980s, when they annihilated 250 Russian soldiers in a day, making the Shah-i-Kot the Russians' most costly field of battle since World War II.

Defenders of the Shah-i-Kot had never tasted defeat. Over the course of 165 years, they had developed and improved their fortifications, digging myriad caves and reinforcing them with concrete, stocking them with weapons, food, and other supplies. Some caves even contained libraries and kitchens. Precisely placed mirrors conveyed sunlight to the deepest interiors. They coordinated these positions with interlocking weapons firing lanes, having long ago calibrated and sighted their Russian- and Chinese-made 82 mm mortars, 57 mm recoilless rifles, RPGs, and machine guns. The overlooks offered the defenders an advantage of ambush and surprise. Historically, invading ground troops had marched into the valley and did not march out. Defenders swept down from the steep walls of the eastern mountains; on the western side, they fought from fortifications on sheer heights along the Whale. The valley trapped invaders in a perfect killing zone. And if bullets did not kill their enemies, they fell to altitude sickness and hypothermia at 8,500 feet above sea level on the valley floor.

The Chechens on Takur Ghar had already fled a secessionist war in their own country that had ground to a stalemate the year before, the latest spasm of a conflict with the Russians that dated from the late eighteenth century. With the Sufi-influenced Sunni Chechens fighting the "infidel" Russians, mujahideen from Arab countries had supported their jihad. Osama bin Laden and al-Qaeda had supplied the funds. Through the late 1980s and early 1990s, Chechen mujahideen fighters had migrated to assist the Afghans against their common enemy. And when the Russians retreated from Afghanistan, the Chechens, with no home to return to, had stayed on, believing in a larger jihad to convert the world. Bin Laden found these veteran fighters easy recruits. He paid them well and gave them a renewed purpose. They had settled in al-Qaeda training camps like Zhawar Kili al-Badr, where bin Laden officially had declared war on America in 1998.

In receipt of intelligence about al-Qaeda moving into the Shah-i-Kot from Tora Bora, CENTCOM ordered the commanders in Afghanistan to get out of their garrisons and find enemy to kill. The 101st Airborne and the 10th Mountain divisions were sitting in the Afghan city of Kandahar and farther north in the country of Uzbekistan, doing nothing. With a desire to get in the fight, the 10th Mountain Division's CO, General Hagenbeck, agreed to lead Afghan forces in the first large offensive operation with conventional forces in the war.

As the plan took shape, elements of the Afghan National Army under General Zia Lodin would form a hammer to pound Taliban and al-Qaeda forces against the anvil of the 10th Mountain and the 101st Airborne divisions. Under the heat of pursuit, enemy forces would run right into the muzzles of waiting American guns. The enemy's decision to flee was essential to the strategy's success. Taliban and al-Qaeda had always run in the past when confronted with a choice between fight and flight. There was no reason to believe they would behave differently this time.

The American planners, of course, hoped to use the element of surprise, but they conceded that before Operation Anaconda even began. Overflights of intelligence-gathering aircraft had warned al-Qaeda and the Taliban of the Americans' interest, if not their intent. They had taken up fortified positions on the flanks of the eastern mountains and the western flank of the Whale, and they spread out, waiting for the Americans to arrive.

The Chechen al-Qaeda fighters linked up on the peak of Takur Ghar with Taliban fighters from Afghanistan's Pushtun and Dari ethnic groups, who knew the terrain from long use and had already manned the bunkers on the peak, overseeing weapons hidden in bulging caches—grenades, RPGs, and ammo for machine guns and mortars. The Chechens, once they reached the summit, worked a command and control network from under a tattered green tarp stretched between a fir tree and a rock outcropping. They used reliable radios, no more complicated than over-the-counter RadioShack walkie-talkies, to coordinate a 360-degree defensive perimeter. They were ready for whatever came up at them, or came down on them from the skies, with a commitment to stay, a ferocity fueled by anger, and a battle experience that American forces had not faced since Vietnam.

3

A S HE GUIDED RAZOR 04 IN TO LAND, FRIEL
looked off the nose and saw muzzle flashes in the
early twilight, about 100 yards out. He maneuvered
the Chinook to a level spot on the ridge to the west of the low
rock outcrop, the bunkers, and the fir trees. Through his NVGs
he saw the rapid muzzle flash of the DShK about 75 feet off the
left front. He hovered 40 feet over the snowy ground and
pushed down the thrust to position the Chinook in a swale
with a ridge partly protecting the bird from machine-gun
fire.

"We're taking fire from the eleven o'clock," the left door
gunner reported.

Friel and his copilot continued to lower the huge aircraft. "Is it effective?" Friel asked.

"Hell, yes," the gunner replied.

"Then return fire!"

The gunner fired only a few rounds before his gun jammed.

The ramp went down. MAKO 30 went out, and Friel pulled power. In a hail of bullets, the Chinook dropped off the edge of the peak to the north and in seconds was gaining altitude out of the enemy's gun range. As they waited to see whether they needed to go back down for MAKO 30, the cockpit crew watched the fuel gauges, until they were down to 1,000 pounds, and then vectored for Gardez, which they reached with empty tanks, only later realizing that bullets had punctured their tanks in several places, as well as a bundle of circuits that controlled the left engine. At Gardez, the shot-up helo was declared non-mission-capable and brought back to Bagram on the end of a hook.

On the LZ, MAKO 30 went out while the ramp was going down—Turbo and Randy moved to the high ground off to the west, while Kyle and Brett, carrying an M-60 machine gun, walked (thigh-deep snow prevented them from running) along the right side of the helo and up the slope to the low rock outcrop on the peak. Slab was the first to leave the helo off the right ramp. He took one step, sank in the snow, and fell on his face. Chapman, paired with Slab, jumped over him and headed toward what he probably thought was cover on the high ground in which to hunker down and get communications with the gunship. He walked up roughly on line with Kyle and Brett to his left, then veered at a slight angle to his right, unknowingly heading straight to bunker #1 on the peak. The trees looked like they would provide cover. To his rear, a fairly broad snowfield offered nothing to hide behind; Turbo and Randy were running under fire. Chapman was doing what he was told to.

At first, the enemy shot only at the helo. But the instant Friel dropped the bird over the northern peak and toward the valley below, the enemy's guns went silent for several moments, as if they were assessing this new threat. In this silence, MAKO 30 made quick progress toward cover in three directions. As they moved, the enemy opened fire with intense bursts of automatic weapons and a recoilless rifle from three different directions—from the command and control area to the northwest, from the southwest, and from the north.

Chapman moved up in the direction of the peak. When he reached the top, he came on a bunker (bunker #1) hidden under a canvas tarp, and he poured 5.56 mm fire at three enemy hiding there. He was shooting at very close range. If Chapman had not taken this initiative and cleared the bunker when he did, the enemy almost certainly would have opened up on Slab, Kyle, and Brett, who were coming up the slope, Kyle and Brett on line with Chapman and to his left, and Slab some twenty paces behind. The whole team might have been killed outright if not for Chapman's actions.

After he'd wiped the snow off his face, Slab ran after Chapman. He caught up with him after Chapman had cleared bunker #1 and was kneeling on its ledge. A belt-fed machine gun erupted seemingly out of nowhere. The fire came from another concealed bunker, only about 20 feet behind bunker #1. Slab sought cover behind the right edge of the low rock outcrop. A few feet away from Slab, Chapman ducked behind a stubby tree, and the bullets split the air between them. Branches and dark-colored tarpaulins helped conceal the gun, but the muzzle threw yellow-orange flame in their direction. Chapman was on one knee inches to the right of the line of fire, and Slab was the same distance to the left, behind the outcrop.

"What do you have?" Slab yelled at him.

"I'm not sure," Chapman said.

Turbo and Randy found themselves a fight about 75 yards down the slope from Slab and Chapman and slightly to the west of their position in an area behind a hill. Kyle and Brett were fighting to Slab's left by only a few feet. They also were seeking cover behind the low rock outcrop, but they were firing to their left while trying to move around the left side of the outcrop to flank bunker #2. Slab and Chapman were facing a murderous hail of bullets trying to give Kyle and Brett suppressing fire, which would allow them to get around the rock and fire into the second bunker, but the intensity of the machine-gun fire pinned Slab and Chapman down, giving them little opportunity to fire their guns. Kyle and Brett sheltered behind the outcrop instead of flanking, and engaged to their direct left, over near the DShK emplacement and the command and control tents.

Slab was thinking, *Hey, there's got to be more than six dudes up here.*

Slab knew that he had to take out bunker #2. He tried firing a fragmentation grenade; the frag exploded but the machine gun kept shooting. His second grenade hit the canvas covering the bunker, rolled down behind the bunker, and blew up without effect. Slab looked over at Chapman. He was on his knees firing at bunker #2.

Suddenly, Chapman yelled, "Who did that?" or "Where did that come from?" loud enough for Slab to hear him over the gunfire. Slab looked and saw the glow of Chapman's NVGs looking back at him. He was thinking, *What the hell is he talking about?*

Chapman was down.

At first, Slab did not know what had happened to his radioman. He was distracted, trying to load his M-203 grenade launcher. In another instant, he looked again and saw Chapman lying on his side with his gun across his body, the muzzle pointed in the direction of bunker #2. The red aiming laser was moving up and down with his labored breathing. It was unmistakable in the dark. He was wounded but alive. Where a tree split the tiny red beam, the movement of Chapman's chest splashed fractured light in the branches. Chapman had his legs pulled up under him in a fetal position, and he was not moving or talking.

Slab's instinct was to help Chapman, but first he had to win this fight. For him to risk his life now to check on Chapman, Slab felt, was taking a chance with everyone else's life. There would be time to go back and check him in a few minutes. Slab was not afraid of what odds he faced now. The moments turned in slow motion. He thought, *One thing at a time.*

He fired the M-203, knowing that bunker #2, about 20 feet away, was inside the 40 mm grenade's arming range. This was a safety feature that had no place where Slab was now. The grenade had no effect. He hoped another shot might explode, so he fired again and ducked back behind the rock to avoid enemy fire. The grenade went straight through the tree branches beside bunker #2 and detonated harmlessly. He loaded a third grenade, put the launcher's sight right on the enemy's muzzle flash, and pulled the trigger. He watched the round hit in the snow underneath the muzzle. It too didn't go off.

He had six grenades left. He turned to his left and shot four grenades at the enemy firing from his left and rear, down near where Turbo and Randy were engaging the enemy. He turned right and shot two grenades to his upper left, toward the DShK position. Then, with the rounds spent, he threw the M-203 down in the snow.

What went through his head was, *This isn't working.*

What wasn't working was Kyle and Brett's flanking maneuver. Enemy fire from near the DShK emplacement stopped them from getting around the rock outcrop and in line to fire into bunker #2. Rounds were hitting around them from their left, and they had to stay low behind the rock to avoid being hit; therefore, they still could not attempt a flanking maneuver on bunker #2. Slab heard the cracks of the bullets against the rocks. He knew what was happening to Kyle and Brett. Snow was popping up around him. Kyle and Brett were trying to suppress two points now—near the DShK and bunker #2—at the same time. Everybody had their own fight, and nobody was winning.

Slab went over to Brett. "Get up on top of the rock and fire point blank into the bunker," he told him. If the M-60 machinegun fire did not kill them, it would at least force the enemy in the bunker to hunker down, and Slab was going to peel around the left side of the rock with Kyle, shooting into bunker #2 and, he hoped, taking it in one quick assault.

Slab told Brett, "When you see us with our lasers over there, shift your fire."

Brett replied, "Roger that."

Brett started shooting from the top of the rock, kneeling down, pouring M-60 fire on the bunker. The hot brass from spent 7.62 mm cartridges hit Slab in the face. He waited to come out firing from behind the rock. Brett was kneeling down but stood up to get a better downward angle. He leaned into the gun, firing at point-blank range.

Slab came out from behind the rock with Kyle to assault the bunker. At that instant a frag grenade thrown from bunker #2 exploded in front of Brett and wounded his foot. Slab looked up as an enemy fighter rolled out of bunker #2 with an AK-47 and shot Brett twice in the legs. The bullets pierced the flesh in his thighs without striking bone, and Brett tumbled off the rock, yelling, "I'm hit!"

"Are you hit in the chest?" Slab called. If Brett was

wounded there, the odds were even that the wound would be critical. Slab knew what he was doing. If he had to break contact under intense fire, he could not take anyone with him who could not move under his own power.

Brett replied, "No, I'm hit in the legs."

For the second time, Slab thought, *This is not working.*

He looked over at Chapman, on his right, through his NVGs. The laser beam across his chest was no longer moving with the labor of his breathing. Slab rolled closer to his right to see, utterly to his surprise, a donkey. He thought, *Jesus Christ, there's a fucking donkey? The gunship didn't see his heat?* He shot twice, and it slumped, its breath going out with an *ommmppphhh*. Cruelty played no part—Slab needed the donkey for cover from fire from bunker #2. He took a round in his pants cargo pocket that shattered his medical kit. A bullet grazed Kyle's knee, burning the skin above the cap; another round shot an eyelet off his boots.

"Man, I think I got hit," he told Slab.

Slab thought, *We are taking way too much fire from the DShK and the bunker. There are more than six dudes up here. I don't have Chappy or Neil anymore. And I got Brett wounded with the 60 down.*

He called for the team to break contact, without knowing the terrain; he was taking fire from three directions, and east was the closest way out. He would have to send Brett first. He asked him, "Can you move?"

"Yeah."

Slab moved behind a tree and crawled over Chapman's feet

in front of bunker #1. He did not have time to check his pulse and did not yell to see if he was conscious because he was apprehensive about identifying his exact position. He looked at Chapman closely, thinking that with the position he was lying in, he must be dead. He saw no movement. He took a last look and decided that Chappy was dead. And even if he wasn't, Slab couldn't drag him where he was going. He was worried whether Brett had broken contact. They were taking fire from the south to the left and from bunker #2.

Slab was experiencing a high-speed stream of consciousness. *Chappy's there. Those guys are there, engaging there, and we need to deal with this first, Chappy's down, OK, looks like he's still breathing. OK, back engaging this problem here, flank this way here, with Brett up on top, engaging this here, tell Brett we're going to roll off the back, get with Kyle, Brett gets hit, OK, what's up with that? OK, Chappy's over there. Crap. His laser is not moving now. All right, I'll try . . . one thing at a time. Muzzle flashes and bullets overhead, past my head. We're not winning this one here. We're not going to do the same thing again; time to move. Go back over to Chappy's position. OK, he is still not moving. I crawl right over him. There probably is a possibility that . . . Yeah, maybe he got wounded in the legs and he was just lying there regaining his breath 'cause it hurt like a motherfucker, you know, but he would have been breathing like crazy, you know? Heck, I crawled right over the top of him. I mean . . . you'd think he'd say something. Give me something, a grunt, a groan. Give me some sign of life. There's nothing there. There just isn't.*

An open space between Brett, Kyle, and Slab and the

eastern ridge, about 20 feet away, provided the enemy machine gunner in bunker #2 with a direct line of fire at MAKO 30 as they broke contact. Slab threw a smoke grenade to disguise their movement. He saw Brett disappear over the edge and to safety. He looked down below to the southwest about 80 yards. Randy's NVGs shone in the fading darkness. Slab gave him a hand signal and pointed out the direction east. Randy understood what he was telling him. Slab continued firing at the bunker while running for the ledge. If he could get his team together again out of the line of fire, they could regroup. As things stood, the team was not going to survive. He and Kyle were likely to be the next two casualties. And that would leave only Turbo and Randy to carry on the fight. Slab wanted to get out of the way for the moment, the gunship could give them covering fire, and then, after assessing Brett's wounds, he'd restart the fight.

From his position, he gave covering fire to Kyle, who moved through the grenade's smoke. Then both Kyle and Slab turned their guns to cover Turbo and Randy, who had to cross the open saddle south of the peak to reach the ledge, 50 yards across open ground through deep snow. The machine gun in bunker #2 fired through the smoke. Slab heard Turbo yell and saw him fall into Randy, who grabbed him and dragged him over to a tree stump near the ledge. A few minutes later when they joined up, Slab looked at Turbo. He was in immense pain. The bullet had nearly amputated his leg above the ankle.

Together again, Randy took a head count. "Where's Chappy?"

Slab said, "He's dead."*

MAKO 30 had fought on Takur Ghar for twenty-two minutes.

---

* Thirty-eight minutes after Slab and his team slipped away under fire, a series of curious, even mysterious, events occurred on Takur Ghar that defied resolution. Such was the fog of war even in the era of the Predator.

As seen through a Predator's murky lens at 0552 local time, an individual, A, presumably an al-Qaeda fighter who had survived the firefight just ended, slowly crawled from a concealed position about 25 yards southeast of the peak and began to cross the open ground beneath bunker #1 where Chapman had been killed; A presumably was trying to flank bunker #1 by surreptitiously maneuvering around and behind the low rock outcrop with the intent to come up behind bunker #1 and kill whoever occupied it. As A continued to make slow progress through the dim new light of day, another individual, B, also presumably an al-Qaeda fighter, emerged from hiding almost directly east of bunker #1 about 25 yards away. B fired an RPG at bunker #1. In response, A began to engage B at 0607 local time with an automatic rifle. An individual in bunker #1 then killed B with rifle fire.

Who was fighting from bunker #1, long after Slab and his team broke contact, and who in bunker #1 did A and B want to kill?

The most likely interpretation described a spasm of enemy fighting enemy after a brutal, close, and extended firefight with MAKO 30. An enemy fighter may have reoccupied bunker #1 after MAKO 30's withdrawal and fired on other enemy forces occupying positions roughly in the same location from which Slab and his team had exited the mountaintop. High-altitude mountain air can distort the location, distance, and direction of gunshot reports. Therefore, the enemy may have mistaken his comrades' gunfire for that of MAKO 30.

Another scenario introduced the Lazarus syndrome, which was hardly new to warfare. Could Roberts have been alive or miraculously come back to life? And could he then have taken the fight to the enemy from bunker #1? That scenario seemed unlikely. Roberts' body did not move from the moment he died of his wounds one hour and twenty-five minutes earlier.

Then could Chapman have been resurrected and slithered into bunker #1 and fought alone? Chapman may have been wounded only in the legs when Slab last saw him; Slab did not have time to check him physically, but a military coroner later reported that Chapman's wounds would have been "immediately fatal." He could not have survived more than minutes, and certainly not long enough to fight the enemy an hour later.

Viewing the archived Predator feeds, commanders wanted to see what they believed to be true—indeed, what they needed to be true. The SEALs wanted to see Roberts come alive and "take" it to the enemy. At Roberts' funeral service in Virginia

Beach, his commander told grieving relatives and teammates, "Neil turns on his beacon and low-crawls to a position under fire. Neil takes the offensive, firing and maneuvering against the enemy, and allegedly storms a machine-gun nest. Neil was shot several times but continued the fight."

Others resurrected Chapman, because his body was found in bunker #1 at the end of the day, raising the question of how it got there—whether he crawled into it, whether his body was later blown into the bunker by powerful concussive forces, or whether an enemy fighter dragged him into the bunker to search his body for weapons or booty, or to strip him of his clothing.

The truth will never be known.

4

Through the cockpit window, Turner had a skybox seat to a breathtaking "firefight in a phone booth." Bright tracer bullets and red lasers, like a futuristic war, had cut through the darkness down below. Infrared sensors showed the fighting, but from his altitude Turner could not tell who was who. He wanted to fire his weapons, but a 105 mm round in the middle of the peak would have a blast effect that could kill everybody, including Slab and his team. With his guns on safe, Turner watched "a very ugly show with no way to help." His earphones filled with seven or eight voices of his crew offering suggestions. Turner told them, "Hold fire."

Slab reported his situation on his MBITR radio. He said, "Hey, we're calling for fire. We're trying to get fire on top of the mountain. We're trying to protect ourselves. There's firing overhead. Two guys are down. We broke contact. We've come off the cliff. We dragged our guys off. We're up here. We need extract." He called for a quick reaction force (QRF), a platoon of Rangers continuously on standby at Bagram for just this kind of mission. "We need the QRF up here. I got two guys wounded and am down to three guys shooting. We're kind of hiding on the edge of a little precipice." Slab made his position clear. "I don't care how close; I know how you shoot. I know your accuracy ranges and I want you to drop on this target I'm telling you about. It's the only chance we got. I know how to call for fire and I know I'm danger close, but I'll telling you I need the fire now."

"There's no friendlies up top?" Turner's gunship asked.

"No," Slab replied.

In the cockpit, Turner thought he heard Slab say that he "had Roberts" and heard him ask, "Do you have him?" meaning, he guessed, did the gunship have Roberts sighted on the peak? The question made no sense to Turner.

Slab had not seen Roberts on the peak, and neither had anyone else in MAKO 30. Slab said, "I want guns on two big clusters of trees up there. Only two are up there near a big rock." Slab told Kyle to turn his strobe on. "You got the strobe?"

"Yeah, I got the strobe," Turner's gunship replied; with the strobe showing brightly the position of MAKO 30, the gunship had the assurance at least that they were not firing on them.

"Put fire on a big clump of trees 50 meters to our west."

The gunship fired about thirty seconds after Slab's request. Marr asked Slab to correct fire. Slab thought, *How can I correct fire? That's happening up above me over the crest.* He said, "I can't correct. You have to do your own firing." He repeated, "Big rock, bunker, trees and bunker and trees."

The gunship continued to fire. Marr asked, "Do you have anybody to your south?"

"No. I have all my guys."

"I have two or three guys moving to the south."

"They are not mine."

"Roger that."

Marr was referring to the huge rock near the rustic mosque 250 feet south of the peak. The gunship fired several rounds—it would eventually shoot seventy-five rounds of 105 mm altogether. Marr told Slab, "They aren't moving anymore."

Slab knew the sound a gunship made when it was firing 105 mm shells. One big thump of the gun going off was followed quickly by the bang of the explosion. Perched on the side of the mountain, listening to the cadences of thump-bang, suddenly he heard only the bang. Rounds were dropping close. Debris from the blasts showered down on him and his team. He called the gunship, "Do you have our location?"

"Roger that."

"Are you shooting?"

"No. Whoever it is, that's not us."

Marr checked the screens. A heat signature from a mortar tube to the southwest meant al-Qaeda mortarmen were lobbing 82 mm shells on the peak in a purely random manner, seemingly not concerned about hitting their own fighters. But they were getting close to MAKO 30, close enough anyway for Slab to mistake them for the gunship's 105 mm fire.

The mortar rounds added a complication to a deteriorating position. Slab wanted to hold as much high ground as possible. He had two wounded. Mortar rounds, he felt, were going to hit on target eventually. He had to move his team away from the mortars. He could not go back up on the ridge. He had to keep moving. But he could not move to his left or right without leaving protective cover.

Randy told him, "We can't lose elevation."

Slab replied, "We can't stay here with mortars coming in," and thought, *Murphy's law is still with us.*

They moved down the mountainside, but nobody could move down such an extreme slope and maintain control. The snow was deep, and Slab thought that if people were not trying to kill him, the descent might even have been fun. Brett went first. He took two leaps and slid on his butt 60 yards straight down to the next outcropping, where the rocks stopped him. Turbo went down next. Slab thought that he would not want even to ski down the incline, like a double-diamond run at a Colorado ski resort. Slab, Kyle, and Randy gave Turbo covering fire. The enemy was continuing to shoot down at them from the peak. Kyle and Randy went next. By now the ruts in the snow were icy slick. Slab slid down fast as a bobsledder. If Randy had not reached out to swing him in, he might not have stopped until the bottom. Strange though it seemed, Slab was grateful for the snow. Without it, covering open distances would have taken longer and exposed them to fire. He believed it saved their lives.

When they found themselves behind a collection of large rocks on a level shelf, Slab paused to check Turbo's wound. He did not take off Turbo's boot for fear that the wound would open up. The amount of blood he had lost already meant that his life was ebbing. The boot's insulation and the snow that had jammed in his boot top served as a compress and bandage. Slab, a trained medic, opted to go with the boot instead of a tourniquet. Turbo was screaming in pain. Randy told him, "You've got to knock that off." Turbo fell silent, instantly realizing the danger his cries might put them in. Desolate and wondering what could go wrong next, they stayed among the rocks for thirty minutes, watching the sun come up.

5

IN TURNER'S GUNSHIP, MARR WAS THINKING, *As if the pucker factor isn't high enough already.*

They were being ordered to go home—now.

Marr thought, *No.* His gunship would not leave MAKO 30 unprotected, and his gunship was all that Slab and the team had as cover. The gunships had failed MAKO 30 twice now, and Marr wasn't looking for a hat trick. He thought, *It's our decision while we're in the aircraft, unless the commanders want to come repo it.*

It was not the response that his commanders wanted to hear.

Marr thought, *Our boss may not like it, but we are not leaving.*

His commanders assumed that the gunship had not heard their order. The gunship was not heading for home. Part of the reason: Masirah was ordering them to stay on station; they were instructing Turner to disobey a direct order (from his own command) in wartime and to follow another direct order, placing him in an impossible position of not knowing which order to obey.

Commanders continued to pimp Turner to leave. Earlier, they had asked for his bingo—the time at which gunships were required to pull off to refuel. Marr figured their fuel loads. The minutes went by. The light brightened in the east. Reasons for disobeying were wearing thin with command. They'd hit the thirty-minutes-to-daylight warning window, and Turner's command demanded to know his intentions. His answer depended on whether other close air support, called "daylight CAS"—F-15s, F-18s, and A-10s—could be found to replace him. An AWACS (airborne warning and control system, a large airplane with a saucer on top that served as an air control and communications platform) reported to Turner that F-18s would soon be available off the carrier USS *Kitty Hawk* in the Arabian Sea, but not soon enough. F-16s and F-15Es were logged to arrive on station from their base in Kuwait, and Turner radioed them with Slab's grid coordinates. But having a specific destination and reaching the destination in time for a seamless transfer were different factors. Turner could do the math in his head: the jets would not arrive in time—not even close.

Turner decided to stretch the thirty-minute rule,

regardless, until the F-15s were closer in to give Slab and his team protection, or until his fuel supply forced him to pull away. In those moments, like Slab before him, he was caught between the forces of necessity and prudence. He thought of reasons why he should leave, but in the end, there was only one—Spirit 03, a lesson that was drummed into the thinking of every gunship pilot. It meant the difference between life and death.

The memory of the incident never left Turner. It had occurred during the first Gulf War, on the morning of January 31, 1991, when Spirit 03, a Spectre gunship, was about to end its mission and head back to its base. Daybreak was dawning. An embattled unit of Marines asked Spirit 03 to delay its return long enough to destroy a last enemy missile battery. Knowing the risks, the crew prepared to do what they'd been asked. As a consequence, an Iraqi on the ground was able to see Spirit 03. He shot an SA-7 "Grail" surface-to-air missile that struck Spirit 03, which then crashed in the waters of the Persian Gulf, killing all fourteen crew members. Those dead men, hardly abstractions, were friends and neighbors of Turner's crew. They had broken the rule.

Turner reminded himself that this was not his decision. *A soldier gets told to charge the machine-gun nest and he does, and he gets told to retreat and he does that too.* Yet as an Air Force pilot in charge of his aircraft, he had the right to decide.

Still, flying in circles at low altitudes and low speeds in almost full daylight made the lumbering gunship a target as obvious and vulnerable as the Goodyear blimp over a football stadium. Turner had been shot at during his deployment to Afghanistan—AAA and, he believed, MANPADs (man-portable air defense systems)—but he had never made his gunship a target during daylight. As if to underscore his fear, Turner's electronic warfare officer (EWO) reported that a MANPAD—a Russian SA-7 antiaircraft missile—was in the air and streaking toward them from the southeast. Turner requested a threat assessment. The EWO reported that the missile was out of range and that an avoidance maneuver was unnecessary.

Masirah came up on his radio again. Six or eight voices were issuing conflicting orders at once. Turner was told to disregard the command from his *other* commander, the one back at his home base, the one who had told him to obey the thirty-minute rule, and get the hell out. The word that Turner was hearing now, Masirah wanted him to remain on station over the mountain until he "ran out of gas or bullets, period!" In short, disregard "the whole daylight thing."

Turner had no problem with that per se. But the conflicting guidance frayed his nerves. He told both commands, "You guys need to get on the phone together and figure out what you want us to do." They did that, throwing rank around on the radio and creating further confusion while raising the level of tension. Turner sat back listening to the sounds of high-level shit hitting the fan.

His commander told him, "You are on RTB [return to base] now."

He was past the thirty-minute window and in receipt of a direct order.

Marr radioed Slab, "You got daylight CAS coming in."

Slab called and said, "Don't leave us."

The gunship had a two-hour flight home with no refueling tanker to hook up to. Their bingo was now.

Turner thought, *Hey, pay attention*. An AWACS called to ask if he had seen a second MANPAD, this one no closer than the first and out of range, but a threat all the same. His crew had missed sighting it, and Turner knew why. The blinding flames behind antiaircraft missiles were harder to see in broad daylight.

AWACs reported that two Air Force F-15E Strike Eagles inbound from Kuwait were delayed on a tanker. Turner did some quick mental math. The fighters were thirty minutes out.

Marr listened over the net. The traffic on the radio was enough to give him a headache, and it wasn't helping. Knowing what he was doing, he reached up and turned the radio receiver switch to the off position. Marr was saying, "We stay until *we* determine what the right time is to leave."

Turner thought, *We are not doing this because we think they are not right in ordering us; we are doing it because we know from talking to Slab that we are the only friends he's got. He's in a hurt locker.*

Minutes went by. The sky brightened. Turner put his game face on. Gas, not daylight or the conflicting orders, decided for him. But that didn't quell his anxiety and guilt. No matter how correct and even necessary his decision to leave may have been, he was putting MAKO 30 at greater risk.

On his turn out, Turner called Slab to tell him goodbye.

Slab wanted to know about the QRF. Turner knew that the Rangers had loaded aboard the Chinooks, and he called to ask about their status.

"An hour," he was told. Other voices on his net quickly reported the QRF's arrival "within" an hour, "a couple of hours."

Vectoring for home, Turner relayed to the AWACs grid coordinates for an offset LZ off the peak. His crew thought they had made the point. They asked the AWACS to relay the offset grid coordinates to the QRF, so that they too would not land on the peak.

Turner said, "Don't let them go into that first one. Two helicopters have gone in there and two have gotten shot up. Don't let them go back to the original LZ."

Finally, when the gunship was quiet, Marr thought, *We disobeyed orders for thirty minutes . . . we did not abandon them.*

The flight home was long and somber. Every man in the crew dreaded the news that might greet them when they landed.

6

ITH THE GUNSHIP A SPECK IN THE MORNING sky, Slab hunkered behind a cluster of boulders 120 feet down the side of the mountain. He could not get back on the peak now, with Turbo and Brett to keep alive. He had to wait for the arrival of the QRF. His team was in a hot spot, with enemy soldiers on the peak harassing them with rifle fire and terrain below them that was unknown and terrifying.

About fifteen minutes went by without the gunship to protect them. Then a pair of F-15 Eagles screamed past the mountain. Slab dialed the close air support frequency on his MBITR radio and asked the F-15 pilots what they had been told. "Nothing," the lead pilot replied. Slab went through it with him. He could not remember the grid coordinates for the top of the mountain. He pulled out his GPS. On the LED was the grid for where he was sitting. He needed CAS quickly on the peak. He gave the pilot his grid, asking for the bombs to be dropped 200 feet to the west and north of his location.

"Roger that. Inbound those coordinates in thirty seconds."

Slab thought, *Why did I do that?* Of many cardinal rules that ground troops follow, the first one is never to give their positions to fixed-wing aircraft. Slab called back and said, "Abort, abort, abort. Stand by."

Slab took a breather. With his GPS in his palm, he calculated the grid for the top and passed it to the fast movers.

"Roger that."

The F-15 came in and dropped a bomb that exploded more than 3 miles away in the valley to the northeast.

The pilot asked Slab, "Can you adjust for that?"

"How about four clicks out?" Slab was thinking, *I'm done with grids.* He said, "Look up. Can you see the tallest mountain out here?"

"Roger that."

"It's the only one with a peak totally covered in snow. You got it?"

"Roger."

"The ridge on top runs north to south."

The pilot said, "Contact." He saw it.

"I am on eastern edge of that slope, midway down the mountain."

"Contact."

"Enemy is on top in the trees."

"Roger."

"I want you to drop your bombs from the ridge line west and your final run in heading will be from your west."

If the pilot missed, the bomb would go over MAKO 30's head, and if it fell short, it would not matter.

"Roger that."

The F-15s dropped bombs and Slab heard them explode, but from his position, he could not know where they fell, or to what effect. The pilot asked him to correct.

Slab said, "I can't correct." He relayed through the F-15 to an AWACS. "What's the status on that QRF?"

In reply, he was told that the QRF was two minutes out, then forty minutes out. He didn't know when they would reach the mountain. The F-15 pilot radioed to him that he had to leave for fuel.

A quarter hour later, Slab saw a Chinook with a refueling probe, a Special Operations MH-47E, fly straight up the valley and over the top of the mountain. He tried to call the helo, but his radio was on the CAS frequency, not the helo frequency. Slab had no idea what the helo was doing. It circled and came back around.

Sitting next to Slab, Kyle looked and said, "I hope they are not landing on top."

IV
"Talk to Me, Buddy"

1

ARMY RANGER CAPTAIN NATE SELF HAD STARDUST on his shoulders. Nothing else explained his success or the uncommon grace with which he accepted it. He was soft-spoken, unrushed, a handsome young man with dark hair, a ready smile, a razor-sharp wit, and an eye for mischief. If he had ambition, he was a master of disguising it. He preferred to believe he was in search of fun.

He came from rural central Texas, outside Waco, a small town where people said "hi" or "howdy" and knew everybody else. It was a clichéd kind of place, yet real. Families practiced their faith, and the Selfs attended Baptist services regularly on Wednesdays and Sundays. They worked at taking in stride what came with life—the good, the bad, and, most trying for a young person like Nate, the boring. His mom was employed at a local hospital. His dad did what was necessary, from insurance sales to cabinet making. Weekends, he propped young Nate on the gas tank of his Honda Gold Wing motorcycle, and father and son would ride the roads across the range. The family knew hard times. Nate did what his parents expected of him, with time left over to do what he wanted—wandering the woods and plains for hours after school and not coming back until dark with a couple of dead snakes or birds he'd shot with his BB gun. What he wanted also meant a girlfriend named Julie, who'd been his sweetheart since elementary school, and whom in time he would marry.

He went to a high school with fifty-six students in his class. Because of the class size, he could play what sports he liked, not just the ones that chose him, and he was good as a football player, decent at basketball, and just OK at track. He pitched and played outfield and shortstop on a baseball team that was a powerhouse in the state, winning the Level 2A State Championship three years in a row, while Self was in the starting lineup. He ranked second in his class, the salutatorian, though he emphasized with puckish understatement that he had only fifty-four other kids to beat.

When he turned sixteen, he bought a truck with money he'd saved working in Crawford on a ranch that President George W. Bush would eventually buy and use for his western White House. On the ranch, Self "messed" with cattle, vaccinating and castrating them; he built fence, mowed, hayed, and bucked bales. His truck was a '65 Chevy, light blue with a white top, a wood bed, three on the floor, and a V8 305 under the hood. One morning later on, after a round of golf with a friend, he was driving on a dirt road, showing off, and the truck turned sideways and flipped 360 degrees in the air, landing back on four wheels with a heavy thump. Nate started the engine again and drove off, noting with pleasure that his golf clubs and a drinks cooler were still sitting in the truck's bed. "Gorgeous," he said.

The military was not a Self family tradition, and beyond personalizing G.I. Joes in the backyard, Nathan never gave it a thought growing up. But when he was pondering a choice of college, he knew he wasn't going to Baylor, ten minutes from his house. His mother and father had married while attending Baylor, his sister went to Baylor, his girlfriend Julie's parents had gone to Baylor, Julie would graduate from Baylor, and one of her sisters would soon be a Baylor alum too. Baylor was expensive. Self's family and Julie's family had Baylor bills stacked "up to here." One day, the fall of his senior year, Nate received a postcard in the mail from the U.S. Military Academy at West Point that he assumed was sent randomly to millions of other high school seniors as well. The price of tuition and room and board—free—attracted him. He returned the card. Reading materials from West Point soon arrived. To Nate, West Point was about the "education available, challenges presented, opportunities, and the chance to see the world and serve." He applied and was accepted on the early action program. It was his only application to a college. But he had agreed to attend a baseball tryout organized by his high school coach, who had sent some of the championship team's film to one or two Ivy League schools. Harvard invited Nate and his family to visit Boston on an expense-paid trip, and Nate was excited to go, if for no other reason than to see a city he had only read about in history books. But his father asked why they should bother. His father's mind was settled. Nate was going to West Point. And that was fine with Nate.

He and Julie, who were engaged in high school, romanced long distance while he was at West Point. Nate did well there, graduating, he says, "in the top 10 percent," which could mean he was first in his class, though he would never voluntarily admit such an achievement to a stranger. Most proudly, he played lightweight football and junior varsity baseball.

With graduation came five years of active service. He chose infantry because it was where he could "make the most impact." He and Julie were married while he was training at Ft. Benning. For a first assignment, he picked Germany, to be close to the action in Bosnia, where he worked with young Ranger NCOs who inspired him to try for the best the Army had to offer, with the most esprit, a long and proud tradition, and stringent qualifications for acceptance. Self's commander in Germany unselfishly stood aside to allow his transfer to the 1st Ranger Battalion, in October 2000, in Savannah, Georgia.

Self was a natural, instinctive leader whom his men adored partly for his trait of acting "a little immature at times." He was no fire breather, trusting his NCOs to supply that heat. He maintained high standards, which he enforced with reserve and calm. He relied on his relationships with his men and on his personality to create a climate in his platoon in which the men respected what he wanted done. That was how he wanted his commands to fall out. He used to say he had failed if he could only get his men to do what he wanted by being hard on them. He created a natural balance of discipline and camaraderie, earning respect while sharing his life with the men in his platoon.

In Afghanistan, one of his sergeants refused to eat MREs (meals ready to eat), the food that the military supplies troops in combat. The sergeant preferred to eat the food that his family mailed from home. He never tired of the taste of peanut butter. Self worked at sneaking MREs into his food from home as a practical joke, with the platoon waiting to see whether the sergeant could taste the difference. (He never did.) Once, Self loaded the sergeant's body armor pouches with a gallon of Army fruit cocktail that sloshed when he was called out on a practice alert, to the joy of his squad.

They had reached Afghanistan on New Year's Day, 2002. Their mission was to form a quick reaction force, a platoon that was ready on a minute's notice to rescue SEALs and DELTAs of the secret Task Force 11 and coalition special operations troops. The work was boring and only potentially thrilling. If the SEALs were the stars of the drama, rehearsed and aware of their stage, the QRF was the understudy, sent in at the last moment, often without a script and unfamiliar with the stage and the other actors. They were the players of last resort, on whom everyone more glamorous relied. To lead a

QRF required a subordination of ego and a willingness to do anything that was required, no matter how dangerous or boring.

The thirty-five men in the QRF were assigned two helicopters, both from the 160th SOAR. While the Rangers waited in their tents at Bagram for the alarm to ring, they prepared, practiced, and planned for four principal missions: medevac, reinforcing a unit fighting the enemy, combat search and rescue, and protecting downed helicopters and their crews. In anticipation, they charged their batteries, set frequencies, and readied clothing and gear to be thrown aboard a waiting helo. They rehearsed to reach Bagram's flight line in fifteen minutes from wakeup. They slept in their clothes.

As the weeks went by, Self had worried that his men might be losing their edge, in particular their shooting skills. He located an abandoned al-Qaeda training site called Tarnak Farm, near Kandahar, where his men could shoot live ammunition and practice team tactics and movement. For two weeks in early February, he and half his platoon trained on individual marksmanship, clearing out buildings on an imaginary enemy objective. The platoon shot the ammunition they were allotted, and their proficiency improved; they were again ready for anything demanded of a QRF.

On March 3, Self had already returned from Tarnak Farm to Bagram with half his platoon, while the other half continued to train at the Farm. His men slipped back into the routine, still yearning for a real fight before their deployment to Afghanistan ended. After months and years of war games, they were at last in a war—but so far it had the same boredom to offer as being back in Savannah. The only differences here were that they lived in tents, ate MREs, and slept on cots in cramped quarters that they had partitioned for "privacy" with imaginary lines. Outside on the base perimeter, hardscrabble fields were sown with Soviet land mines. Long concrete runways weathered in the harsh winter snow and cold; off the runways, against a picturesque backdrop of high mountains, abandoned Russian MiG-21s and MiG-18s gave the base the look of a junkyard. They were close to war but far enough away to be in danger of missing it.

The order for Self's QRF to spin up, if it ever came, would be issued from Masirah through Bagram's tactical operations center (TOC), the local hub of special operations, commanded by General Trebon. The TOC was located in a dilapidated space near a former Soviet air control tower. Inside, plaster hung down from the ceiling, and the broken-out windows contrasted sharply with the radios capable of hearing a complex array of SATCOM communications and feeds, computer monitors and consoles on temporary stands, telephones, and charts and tables for maps.

For Self and his half-platoon, nothing special was anticipated on the night of March 3 and 4. Earlier, when a special operations safe house at Gardez received threats of an imminent attack, he had checked the overhead imagery and drew up a course of action, but just as he was about to order his men out, word came down that the QRF was not needed after all, and he put his soldiers back to bed. He could not sleep that night and was in the TOC working on manifests at a computer and listening with half an ear to radio traffic when a call on the net alerted him. A helicopter was down, either due to maintenance or an RPG—both causes were mentioned. The 160th SOAR was part of Self's QRF responsibility. He approached his commander, an S-3 operations officer and a fellow Ranger—indeed, the ranking Ranger at Bagram—and said, "I don't know if you've heard about this. But I'm going to get my guys ready."

At the tents, where the men were sleeping, his alarm call was met with sleepy complaints.

"Yeah, you know how it goes, Captain . . . ," one of his squad leaders, Staff Sergeant Ray DePouli, told him, and rolled over.

Self said, "No, there's a *task force* helicopter down."

The Rangers woke up fast hearing that, thinking this might finally be the real deal. Maybe this was their invitation to a fight. Self left them to get ready and move out to the flight line. He returned to the TOC and listened to the radio. Now he was hearing that a soldier had fallen out of a helicopter. He did not know the downed helicopter was in any way related to this man who fell. He assumed the events were separate and co-incidental, but his QRF might have to deal with each one anyway.

"What's the mission?" he asked his S-3.

"Bird down. Trying to divert either a gunship or a Predator over it to get a feed so I can see it here. Downed aircraft, and we got a guy who fell out of a helicopter."

Self ran back to the tents. "Two things going on," he told his men. "Not sure what the mission will be yet."

Nobody was sure. The TOC had the downed helo's call sign and frequency and the knowledge only that it was down on the valley floor. No one in the TOC knew that it had crash-landed seven miles away from where it was shot up on the mountain peak. And when Jason Friel went to pick up the pilots, crew, and customers of the downed bird, the TOC finally formed a partial but by no means a complete picture of events. The scene on the valley floor, imaged by the Predator, looked altogether peaceful: one helicopter down in a flat area, people walking from the wrecked helo to the rescue helo. *Not like they are under fire,* Self thought. He asked his S-3, "Are we just going to leave the helo there?"

"Yeah, and you guys are going to secure it until we figure out what we are going to do with it," his S-3 told him.

"What about the guy who fell out?"

"We don't know."

Self thought, *Some poor kid just fell out while flying along and he's somewhere in the valley, probably dead, on the ground.* But when he returned to the TOC a second time, he was told about a strobe near the fallen SEAL. "You may have to go link up with him and rescue him," he was told.

Self had no idea that the crashed helicopter, Razor 03, and Roberts' helicopter were the same aircraft. He knew the map coordinates for Razor 03, with no reference to a higher elevation, much less a mountain peak. He studied imagery for the valley and was excited to get moving. Neither he nor his men had ever seen combat before. Now, even though the words "hot" or "in contact" were never mentioned, the QRF was going to get some of what they wished for.

Self had told his men to gear up and prepare to land on a flat valley floor, with no enemy sighted at the moment to worry about. They were going to stand watch over an empty helicopter. He added that they should be ready to fight any enemy who tried to take away the helicopter, and as ridiculous as that sounded later, it seemed potentially real and thrilling at the time. His QRF would wait on the ground until a salvage helo came to pull out the downed helo, or until it was blown up and destroyed. Self was ordered to disable the helo's guns and the radios and remove any sensitive materials left behind by the crew. He walked out of the TOC carrying his notebook with the grid coordinates and GPS headings. He had no coordinates for the peak.

On the flight line in the dark, the helo crews did not know who was going where to do what. Of SOAR's two Chinooks on the line, one was getting ready to transport fuel to Gardez in a blivet (a plastic bladder for fuel that is tailored to fit in the Chinook's back cabin). That left only one other helo to carry about 25 Rangers and Special Tactics airmen of the QRF, men who were milling around the helo waiting to get aboard. With that number of men and only one helo, Self told himself, *This doesn't make sense.*

The men from AF Special Tactics (STS) who were getting on the helicopter were strangers to Self. He asked them what they thought they were doing. "Flying with the QRF," one of them, Gabe Brown, replied.

"I don't even know who you are," Self told him. "Get off. I got my own guys."

A bizarre calculation went through Self's mind. *Team of four STS, and I'm expecting a team of three. I have room for thirteen including those guys. I'm only getting one aircraft. Nobody is at the wreckage site. Why do I want parajumpers and a combat controller when I already have a guy who can talk to aircraft? I need as many shooters on the ground as possible, not AF guys sitting around.*

"I don't need these guys," he told his commander at the TOC. "I got my own guys."

"Hold on," the word came back. "You may have to fly with the capability"—meaning take everybody.

Self asked, "Man, isn't the mission the downed aircraft?"

"We don't know yet. We don't know." A minute later, his commander told him, "Cut one of those guys off. Take three of them."

Self had to choose ten shooters, and the rest would follow in another helo; indeed, a crew was removing the blivet from the other helo to make room for them. Self would lead the way with his first squad, which he considered his best. "You're going with me," he told them. He asked for Marc Anderson's machine-gun team also, because he thought of them as his best. He had his own TACP (Air Force tactical air control party), Kevin Vance, to talk on radio. But Self thought the two AF parajumpers (PJs), Keary Miller and Jason Cunningham, and the AF combat controller, Gabe Brown, were pure fluff. Brown, Miller, and Cunningham climbed aboard and made themselves look small and inconspicuous in the middle of the helo. Self ordered his second squad leader, "Get down there to the helo crash site in the valley somehow."

The word came down to Self: "You can go now."

As his helo, code named Razor 01, was spinning up and about ready to leave, a Ranger captain hurried up to the flight line in a Humvee and told Self, "You are flying to Gardez, and when you get there, we'll give further instructions. Get this flight down there. Then you are ten minutes away from whatever we need you to do."

Self jumped on board the helo, and only then did he see Gabe Brown, the extra Air Force CCT, and two PJs sitting on the floor. "I thought I told you guys to get off," he said.

"Our equipment is already on," Brown replied for the three of them. "They decided we'd just go with you."

Who's "they"? Self wondered, thinking, Here we go again. Now he had one STS team who were strangers, but who were briefed on the mission. And he also had his usual team with whom he felt comfortable. He told the strangers, "Hey, Vance is going to talk for me. Who's the CCT here?"

Gabe Brown raised his arm.

Self pointed to Vance and said, "He's the fires guy," meaning that Vance, who trained and lived with Self's platoon at Hunter Army Air Field in Savannah, could call in close air support if any was needed. Self was choosing the man he knew and had worked with; without trust, the coordination of close air support could be worse than a nightmare.

Self also wondered why he needed the PJs Keary Miller and Jason Cunningham—PJs rescued sailors drowning at sea, didn't they? What value did they add to a real fight? He gave up, saying to himself, *It's too late now.*

Once in the air, Masirah radioed to tell Self what they wanted him to do. When they landed at Gardez, together on the radios they would "scratch in the sand" a plan to rescue Roberts and secure Razor 03. The radio in Self's ear crackled with questions from call signs he did not recognize about when the QRF—*his* QRF—would reach "here." He had no idea where "here" was, unless the reference meant Gardez. He thought he would be going eventually to the valley crash site, until he heard a call sign he recognized as the SEALs in MAKO 30 talking about a missing person. Self thought, *It's probably part of the reconnaissance effort, and MAKO 30 was nearby and going to find this guy who fell out.* He thought that maybe he would link up with the SEALs and everyone, including the lost man, would return to Bagram in the same helo. The SEALs, he heard on the radio, were "in contact with the enemy."

Self wrote with a grease pencil on a Plexiglas light board and passed the board around the back of the darkened helo. He was seated on the floor up front by the cockpit hatchway. Beside him was the SOAR crewman and medic, Cory Lamereaux, and next to him, standing up in the right side door was the mini gunner, Phil Svitak. One of Self's squad leaders, Staff Sergeant Ray DePouli, was riding near the ramp, and his men and their gear occupied the body of the aircraft on the floor.

Over the next fifty minutes, the plan changed twice. Self's QRF was told not to land at the crash site *or* at Gardez. They were told now to "pick up the SEAL sniper team in contact with the enemy, including this guy who fell off." Self wrote on his light board, "MAKO 30 in vicinity of the LZ in contact with enemy. We are going to land and conduct an extraction on hot LZ." He thought for a moment, then wrote, "Watch your fires. There are friendlies on the LZ." He told DePouli over the ICS radio, "I envision this being, we land, get off, link up with them, put them on, and fly away."

He envisioned wrong.

Self rose up on a knee on the helo floor and looked out a window. The darkness was fading fast with the rising sun. The Chinook was flying "nap of the earth," only feet above the ground following the contours, along a north-to-south crest. The Rangers started putting away their NVGs. Self was struggling to find out where they were going to pick up the SEAL sniper team. He unfolded a map and looked for the grid coordinates, while listening to the ICS for updates.

The plan called for the helo to drop off Self's half of the QRF, called Chalk 1, at an offset location a few hundred yards away from and a couple hundred yards below the peak; in-filtrations followed the same pattern, whether they were manned by a QRF or by reconnaissance-sniper teams. The other half of Self's QRF, Chalk 2, would land on its own offset LZ. The chalks would link up on the peak and turn to the task of rescuing Roberts and defending the SEALs.

Razor 01's SATCOM radio inexplicably failed, and all

communications now had to be relayed through their line-of-sight radio with an AWACS in the area, which was communicating with Masirah and Bagram. The AWACS sent grid coordinates to the helo, but choppy communications made understanding them difficult. Up front in the cockpit, Razor 01's air mission commander, Chief Warrant Officer Don Tabron, was sitting in the jump seat recording the grids on a notepad. He asked the AWACS, "Read the grid back to me." He listened and asked, "Are you sure? Have Masirah read it back again. Have Masirah send it again, whoever it was that sent it. Have him send it again."

Now, effectively, they were lost in a maze of conflicting grid coordinates. There was little they could do in the helo to clear the air. Tabron was trying to sort out the coordinates to ensure that he had the right one, but he worried less about finding the right one than about flying toward the wrong one.

Closer to the peak, Self stared out the side window searching for an LZ. The helo circled the peak once, then twice, turning hard. Tabron was asking the AWACS, "Where *is* the LZ? I don't see it. Where is it?" By now, the AWACS, too, was confused.

In the cabin, Self sensed that something was very wrong. While planning for one set of grid coordinates, he had received a different set, and wrote those numbers down to load into his Garmin GPS. But before he located a map set, he was passed yet another grid; a grid was sent again, and it changed again. Meanwhile, maneuver turbulence of a helo flying nap-of-the-earth was throwing him around the cabin, making it impossible to concentrate and study maps, much less specific grids. Razor 01 was less than two minutes to touchdown. Time had nearly run out. Self was going where he was being taken, and that was that. When he jumped off the helo he assumed that he would find the SEALs and Roberts waiting for him. *Why else would we be going in there?*

Flying over the peak, Self studied the terrain through the left side window. A Ranger kneeling beside him, Matt Commons, the M-240 machine gunner, turned to him and said, "Sir, it's a great day to be a Ranger."

The aircraft leveled out and powered into a hover. Self quickly scanned the terrain and thought with alarm, *There are no Americans here!* Weren't they meant to be waiting and ready to go? Was the helo about to land at the wrong LZ? Was that why the Americans were not there? Through the ICS, Self heard the pilot asking, "Where's this LZ?"

Self tried to calm himself, thinking, *They just are picking a place in the vicinity where the SEALs got shot up.* His next thought came with a kind of amazed disbelief: *We are going to land on the same LZ where 03 and 04 were shot up!*

2

RAZOR 01'S PILOT, WHO MINUTES AGO HAD ASKED, "Where's the LZ?" was Chief Warrant Officer Greg Calvert. From the first moment he had spun up the helo at Bagram with the QRF that morning, he knew only that somebody had been "displaced" on the ground. He'd waited to be told where the man had fallen off, but was never told. He heard that Predator feeds showed the lost man to be alive. Initially, he envisioned him waiting on the valley floor, near Mack's downed aircraft, but now he wasn't sure of anything.

After leaving Bagram, Masirah had ordered Calvert to go to new grid coordinates. When his copilot checked the grids, he reacted with surprise and told Calvert, "That's not where they told us Al was." Calvert had looked out the window. He was sitting on the right of the cockpit. He could see Mack's crippled helo on the ground. "This isn't right," his copilot told him. "They're giving us coordinates on *top* of a mountain."

Now, with two different grid coordinates noted on his pad, Calvert had to decide which one to choose. He said to himself, *We got people on top of the mountain. This is no longer a QRF for the aircraft but a recovery and rescue operation of personnel.* He was looking at a mountain peak and a valley floor, and he decided that the SEALs needed the QRF more urgently than an abandoned helo did.

His copilot asked him, "Is the mountaintop where they got shot up?"

Calvert had no idea. He had no way to find out, either. He quickly tried to recycle the radio. He said to himself, *We never have problems with our SATCOM. We just* don't *have problems with our radios.* He came to the conclusion that his radios worked fine and that the problems came from the outside. He thought, *Maybe they are jamming.* He tried to contact a gunship to act as a relay. The gunships were gone for the day. Using his short-range line-of-sight radio, he contacted the AWACS. The breakdown was starting to anger him. It could cost him and his customers their lives.

Relaying through the AWACS, Masirah told Calvert to get up to the mountain. Nothing was mentioned about an offset LZ or about the SEALs and Roberts.

Calvert thought, *All these people on a mountain 10,240 feet high, instead of on an 8,000-foot valley floor?* He trusted that

Masirah had a clear picture. He had no reason to think this was going to be anything other than a normal drop at a cold LZ. This was his first time in combat, and he thought, *Maybe this is how it goes.*

A T THE UNIVERSITY OF LOUISVILLE, BY HIS OWN sober reckoning, Greg Calvert had majored in soccer and beer. By the spring of his freshman year, he was ready to be "recaged," which for him meant a trip to the Army's local recruiting office. He trained as an infantry medic, then a flight medic. One day while riding as a passenger in a helicopter, he knew he was meant to become a pilot because, from where he was perched on the hard, cold floor, the seats in the cockpit looked cushy. He was smart and restless, and he made the transition from medicine to aviation look almost easy. After flight school, he trained in Black Hawks, Hueys, and Cobras, and then in 1999 he decided that he had the experience, flair, and knowledge to join the 160th Special Operations Regiment (SOAR). He had heard the rumors about SOAR that he found appealing. Depending on who was talking, their pilots were either consummate professionals or consummate cowboys, and Calvert thought of himself as both.

He had a nature that seemed tailored for SOAR, with boyish charm, boundless enthusiasm, and emotional currents that made him special and different. To those who wondered which extreme was true, whether SOAR's pilots were professionals or cowboys, he'd say, "Ones who think the latter don't have the *cojones* to try out themselves." Despite the inherent challenge, he was a gentleman, with the bluish blood in his veins of Lord Baltimore—from the line of the dissolute second son, James, whom his father had banished to Canada. With an average build, almost on the thin side, red hair and freckles, and a tenacious will, Calvert was a pilot to be counted on. His sense of humor, irony, and the ridiculous gave him a perspective few men achieve.

In imagining himself in SOAR, he saw Cobras and Black Hawks, especially Direct Action Penetrators (special-ops Black Hawks modified for attack missions, armed infiltrations and such). In short, he imagined glamour and romance. Chinooks, the ugly eggbeaters, did not have a slot in his dreams. Finally accepted as a full member of SOAR, the pinnacle of excitement and derring-do, he was assigned to an eggbeater.

When he reached Uzbekistan in December, he had arrived

in his first real war, ready to take it to the enemy. Instead, he flew "fat cows" and named his helo the "Flying J," after the chain of gas stations. His Chinook hauled 800-gallon rubber Robbie tanks. He flew in, peeled off, landed, got out and set up a one-man defensive perimeter, and waited to pump gas. And when the tank was empty, he rolled up the blivet and flew away. His excitement came by association; for instance, he had "passed gas" in support of quelling the prison uprising at Mazar-i-Sharif to Direct Action Penetrators, the sexy helos. When they flew away into battle, he was still a mobile FARP (forward area refueling point), and it sucked.

Then by chance, someone in somebody's family died, and that somebody was sent home. It was Christmas 2001, and Calvert volunteered to take his place on temporary assignment. He had packed accordingly, and now, weeks later, at the start of Operation Anaconda, he was assigned to fly the quick reaction force for Task Force 11. He was briefed. He met Captain Nate Self and shook his hand, but he did not think that anything glamorous or thrilling would come of the assignment. Nothing ever did. QRF was purely second string. With QRF he was still "waiting for something to happen. You were not the happening itself."

On the night of March 3, Calvert had pitched in to insert and take out special observation teams in the mountains overlooking the Shah-i-Kot valley. He'd flown to Gardez to flip-flop his Chinook when his friend Al Mack's helo had been declared non-mission-operable. He had ferried the broken helo back to Bagram, catching a nap in the cabin while a maintenance pilot took the controls. About halfway to Bagram, he plugged in a headset and heard "bits and pieces" about the plight of Jason Friel's helo carrying the SEALs back to the peak.

At Bagram, minutes after landing, Calvert was reassigned a healthy Chinook, code-named Razor 01, with "FDNY" and an arrow with a bolt of lightning painted on the hull in muted grays. A ground crew had started to outfit the Chinook with a Robbie tank, but the crew returned to take out the same tank. Calvert was fuming. He wanted to get back over the Shah-i-Kot valley believing that Al Mack and his crew at the crash site needed him to pick them up.

"Let's go!" Calvert was shouting at the ground crew. "We have to move."

He took off minutes later carrying as customers Nate Self's half of the QRF—Chalk 1, made up of ten Rangers and four Air Force men. The other half of the QRF—Chalk 2—was composed of ten Rangers and left minutes later aboard Razor 02.

4

ON FINAL APPROACH TO TAKUR GHAR, CALVERT
brought the Chinook in too slow, and his copilot,
Chief Warrent Officer Chuck Gant, told him, "Keep
your speed up. Keep your speed up. A little bit more."

The cockpit crew was looking out, front and sides, and
the crew in the back watched on both sides and to the rear
in the dawning light. That they could see no enemy soldiers on
the peak indicated that Turner's gunship had killed those who
were still alive after the firefight with Slab and his team. Calvert
came up on the peak from the south, over the saddle. He
picked out a landing direction for a level place below the crest.
He swung out to the left and came back around down the

mountain, and now he was moving up the spur, so the nose of the Chinook would stay out of a line of fire that he thought could come from the peak. He executed a swift "pop at the top" at 90 mph, and right before the top, he flared, leveled, and came straight down, like dropping on the deck of a ship. Over the snowy shelf, he bled off airspeed and started a cyclic climb by pulling off the stick but keeping the power on; the Chinook was now maxed out on power with the weight of the passengers at 10,240 feet. He was holding power, bleeding off airspeed. He could feel his copilot join him on the controls, just in case.

Fifty feet above the ground, as soon as Calvert flared the Chinook, bullets crashed through the chin bubble. In the right seat, he watched as holes pinged through the windshield glass. Two bullets hit his helmet and jerked his head left, as if a hammer had slammed his skull. In the same spray of fire, he was shot eight times across his chest, one bullet lodging in the Kevlar armor while seven flecked off.

On the controls, he increased the Chinook's speed; he was aborting the landing. He pulled power and was nosing the bird up when he heard the tortured shredding of the right engine's turbine blades. The left engine surged to pick up the load left by the disintegrating engine. Calvert had to gain airspeed if he wanted to get out of there. He nosed the helo over. Only seconds had gone by since the first shots. He was not going to make it over the ridge. The shelf that overlooked the valley stood too high. To his right, the enemy was pounding the helo with machine-gun and RPG fire.

He was going through a decision process—whether to attempt a go-around or make the landing. The smartest course of action now was to land.

A bullet hit copilot Chuck Gant in the right thigh. He was holding the controls with Calvert, who said only, "Not going to make it. Got to land." He threw the helo in a flare, careful not to raise the thrust, to bleed off any inertia in the blades. He nosed the Chinook over and pulled it back. As they went down, he held the cyclic neutral. "Oh, shit, this's going to hurt," he shouted. The heat from continuous blast of the right door mini gun warmed his cheek through the open side window. The helo hit the ground at 500 feet per minute into a 20-degree slope. He pushed the controls to the left and pulled thrust left in the engine. Calvert thought it "was the best goddamned landing I have ever done in my life."

Phil Svitak, the right mini gunner, yelled, "Troops firing two o'clock, engaging."

"Guy at three o'clock," Calvert called out to him.

The helo was taking rounds from both ends and sides. The left door gunner, Dave Dube, was hit in the leg with a round that shattered his knife, piercing his flesh with metal shards. Svitak's mini gun went silent. A boot flew past Calvert's face and brushed his helmet. The air mission commander in the jump seat, Don Tabron, rolled out the back of the helo. Gant had pulled the engines' stop switches, and he slapped Calvert's shoulder before he popped the left emergency panel door and dropped out onto the snow. Bullets shredded the cockpit's plastic and metal, glass and insulation. The back ramp would be down and the Rangers would be running off, Calvert thought. If he failed to hold the helo into the slope now, the Chinook would roll over on the Rangers, whom he presumed were already out and would be huddling by the aircraft.

Calvert held his hands on the controls until the helo stabilized on the incline. As the blades churned down, the aircraft wobbled dangerously, but because of Calvert, it did not roll over. The aircraft settled, and with the rotor brake on, the blades stopped. Calvert said to himself, "OK, it's down, it's stable."

He peered through the blown-out windshield. An enemy stared at him over the low rock outcrop, the same low formation on which earlier Brett had been shot in the legs. Calvert held the stick with his knees and brought up his M-4 rifle, in which he already had chambered a round. He flipped off the safety without thinking and fired two bursts out the Dairy Queen, the side slide window. He reached up for the emergency handle with his left hand as he fired another burst from his M-4. He kicked out the bottom of the door, and suddenly, when he reached back to get his weapon, his hand was on fire. Three bullets had hit him—one of them an orange tracer coated with burning phosphorous. He was also hit in the left leg. Two bullets had lodged in the muscle of the web between his thumb and forefinger. A single tendon and ulna held his hand to his arm. With his radial artery severed, deep red blood pulsed three feet in the air, spraying the cockpit consoles with a curtain of blood. In disbelief, he stared at his glowing, smoking hand. His glove covered his fingers, but the impact somehow had turned the glove inside out.

In the gunfire, an electrical fire burst from the cockpit's right side panels. Reaching up with his good hand, Calvert felt where his face was burned and blistering from the heat. Acting out of purely primitive survival instinct, he put his M-4 on the center console between the pilots' seats and rolled over to protect himself. He tried to stop the bleeding in his hand by holding a pressure point, but he was losing blood too fast. At this rate of loss, he had less than four minutes before he would bleed out. The jump seat was set in an up position where Tabron had left it blocking the companionway to the cabin, and Calvert crawled over the center console and the seat. The bat belt on his flight jumpsuit snagged on a toggle switch. He could not move. He kicked against the panel and when the snag broke suddenly, he flew out of the cockpit back into the cabin like he'd been expelled. He was thinking, *Now what?*

5

ORDINARILY, SOAR MEDIC CORY LAMEREAUX positioned himself beside the right mini gunner; this morning it was Phil Svitak. Lamereaux's med-ruck casualty evacuation package—a compartmented duffle that held his medical requirements for the field, right up to but not including surgical instruments—filled a space between Svitak and the companionway to the cockpit. Lamereaux tried to stay out of Svitak's way. His job was in the aircraft, working as an EMS technician treating casualties carried from the field while the helicopter was transporting them to a forward surgical team. He kept wounded men alive and stable in transit.

On the final approach, he was holding on, looking over

Svitak's shoulder to help with ground surveillance. Lamereaux knew Svitak from other missions and he was surprised when he told him suddenly, "Doc, move back!" Lamereaux gave him a questioning look; he thought he got along with Svitak.

Svitak leaned into his mini gun, searching the peak for targets. Lamereaux moved to Svitak's right, forward to look out the first cabin window. He squatted down and grasped a bar on the bulkhead to brace himself. He peered down at a panorama of smoldering fires and blackened gouges where explosives had charred the earth. The pilot was flying in slow, Lamereaux thought, into a sloped landing on a saddle of snow, but otherwise this was shaping up as routine.

Immediately, there was a boom and an engine whined out of control, redlining its RPMs. Ten or fifteen feet off the ground, the helo nosed over and crashed. Enemy fire poured into the cabin. Like everyone else, the crash threw Lamereaux forward and down on the floor. Stunned for several seconds, he was on his back, with blood pooling in his eye sockets. He shook his head, telling himself, with more hope than certainty, "Hey, I'm OK. I'm OK." He had taken three rounds to his flight helmet. The impact had knocked him back. One bullet had penetrated his nonballistic flight helmet, stopping just short of his skull but piercing his scalp. A shard of flying metal had lacerated his eyebrow with a quarter-inch cut that bled profusely, accounting for the blood in his eye sockets. When he figured out the nature of his own wounds, he thought, *Thank God I'm OK.*

The enemy was targeting the Chinook. It was dawn, and

the huge machine was hard to miss where it had landed, out in the open in a natural bowl layered in snow. The enemy's intent was to kill the *aircraft*. Their every weapon, except the 12.7 mm DShK, was dialed on automatic and putting fire into the bird. Only a movie—say, the final scene of *Bonnie and Clyde*, when the law riddles the outlaws' sedan—could describe how bullets and other fires from a recoilless rifle and grenades shredded the helo. The ambush shocked the QRF and crew of Razor 01, but the enemy fighters' true shock must have been greater—that *their* enemy had sent a third plump target down the sights of their guns.

A bedlam of bullets thundered against the metal walls and sounded over the panicked shouts of men, their screams of pain, and the rumble of chaos and commotion. The impact had thrown the QRF down and forward in a single violent motion. As the Rangers struggled to unhook safety harnesses from the floor, a horrible reality began to dawn: they were trapped targets in a large, unprotected shooting gallery. Bullets came through the cabin interior from three or four directions. That this was happening to them now created an atmosphere of incredulity, as old as armed combat; they had read about this moment as thrilling. But now, there was no romance and no charge. They reacted to the immediacy of violent death with animal instincts and the habits of training.

Svitak was hit while the helo was still flaring. Two rounds from an AK-47 caught him an inch below his armor. He was thrown straight back, as though he'd been slammed by a truck.

Lamereaux leaned over him. *Shake and shock*, he thought.

"Talk to me, buddy," he yelled in his face. Svitak had saved Lamereaux's life by telling him to back away from the door. He was pale, almost ashen. Lamereaux tested his carotid artery for a pulse and felt a faint beat. He swept him for blood, checking his body for injuries, and could not find a mortal wound. Svitak was dressed in a thick, form-fitting cold-weather suit called a Mustang. Lamereaux turned away from him for an instant to move up closer to the bulkhead; bullets cracked past him through the companionway between the cockpit and the cabin, and over him through the right gunner's door. In a crouch, he swiveled around to Svitak and again checked his carotid. Svitak had no pulse. He was dead. Lamereaux did not attempt CPR. He needed to aid the next wounded guy. That was how it went.

He looked to his left. The door mini gunner across from Svitak, Dave Dube, was slumped against the forward bulkhead beside the companionway, his face pale, his legs akimbo in front of his body. Lamereaux was crawling to help him when Calvert shot out of the cockpit and landed face-to-face with him on the floor, screaming, "I'm hit, I'm hit!"

A gout of arterial blood spewed from Calvert's wrist. Lamereaux had seen this kind of thing in movies, but in actuality, the sight was hard to believe—a stream of bright red blood, pulsing stronger, then weaker, with each beat of his heart. He reached in his medic's vest for a tourniquet. From reading medical books, he knew that he had two or three minutes to bring the bleeding under control, or Calvert would die. Lamereaux was thinking, methodically, *Occlude all blood flow.*

The two elbow bones protected the arteries. In trauma care, a tourniquet was usually applied above the elbow to pinch off the bleeding by pressing the artery against the bone. But victims with this kind of care, as a result, often lost their arms below the tourniquets to amputation. Lamereaux thought to tie off Calvert's arm *below* his elbow. At least he'd try it there. He might lose his hand, which was lost anyway, as far as Lamereaux could tell, but not his arm. The stanched wound oozed blood, and he further applied a pressure dressing to the hole in Calvert's wrist.

Calvert was in shock. His hand was all but gone. The pressure of the tourniquet bore down on the nerves in his arm. "Goddamn, Cory, that hurts," he told him, between screams of pain, as Lamereaux cranked down harder on the tourniquet. Calvert thought he would pass out from the agony.

"You got your morphine?" Lamereaux asked him.

Calvert carried a 10 mg Tubex of morphine sulfate in his jumpsuit sleeve pocket. "Yeah," he replied.

"Give it to me." He grabbed the vial, and Calvert never saw it again; morphine at that altitude and in the cold threatened his life almost as much as his wound.

Calvert had the presence of mind, despite the pain of his injuries, to ask one of the Rangers to give him all the survival radios. Using the radios one at a time, he broadcast, "Razor 01 is down! Razor 01 is down!" He gave their grid coordinates, then added, "Numerous casualties and taking fire." He got no reply, but he knew that someone would hear it.

The left gunner, Dube, looked worrisomely pale and was

sweating in the cold. Clearly in shock, he was staring straight ahead at nothing. As Lamereaux was turning to attend to him, he heard a crew chief back in the cabin yell, "Two patients off the tail," and he knew others were either wounded or dead. They were in a hurt locker, and unless somebody did something soon, with the bullets flying down the length of the helo and through its sides, they would all be dead.

Halfway down the cabin, crawling on his stomach, Lamereaux came on Private First Class Marc Anderson. He was a big guy, the M-240 machine gunner. Without checking him, Lamereaux guessed he was dead. He had been struck in the heart even as the helo was hitting the ground. The PJ, Jason Cunningham, was working on him. But clearly, only seconds after crashing, his death was apparent in spite of everything Cunningham was trying to do.

Lamereaux turned back around to attend to Dube at the front end of the helo. He lowered his head as bullets pierced the bird's walls and flew through the companionway and down the length of the fuselage. Daylight popped in the cabin's walls one bullet at a time, like a cartoonish new day dawning as seen from the inside of a colander. Bullet-blasted padding on the walls filled the air with drifting material, like a snowfall. Lamereaux pressed himself flat on his stomach. The helo's left-side external self-sealing gas tank was absorbing most of the bullets from that direction, and Lamereaux felt protected as long as he stayed low. He was gathering stock when an RPG flew through the opened right cabin door where Svitak had been standing and exploded against the left interior wall inches from Calvert, Dube, and Lamereaux. The RPG struck a high-altitude oxygen bottle, which exploded, spraying shrapnel in every direction. A fire in the soundproofing started to burn its way along the wall.

A crew chief on the ramp shouted, "Man, you *gotta* put that fire out."

"Yeah, OK." Lamereaux looked at an empty fixture on the bulkhead where he expected to find an extinguisher. "Throw me the one from the back," he shouted.

The fire was spreading fast along the insulation. Lamereaux rose up on a knee, leaving the modest protection of the level of the external gas tank. He sprayed the fire for several dangerous seconds with the extinguisher's foam until he was satisfied that the flames would not spread. The cabin was choked with acrid smoke. With the enemy's bullets cutting the air down the length of the aircraft, and the fire, Lamereaux needed to shift the casualties outside, and yet the Rangers who had run out of the helo were taking hits. Waiting in the cabin, he thought, *Well, at least the fuel tanks haven't blown up yet.*

6

RAY DePOULI, THE RANGER PLATOON SERGEANT, had never felt such turbulence as when the right engine was hit. He saw a ball of flame and heard the enemy's machine gun rake the helo's right side. For some reason, he had thought they were still flying at 5,000 feet. He told himself, *Oh, shit, we're going to crash.* He grabbed the metal rail on the floor that his safety harness was snapped into, and held on, thinking, like a frightened kid over the first huge drop of a roller coaster, *Here we go.*

When they crashed, he saw only light, thinking, *What the hell are we doing? What has happened?*

The crew chief in back by the ramp yelled, "Go!"

DePouli, a hard-nosed NCO from a suburb of Seattle who expected the best out of his men and usually got it, ran five feet straight off the back ramp in the open air. No matter how tough the going, he was never one to complain, and if he had a beef—like a complaint, but without the whining—he had a solution. Standing out on the open snow in the morning twilight, he scanned the terrain to his left and right. The depth of the snow surprised him. He felt a push and was spun around. A 7.62 mm round had hit and lodged in his armor back plate an eighth of an inch from the bottom edge. He recovered from the spin, catching a glint of movement on the ridge to the left of the helo. An al-Qaeda fighter lying on his belly behind a machine gun was pouring rounds straight into the helicopter at close range. DePouli acted out of pure instinct, "going with the motion." He seemed to be viewing himself from a dreamlike distance as he brought up his M-4 rifle to fire. He snapped off the safe and unloaded a thirty-round magazine into the gunner in one continuous burst. He watched the man's head pop with a pink mist. DePouli dropped to one knee to change out the magazine. On his left lay a dead enemy whom either Dave Dube or the left ramp gunner had shot while on final. DePouli pumped rounds into him to be sure he was dead.

He went prone on the snow, watching to the left. Bullets were flying over him. Rangers were balled up on the ramp in their panic and haste to get out of the burning helo. Sean Edwards, the left ramp crew chief, partly blocked the ramp; the crash had slammed him to the steel floor harder than the other passengers and injured his knee. Ranger Specialist Matt Commons lay facedown on the ramp, a pool of blood spreading from a wound in his head into the snow. Ranger Sergeant Bradley Crose was sprawled on his belly with his boots on the ramp, his torso in the snow. He was not moving. Staff Sergeant Josh Walker, running out with DePouli, stopped at Crose. He grabbed him and started to pull off his body armor. "He's dead," he said.

The PJ, Jason Cunningham, checked him. "He's got a pulse," he said. He checked again and shook his head.

With a glance, DePouli had a sinking feeling that Crose wasn't going to make it.

Sergeant Aaron Totten-Lancaster, a twenty-six-year-old blue-eyed SAW gunner from New Jersey, had exited the helo holding the handle on Crose's body armor. A minute before, he'd been thinking about the beauty of these mountains in a sunrise. He knew what to do when they landed. The platoon had rehearsed until the motion was almost mindless, meant to be clean. He thought Crose had slipped on the ramp. He looked down and yelled, "Hey, Sarge. Get up!" With a glance, he knew Crose wasn't getting up. He went to the right side of the aircraft and he kept running. He searched for the enemy and nearly tripped over a dead al-Qaeda fighter as he made his way toward the nose of the helo up by the refueling probe. He saw the copilot, Gant, fall out of the cockpit emergency door. Totten-Lancaster was shoulder-firing his SAW. He needed more stability for accuracy, and he laid the weapon on the snow, but the bipod sank in up to its barrel. He braced the gun against his body, and now he sank in the snow. He was firing from the one o'clock position of the helo. Gant was appealing to him for help. "Hold on a second," Totten-Lancaster told him. "We have to get these guys first." He watched an enemy fighter aim an RPG from around the rock outcrop. Totten-Lancaster was angry about the attack. He smelled the cordite and the overpowering pine oils in the air from bullets shredding the trees. He got down prone and rested his SAW on the helo's emergency door, lying flat on the snow. He heard a blast and at the same instant felt pain in his right leg. His right leg kicked over his left leg. The feeling reminded him of a time when he had grabbed his uncle's electric fence. He didn't think anything more about the wound, but when he got up to run across the snowfield for a rock to hide behind, he fell on his face. His right foot wasn't working. Shrapnel had lodged next to the nerve that controlled its up-and-down movement. He rolled over to the rock, trying to stay under the enemy fire. He was thinking, *We're in trouble because this is a bunker system. We're taking so much small arms fire.*

Chalk 1 of the QRF faced imminent annihilation. They had a downed helo, four KIAs in the first fifteen seconds—Svitak, Commons, Anderson, and Crose—and only five healthy shooters remained to fight against an unknown number of well-armed al-Qaeda and Taliban. The QRF was caught in an ambush in a subzero environment and thin air at an altitude at which no Ranger—indeed, no U.S. troops—had fought before. They could rule out support from the air. The gunships had flown home, with nothing yet to replace them.

7

THE RANGERS HAD NO IDEA WHERE THEY HAD
landed. They could have been on "fucking Mt.
Rushmore." They had "kicked a hornet's nest," just as
the planners of Anaconda had hoped might happen on the valley floor, without realizing until it was too late their peril. Now,
they could not break contact like MAKO 30 had done, not with
their number of casualties. Worst of all, they were fighting
for their existence, and losing the fight, on terrain that put
them in a bull's-eye.

The helo had crashed in a natural bowl of snow and rock.
The enemy fighters enjoyed prepared positions on two-thirds
of the bowl's rim, looking down. Even more perilous, the

distance between the enemy and the Rangers was very narrow—some 60 feet of open ground separated enemy bunkers on the peak from Self and the others behind the rocks. Firing a recoilless rifle, AK-47s, and RPGs, they could hardly miss hitting the helo at a rapid rate from two entrenched positions—behind the low rock outcrop that Slab, Kyle, and Brett had used as cover and from two bunkers dug into a mountain to the immediate right of the outcrop.

It dawned immediately on the Rangers' leader, Nate Self, that they had no choice but to fight their way out. Nobody was coming to help them.

He had felt the helicopter fall out of the sky. He'd been kneeling and was slammed to the steel floor when it hit. When he came to, he was staring at the ceiling through a flurry of shattered insulation. He could *see* the rounds blow through one side and out the other as it hit the insulation. Sparks flew where the RPG had smashed the oxygen tank. And with the fire, he crawled as fast as he could over his Rangers to get out. He had unfastened his snap-link from the floor rail, but the Rangers he climbed over were still snapped in, with their safety lines pulled taught by the impact. Everyone was sprawled everywhere and terrified of dying.

Getting out, he'd crawled past Anderson and seen Commons lying on the ramp. He did not seem real. On the left side, Crose was facedown on the snow. DePouli was shooting to the right uphill. Self tripped and fell in the snow, and his momentum threw him into a somersault. *Falling isn't a bad thing when you are being shot at,* he thought.

With a burst of gunfire across the corner of the ramp cracking over his head, he ran up the right of the helo's pudgy waist bulge in a direct line of enemy fire. Bullets flew over his head and hit the helo. He smelled pine trees, petroleum, aircraft lube, and a fruity essence of cordite. Nothing here seemed real. Self understood what was happening, and yet it seemed as though he had stepped through a screen into a movie that was already playing.

At the moment that he most needed his M-4, it malfunctioned. A round did not extract and was stuck in the receiver. He normally zip-tied a steel ramrod on the side of his weapon to push down the barrel and eject a jammed bullet; he had tried to remember to buy a piece of metal tubing at the Home Depot in Savannah, but he had forgotten in the rush to leave. He jammed his articulated cleaning rod down the barrel; the rod broke off in the weapon. He threw the M-4 aside and ran back to the helo's ramp for Crose's weapon. A bracket on his NVGs had snapped on impact during the crash, and he took Crose's NVGs off his helmet. The enemy fire was intense, and Self was out in the open. He looked down the fuselage toward the refueling boom. Svitak's M-134 mini gun was resting on its mount out the window, and he thought, *I wish we had power to that gun, because it's in perfect position to shoot at the enemy positions.*

Totten-Lancaster was huddled up by the helo's refueling boom in front of Self, and DePouli was at the rear, shooting to the left now. The Air Force tactical air controller, Kevin Vance, came up to join Self, shooting an M-4.

Specialist Anthony Miceli, a SAW gunner from St. Louis and the second youngest American on the peak by a couple of months, ran out of the helo over the bodies of Commons and Crose. He was out in the open and carrying his SAW in both hands below his waist. Bullets from two directions struck him in the same instant: one shot off his SAW's ammo drum, lighting up rounds inside the casing; one hit the lower receiver; one hit the front of the weapon and went through the laser into the gas tube; and a fourth hit the sling. His thumb was nicked. He quickly realized what happened and ditched the SAW, picking up Commons' M-4. He was surprised how he could feel the bullets going by. He lay prone at the nine o'clock of the helo. An RPG came in straight about a foot off the snow and went past him close enough to reach out and touch. He was in the middle of no-man's-land. Rounds were flying over and past his head.

The al-Qaeda fighters dominated the field. They popped up, played cat-and-mouse, leveled bursts of AK-47 fire at the helo profile as much as at the Rangers, and ducked down again in the bunker and behind the outcrop. Completely exposed to the enemy's guns, Self and the others returned fire as best they could. An RPG exploded almost at Self's feet. The snow trapped enough of the blast and shrapnel to save him. He felt a powerful blow to his thigh, as if someone had hit him hard with a long nail welded to the face of a sledgehammer. With adrenaline pumping, he ignored the wound. He thought, *We are going to be here all day long. The sun is just coming up. It's not over the mountains yet. This aircraft is not taking off again. We are in the middle of a fight. There is no way out of it.*

Fragments from the RPG that hit Self also wounded Vance in the shoulder and Totten-Lancaster in the leg. The RPG gunner ducked behind the outcrop, reloaded, and came back up. His next RPG skipped off the helo's ramp but did not explode. He sat down while his assistant gunner slid another RPG into the tube. Self took this opportunity to put distance between himself and the helo. He saw a shelf of rock, 8 feet long and no higher than 3 feet, that stood out in the open to the right of the helo and below the peak about 50 feet. It would have to suffice. He ran toward it, firing uphill. He slipped and struggled to keep his footing in the snow. He felt that he was moving in slow motion. The lack of oxygen in the high mountain air seared his lungs and left him gasping. At the rock, the body of the enemy fighter Svitak had shot from the helo's door freaked Self out. Self didn't trust that he was dead. He was lying there almost like he was alive.

DePouli ran behind Self, who ordered him to move the enemy's body out of the way and stay down behind the shelter of a small pile of rocks about 12 feet to the right. Ranger Private First Class David Gilliam, the squad's M-240 machine gunner, slid over with DePouli. Self felt more comfortable now with two firing positions. DePouli lay on his stomach with his gun resting on the rock. He waited for the enemy with the RPG to rise. When he saw his head, he aimed his M-4 and pulled the trigger. The al-Qaeda fighter flew backward, shot in the middle of his forehead. Where he fell, the RPG lay across his chest.

Now, Vance, Totten-Lancaster, and Staff Sergeant Joshua

Walker joined Self behind the rock. Walker stood up firing. He shouted indignantly for the other Rangers to hear, "Who do these fucking guys fucking think they are?" Self looked at him funny. He said nothing to him, too afraid he might spook. Walker had taken two rounds to his helmet, which had shattered into a kind of surrealist cock's comb of blasted Kevlar.

The Air Force combat controller, Gabe Brown, ran out of the helo and dropped slightly down the saddle about 30 feet behind Self and his team in a shallow defilade. Rounds flew over and past his head as he set out the antenna for his SAT-COM radio. He was carrying his M-4, which he set aside, reminding himself that his weapon, the one that could get them out of this mess, was his radio.

Self yelled over his shoulder to him, "Get me something overhead." Self had no interest in reaching Masirah. *What are they going to do for me on top of this mountain? I know nobody is coming up here to help anytime soon. When it's a matter of just living or dying, who cares if they're mad at me for not letting them know what's going on?*

To make certain that Brown had heard, the Air Force TACP, Kevin Vance, near Self behind the rock, yelled down at Brown, "If you get comms, bring it in on right and hit with guns."

The enemy fighters were still firing into the helo. Maybe they feared it would spin up and fly away. They also directed steady fire at Self's position and lobbed grenades down the hill toward him and the others. These grenades might have taken a devastating toll if the snow had not absorbed their blasts.

The terrain worked heavily in the enemy's favor. Self was almost 100 feet lower than the peak across an open snow field about 50 feet long, with only two paltry outcroppings to hide behind. He and his Rangers were firing up a 55-degree slope. Carrying an M-203, Josh Walker fired 40 mm grenades that either bounced off the face of the low rock outcrop or arced over the enemy's bunkers and exploded down the steep incline to the north. Armed with proximity fuses, M-203 rounds were used for direct fire, and they moved slowly enough through the air to be seen. When lobbed over this short distance, the rounds had a tendency to fall back down to earth near the shooter and roll downhill along the incline. Walker tried to throw the grenades with his arm, but they only dropped in the snow and burst to no effect.

Self took a moment, sheltering below the rock, to assess the field while his men continued their suppressing fire uphill. He looked down the mountain across a wide-open snowfield. He worried that al-Qaeda reinforcements could move up through the trees from that direction. He would never know until the last moment. A ridge at the far edge of the field offered the enemy an ideal concealed position from which to pour fire uphill into Self's back. He saw no signs of the SEALs that his QRF was meant to link up with. He looked to his right. Casualties were lying up behind the ramp. The copilot, Chuck Gant, wounded in the leg, was firing from his side of the helo. Miceli lay prone at the rear firing to the six and nine o'clock of the helo. Self felt threatened from his right flank. He did not know about the cliff, just out of sight.

He was feeling a bit like General George Washington when he wrote to his brother John Augustine Washington from Fort Cumberland on July 18, 1755: "Dear Jack: As I have heard since my arriv'l at this place, a circumstantial acct. of my death and dying speech, I take this early Opportunity of contradicting both, and of assuring you that I now exist and appear in the land of the living by the miraculous care of Providence, that protected me beyond all human expectation; I had 4 Bullets through my Coat, and two Horses shot under me, and yet escaped unhurt."

Of the twenty-one men on the helo when it crashed, the two pilots and the air mission commander were wounded; Svitak was dead; Dave Dube was badly wounded in the leg; Marc Anderson was dead in the aircraft; DePouli was shot in his armor back plate; Brad Crose and Matt Commons were dead on the ramp; Josh Walker was hit in his helmet by two AK-47 rounds without realizing it; Miceli's SAW took four bullets; and Totten-Lancaster, Self, and Vance suffered wounds from the RPG and a grenade.

8

AFTER SOAR MEDIC LAMEREAUX HAD EXTIN-
guished the fire along the helo's left cabin wall, he
turned back to Dube, the left door gunner. To
get to him, he had to cross the open space in the companionway that offered the enemy a clear shot through the aircraft
to the ramp. Nearly every time Lamereaux moved, the
enemy opened up with a swath of deadly fire that, because of
the helo's uphill angle, went high and through the cabin
roof.

Lamereaux talked pointedly to Dube to gauge his mental
status. The gunner was pale and sweaty. To keep his mind alert,
Lamereaux asked him to check himself out for additional

wounds as he bandaged his leg and assessed him from head to toe, front and back.

Next, he turned to Calvert, whose wrist continued to ooze blood. Calvert told him, "My left leg is hurting." Lamereaux cut open his pants and said, "Holy cow, you've been shot in the leg." There was little blood, as Calvert had already lost a significant volume of blood from his wrist wound. Lamereaux hooked him up to an IV. A limited supply of IVs inspired him to think ahead. Already, this soon in the fight, he had a left seat pilot with a serious leg wound. The right seat pilot was shot twice. The left gunner was shot, and a Ranger, Totten-Lancaster, was wounded in the calf. Lamereaux counted four patients. He was thinking, *It's a miracle. Well . . . maybe not—it just could be a lot worse.* He had one oxygen tank, and he started Calvert with that. With Calvert, the loss of red blood cells reduced the oxygen-carrying capacity of his blood to his brain, and he needed as much 100 percent oxygen in this thin air as could be found. When the single bottle ran out, Lamereaux hooked him up to the helo's high altitude system. He also hooked him to a bag of Hespan, a plasma volume expander that medics routinely carry on battlefields. Lamereaux had three patients who were eligible for morphine. He held off for now.

The two other medics on the helo, both of them with the Air Force, worked casualties in the aft end of the cabin. The team leader was Keary Miller, a pararescue PJ. About ten months before, Miller had switched to a reserve unit with the Kentucky National Guard after ten years as a PJ with the 23rd

Special Tactics Squadron. He'd worked in Bosnia, but altogether, the ten years hadn't been what he'd expected when he signed up. He turned his back on active duty for a better quality of life with a growing family; at twenty-nine, it was time to move on. He was giving the Air Force one weekend a month and two weeks in the summer, waiting for a full-time reserve slot to open up. He planned to stay in for twenty on the sidelines, eventually draw a retirement, and enjoy life into the sunset. He was pulled back to active duty after 9/11, and here he was, doing what he had long ago given up ever expecting to do.

The other PJ medic, Jason Cunningham, was someone the doctors and nurses at Bagram treated as an adored younger brother. Cunningham loved medicine—a surgeon at Bagram in the 274th Forward Surgical Team, Army Major Brian Burlingame, met Cunningham one day, and the PJ asked with a smile, "Hey, what can you teach me? Make me smarter." To Burlingame, a general surgeon and West Point graduate, Cunningham was a unifying factor in his medical group. He peppered his medical team with questions that kept them sharp—how to care for the acutely injured in battlefields, different ways of doing the same thing, ways to be smarter, to be more efficient, to travel lighter. The conversations would begin with Jason asking, "Hey, Doc, I'm thinking about this, what do you think?"

Burlingame would answer, "Yeah, Jason, it's a good idea, but if you do it this way, it might be better."

Just before March 4 and the QRF, Cunningham had

worked with Burlingame and his medical team to bring whole blood onto the battlefield. Whole blood can be used to keep wounded men alive longer. The downside to the blood in this form was its perishable nature. Cunningham wanted to have access to the best medical products to save lives, and he was carrying whole blood on the helo when it went down. This was Cunningham's first experience in combat with wounded, and at twenty-six, he thought that he was ready.

Growing up back in Carlsbad, New Mexico, he viewed himself as a silver-spoon boy who, by some horrible cosmic mix-up, had been born in a plastic-spoon family. His parents were rednecks. They worked hard all their lives for every penny; the weeks leading up to Christmas, his mom, Jackie, took the three kids—Jason, an older brother, and a younger sister—out on highway verges scouring for cast-off soft drink bottles and cans to redeem for money to buy presents. On weekends they cut firewood in the Guadalupe Mountains to make extra money. Jason wasn't into manual labor and spent more time trying to give his mother reasons why he shouldn't have to help out than he did cutting wood. Proudly, she thought he was destined for the law.

Jackie was a journeyman sandblaster/painter in the oil fields, and Jason's dad, Red, was a welder. Jason told his friends that his mother was a "painter," as in artiste. Whatever else Jackie was, she was funny, and her children learned a deprecating humor from her.

Jason was vain. He left the house with every hair in its proper place, and he despaired of growing bald at a tender age, like his dad and grandfathers. When he was fifteen, he asked Jackie for hair plugs for his birthday: "I'm *not* losing my hair, Mom."

Weekends, he worked at Michael Lee's pawn shop. In lieu of a salary, he brought home "treasures," like a World War II gas mask that he loved and wore after school doing chores and homework. Eventually when he put it up for sale at a flea market, he priced it at a respectable $25. No buyer was tempted, and by the late afternoon he'd marked it down to $2. A local hunter finally took it off his hands, as a joke, because, he told Cunningham, when he went hunting, a friend's farts smelled so bad in the tent, he needed a gas mask. Cunningham was crushed.

After high school, he joined the Navy, but he never stepped on a boat. He was stationed in Italy, married and divorced his wife, Theresa, retired from the service after four years, and played stud muffin to the girls in Farmington, New Mexico, who fell for his charming smile and penetrating blue eyes. During the days, he worked delivering towels. After ten months of this carefree life, he married his ex-wife again. He elected to return to the service but wanted the kind of challenge that only the SEALs or PJs could offer. He chose the PJs over the SEALs, he said, because he preferred "search and *rescue*" to "search and *destroy*." He weighed 185 pounds and stood 5 feet 11 inches when he graduated as a PJ. He talked incessantly and earned the nickname "Lippy." Life wasn't all about *him* anymore. It was more about his two daughters, Kyla and Hannah, and a marriage he was determined to make work this time around.

After the helo crashed, Cunningham and Miller heard someone yelling, "Get out, get out, go go go."

Cunningham remained in the helo, while Miller followed Crose to the ramp, and Commons followed him. Miller kept moving, orientating in the daylight to figure out where the enemy was firing from. The Rangers in front and behind him were shot. Miller treated his first patient, Commons, on the ramp. He saw an RPG come straight at him and could only look up as the RPG bounced off the helo's roof. The novelty wore off with so many RPGs coming at the helo in the first few minutes. Miller focused on Commons' wounds, first checking his airway. He did a quick shakedown and found no blood. *OK*, he asked himself, *what happened?* He reached under Commons' body armor and his fingers felt where Commons had taken a round that had entered his side and came out through his chest. He moved over to Crose, who was without a pulse and not breathing. He had taken a round in the head under his Kevlar helmet. Miller looked in the helo at Cunningham, who was working hard to treat Anderson. Miller asked him what he needed and Cunningham said that one of the pilots was up under the helo's chin bubble.

Miller worked himself around the side of the helo to Chuck Gant, who was lying out in the open underneath the helo and taking fire. Miller tied a tourniquet on his wounded thigh. He ran back to the ramp for help. Brian Wilson, the right ramp crew chief, came up with him, and they dragged Gant back to the ramp. Miller noticed that Vance's radio/computer was lying on the snow where he'd dropped it while running out of the helo. Self was using Vance as a shooter. Miller carried the radio over to where Gabe Brown was setting up communications. He helped him extend the SATCOM antenna and returned to the helicopter. With an M-203 grenade launcher, he guarded the rear of the helicopter.

9

D ON TABRON, THE 160TH SOAR'S AIR MISSION
commander who had been seated in the cockpit's
jumpseat handling the radios, pitched in to help
with the fight. He thought, *When the special operations guys
are in the air, we're in charge, and when we are on the ground,
they're in charge.*

After he ran off the ramp, he rolled over in the snow and
covered the left side of the helo until shooting from that
direction stopped. He understood the terrain. The al-Qaeda
fighters to the west and southwest had excellent concealment,
and nobody knew their numbers. Tabron had discovered an
oddity of combat: when he was being fired at, his focus

narrowed to a pinprick. It did not matter to him at that moment if a hundred enemy fighters were on the mountain. He only counted the one who was shooting at him.

He was lying on the ground, and the sun was rising over the mountains, reflecting off the brilliant carpet of snow. He was wet and cold. Lamereaux came over and said something to him, and Tabron noticed for the first time that his left index finger was shot off down to the first knuckle. He stared at his gloved hand. A bullet had ricocheted straight up his sleeve, piercing the fabric of his flight suit with five holes. Lamereaux threw him a blanket-sized piece of soundproofing to lie on. He heard someone shout, "Hey, we got the left seat pilot up on the ground there."

Tabron and PJ Miller ran up and grabbed Gant by the strap on his flight vest and dragged him back over the snow to the casualty collection point that Lamereaux, Cunningham, and Miller had set up under the tail of the helo to protect the wounded from the small arms fire from the peak.

Self called for a resupply of ammunition. Tabron and the helo's right ramp crew chief, Brian Wilson, gathered up ammunition from the helicopter and, under cover from shattering bursts of rifle fire from Self and his Rangers, sprinted across the open snow, under fire from the peak. With the snow, the heaviness of the ammo, and the thin air, Tabron felt "like a rabbit in a shooting gallery. You get there and almost collapse, give it to them, catch your breath, and run back to get more."

Wilson brought up the M-203 and the 40 mm grenades,

Petty Officer 1st Class Neil C. Roberts, 32.
(U.S. Navy)

Tech. Sgt. John A. Chapman, 36, in Afghanistan a week before the battle on Takur Ghar.

Enemy's command and control tent. The tarps may have been the reason the gunships failed to notice the enemy presence on the mountain. (USSOCOM)

The DShk heavy machine gun position on Takur Ghar. (USSOCOM)

Artist Don Stivers' rendering of Razor 01 minutes after it was shot down. (Don Stivers)

1 David Gilliam and Ray Depouli
2 Kevin Vance, Nathan Self, Joshua Walker, Aaron Totten-Lancaster
3 Chuck Gant
4 Don Tabron
5 Gabe Brown
6 Keary Miller and Cory Lamereaux
7 Pilots Bartley and Lipina

Sgt. Bradley S. Crose, 27.

Cpl. Matthew A. Commons, 21.

Spc. Marc A. Anderson, 30.

Sgt. Philip J. Svitak, 31.

Sr. Airman Jason D. Cunningham, 26.

and as he was being fired on, he ducked and threw them across the remaining distance. He and Tabron wore down from exhaustion after seven round trips with ammo and guns. During one run with the heavy grenades, Tabron knew he was going to get shot if he didn't protect himself. He decided to roll on the snow, just as Totten-Lancaster had done, over to Self at the rocks, and roll back to the helo. His rolling maneuvers almost certainly kept him alive, bullets snapping safely over his head.

Self was weighing the odds in favor of an assault on the peak. It was going to have to be tried eventually. He saw no other way to clear out the enemy from the high ground than to storm them. DePouli, behind the rocks to Self's right, was searching the sky for the sight of the Chinook with Chalk 2 that had followed them from Bagram. He was thinking, *Fuck! We're up here, guys are wounded and guys are dead. There's only a few of us who can do anything. What's our plan? We started out half a platoon, and now we are a quarter of a platoon. We can accomplish our mission with a bare minimum of guys if we have to. But I'd feel a lot better if Chalk 2 was with us. So, what the hell do we do now?*

Unless the Rangers took the peak, they would be fighting uphill all day long.

DePouli was ready to charge, telling David Gilliam, the machine gunner next to him, "Let's just kill these guys and get the hell out of here."

10

GABE BROWN WAS WORKING HIS END OF THE fight.

With his radio, he was vainly searching for gunships. He next went looking for AWACs. He had line-of-sight communications and SATCOM with which to reach Bagram. Finally, someone answered. It was Masirah, relaying through the AWACS. Brown said, "Hey, this is Slick Zero One, part of the Razor 01 flight." Brown reported what was happening, and the numbers of their KIAs and wounded. Masirah wanted to know what had happened to the SEALs, and if the QRF had contacted them. Brown had no idea what they were talking about. *Men dead and dying up here, and they want to know about the SEALs?* It made no sense to Brown, who was still trying to connect the dots. Masirah passed him the SEALs' line-of-sight frequency and asked him to contact them.

Brown was kneeling in a shallow defilade. Bullets popped and snapped over his head and past his ears. He was scared. But after a few moments he realized, *It's just pops and bangs. I'm not hit. Just keep on going.*

With his calm demeanor, Brown felt almost comfortable in an atmosphere of chaos. When things sucked, he felt, if not the best, then very fine. He admitted to being strung high, but once he'd entered the cone of chaos, something strange came over him. Time slowed down, like it had the time he'd flipped his mom's car on a hairpin turn, and while the car was still rolling, he slowed down the motion in his mind to figure out how to position his body so that he would not fly through the windshield. As a CCT, he loved working on dirt strips with aircraft whipping around and C-130s on short finals and men crossing the runway and the radio quitting on him.

Soon after he'd arrived in Afghanistan he'd been on the very same mission that Slab was on when he rescued the C-130 crewman. Gabe was riding a Chinook over the high Kush, with snowy peaks below. The Chinook was refueling on a tanker, taking gas in midair, and the sun was so bright its reflection off the snow confused the helo's anti-aircraft warning system into thinking the sunlight was a missile and the system automatically popped out defensive flares. He was being thrown around in the mountain turbulence when suddenly he smelled gas. He jumped up, thinking, *Holy shit*. The tanker to which the helo was connected by a refueling boom had plowed into the mountain, with his Chinook still connected. The helo pilot popped rivets in a very tight turn to avoid the tanker's fate.

On the ground, Brown jumped out, up to his crotch in snow. He looked down a steep incline toward the tanker's crash site, dizzy from the altitude and winded. With his radio, he called in help. Seven out of seven crew members survived. On his way back, Brown said, "That was a pretty good mission, for my first one."

His steadiness came from his father, Billy Duane, who died of cancer when Gabe was twelve. The father had flown B-25s and F-86s in Korea, and retired in '71 as an Air Force major. His last six years, fighting cancer, he devoted to being with Gabe, his youngest son. They had fished and hunted and gone camping.

Living in the sticks outside Rolla, Missouri, in a house with six bedrooms and two bathrooms on 3½ acres that backed onto 40 acres of woods, Gabe became the man of the family after his father died. He was clever with his hands. He did not have the toys that other kids played with; he built his own toys. In school, his grades reflected a lack of interest, and he struggled with math. His teacher said he knew the math principles in his head; he could work out problems without knowing he was using algebra. Frankly, his teachers did not understand him. He never wrote a single book report, and was proud of it. He read instruction books that told him how to do real things, like learning magic as "Gabe the Great." He had utter self-confidence. There was nothing he felt that he couldn't do. His mother said, "Most people fail because they don't try. Gabe always tried."

He was a state champion wrestler in high school, despite a tendency to let go at the end of matches. He told his mother, Marie, about a dream that worried him. "Mom, I'm climbing and I'm on a stairs, and I'm climbing and climbing and I get to the top, and I can't push the door open." Marie said, "Gabe, whatever you do, when you get there, get that door open."

He pushed hard. It led him into fistfights at school. He earned a reputation for standing up for himself, no matter how uneven the match. He wrecked three cars, raised endless hell, and, with no father to discipline him, walked the edge of trouble. But he seemed to know "where he could go, how far he could go, and he always stopped." Instead of falling in with a bad crowd, he fell upon an obsession when a friend of his father's gave him a radio-controlled model airplane. He learned to fly from the ground, and he built airplanes from scratch, creating order out of the chaos of a thousand different parts. For an F-15 model, he constructed a working fan jet engine from scratch and singed his eyebrows in its heated exhaust blast. Over time, he flew his creations with skill and daring. He could judge speeds and distances expertly. He knew flight approaches and angles in three dimensions, and he understood how to describe with words what he directed the model airplanes to do. He often awoke early to go out flying before school. He carried a lawn mower battery in a box across the frosted ground to start the airplane's engine, whacking his thumb until it bled. After he flew, he went back to the house, put the airplane away, and waited for the school bus out by the road.

His "priding point" was a capacity to work hard even at a young age. On a haying crew in the summers, he bucked 1,000 and sometimes 1,600 bales in a day, and he'd work forty-eight hours straight. He actually sought out work that no one else his age would touch. He was struggling to find his way with dreams of college that his grades (Cs and Ds) did not support. When graduation came, he followed his father into the Air Force. A recruiter tried to interest him in avionics and spoke to Brown about combat controllers. He said that most young men could not make the grade. Gabe read a brochure about it and thought, *I can do that.* What appealed to him was that combat controllers worked in an independent atmosphere of freedom. That was how he had grown up, to do whatever he wanted without limits imposed by authority.

Awarded the CCT red beret in '94, he first went off to England and then served in Kosovo. He had met Gloria, who was valedictorian of her California high school class. Before agreeing to marry Gabe, she gave him "the speech" about life and the future. She was the stability he was searching for.

Afghanistan was his first combat experience. He listened to the special operators, the A team, as they came in from the field. They had it together, he thought. He learned from them about the practicalities, the stuff that wasn't taught, to tie the air to the ground with his radio. By the time Anaconda began,

Brown was attached to Calvert's Chinook. He thought, *Give me a team leader, give me a helicopter, and if it flies and there is a problem, I'll be there.*

Earlier that night, he'd been awakened and told about a crewman who was missing from a helo. Brown had made his way to the flight line. When Calvert had spun up the helo, Brown kept quiet, chewing sunflower seeds and thinking, *They'll probably fix the problem, and we'll turn around and come home.* He tried to catch a nap. He was cold, but he knew the Chinook's "hot spots." He carried an inflatable pad so he wouldn't have to sit on the cold, bare metal floor. He did not really care whether he was briefed on the mission. No matter where he went and what he would be doing, he knew his job. His radio was secure in his ruck. Reminding himself of a CCT mantra, *The radio is your life*, he was ready for chaos.

He had never been in combat, never had a shot fired at him in anger, never called in close air support on anything other than dummy targets on safe ranges where proximities were carefully guarded and maintained. But now, under fire, he calculated what facts he'd need when and if fighter jets came to help them. He would need to slow down chaos like he had never done before, as the consequences of a single small mistake were unthinkable. He wanted to be concise. He wanted to get the jets in on the targets quickly. He worried about his radio, which could simply lock up if he pushed too many buttons too fast. He was methodical and cautious. He worried about the effects of the extreme cold on his delicate electronic equipment. He carried a Garmin GPS, a civilian model about the size of a microcassette recorder. If its batteries got too cold, it malfunctioned. He switched out its batteries and warmed them against his body.

Minutes ago, he had run off the helo, stepping over the dead in the cabin and over Commons and Crose on the ramp. He ran with his radio to a flat rock where the sun had melted the snow. He shouted to Self, "Hey, Ranger, where is the enemy?"

"The tree," Self shouted back.

"Right. What tree?"

"*That* tree."

From a pocket, Brown whipped out a "J-Fire," a reference for close air support that showed how close to friendly troops bombs could be safely dropped. Brown read in black and white that CAS wasn't going to happen with them sitting this close to the enemy.

AF combat controllers like Brown thought of themselves as different from the enlisted TACPs like Kevin Vance, although both jobs were similar, even if the training wasn't. Brown was not comfortable taking orders from Vance; only the team leader, the CO on the peak, had the authority to issue orders to bring in CAS, and Brown thought that Vance might be giving orders on his own. Every time Brown called up to Self, he got Vance, and he finally said to him, "If I yell 'team leader,' you answer with what he tells you, and we'll go with it" on the assumption that Self had weighed the decision. Brown yelled, "I got fighters. Hey, Rangers! We've got bombs and guns. What do you want?" It was Self's choice, even if the J-Fire book said it was too close for bombs. Brown held up his compass. He had a good run-in heading for the jets.

Self replied, "Go with guns."

11

A IR FORCE LIEUTENANT COLONEL BURT "DIVOT"
Bartley had pulled off a midair refueling from a
tanker, taking on 6,000 pounds of avgas. He was the
commander of the Air Force's 18th Fighter Squadron, attached
to the Iraqi Southern Watch since December 17, flying out of
al-Jabr, Kuwait, three hours' commuting time to Afghanistan
on a good night.

Bartley and his wingman, Air Force Captain Andrew "Rip"
Lipina, flying single-seat F-16 Vipers, carried the radio code
names Clash 71 and Clash 72. Under each Viper's wing that
night hung four laser-guided bombs, and 500 rounds of
internal 20 mm ammunition lay stacked inside the fuselage. A

500-pound GBU-12 bomb loaded with 250 pounds of tritonal, a mixture of TNT and aluminum powder, surrounded by a 250-pound forged steel casing, had a blast pattern that shot hot steel fragments 3,000 feet in every lateral direction. Bartley and Lipina could release all 500 rounds of 20 mm ammunition with a single quick flick of the gun button on the joystick. All this firepower did not come without risks to the men it was meant to support. With the jets moving at speeds of 900 feet per second over the ground, targeting errors were a great danger when only a few feet separated friendly and enemy forces.

Earlier that night, Bartley and Lipina had been briefed just after midnight local time in Kuwait. Aware that a helo was down in the Shah-i-Kot but unaware what their tasks would be over Afghanistan, they took off about 0300 local time, flying across the Arabian Sea and southwestern Pakistan before reaching Afghanistan. They refueled another time and crossed into their area of operation around southeastern Afghanistan. An AWACS told them to "frag"—go to their orbit point and hold. That meant the night looked like it was going to be business as usual, with the expectation that they would fly on station until somebody called them.

A voice from an AWACS came up in Bartley's flight helmet. Troops needed his help at the downed helicopter. He and Lipina started to prepare. A check of their maps told them that Takur Ghar was 200 miles away. Even at a speed of 9.5 miles a minute, Bartley estimated twenty-two minutes to the mountain. He pushed the throttles up to military power against the

Vipers' Q, or aerodynamic limit. He overheard the call sign Slick 01, Gabe Brown's, relaying through AWACS. The casualty figures that Brown reported struck Bartley in his heart. Without his bombs and bullets, the Rangers on the mountain could not hope to evacuate their wounded. The emotion and the stress bore down on him, unlike any other time in his twenty years in aviation.

This would be his first use of the aircraft's weapons for real; Lipina's, too. Lipina was excited. Something big was about to happen. He was thinking, *This is the first time from the get-go of a pretty good chance of using bombs and guns.* To an Air Force fighter pilot, this felt like a dream was coming true.

On previous missions, Bartley had dropped bombs on enemy positions without friendly troops anywhere near the points of impact. He had only trained at close air support, but he had worked CAS with live ammunition and troops in training more than any F-16 pilot in the combat air forces. He had spent three and a half years with the 549th Combat Training Squadron at the National Training Center. At Nellis AFB, he flew CAS on a nearly daily basis, ten exercises a year, each exercise lasting about two and a half weeks, with as many as ten "battles." To him, fate had put him on this course.

Bartley knew enough to know that CAS was the most inefficient way for air forces to engage the enemy. He preferred dropping thousands of pounds of bombs well clear of friendly forces. It was like a mantra. *If you can kill someone with a rifle at a hundred meters, why wait for him to come at you with a pistol or a spear or knife?*

Bartley saw the peak of Takur Ghar out his bubble. He linked with Gabe Brown, who articulated exactly what he wanted Bartley to do. He gave the pilot an attack axis on the mountain to run in on, looking up toward the bunkers over his right shoulder. In a clear, calm voice, Brown described where he wanted the bullets to strafe: two helicopter lengths to the right, at the one o'clock position of the downed helo. Bartley calculated the Chinook's length at 50 feet; therefore, 100 feet separated the enemy bunker from the broken helo. The Rangers, at the helicopter's four o'clock position one helicopter length away, were even closer than danger close.

Bartley's "pepper track," or aiming reference across the ground, was moving at 9 miles a minute. He would be shooting at a target zone 500 feet long and no-room-for-error wide.

He lined up the downed Chinook in his targeting pod. He was off NVGs. It was daylight, around eight o'clock in the morning, and the sun was low on the horizon. He turned 150 degrees to get on the attack axis and rolled down the chute on final for the run. At this altitude, in the mid-20s, he could not make out people on the ground from two or three miles out. He was engaging a position on the ground, diving at 30 degrees. He planned to pull out of the dive at 1,500 feet above the mountain. As he came in the Viper screamed with a sound that curled the air.

At that closer-than-danger-close range, Bartley needed a final clearance before he could shoot. Brown gave him the initials of his name, in essence saying that he accepted the risk of being hit by friendly fire. Bartley would strafe and drop bombs wherever he was told, but he knew that fingers would point at him if there was fratricide.

He rolled in, but Brown did not see him on his first pass in time to give him final clearance, and Bartley did not put bullets on the target. He pulled off, made an immediate turn, and came back around on the same axis in an arc the shape of a kidney bean. On the pass, Bartley had not seen the enemy on the peak. He knew where Brown told him they could be found, but the shattering sound of his engine had almost certainly sent them burrowing into the bottom of their bunkers. He and Brown talked over corrections. On this roll in, Bartley would pop out a couple of self-protection flares to allow Brown to see where he had lined up and was coming from. The two men understood one another; each understood, even this quickly, how the other one thought. In training, some pilots' voices had actually frightened Brown into wishing they would not drop their bombs anywhere near him. But Bartley's was a calm, reassuring tone. Brown was staying easy with an effort, and on the next run, he cleared Bartley hot on final.

Bartley laid a good solid pattern of 250 rounds across the peak, shredding what was left of the fir trees, bullets cracking off the rocks. A 20 mm bullet is about the same length as a man's thumb and about an inch in diameter. The sound of the gun was like popping plastic packing bubbles. Brown ducked down. Snow flew up across the peak, and he smelled the pine scent as the trees splintered. He was watching the Rangers *not* get hit.

With the Viper in a tight turn, Brown yelled to Self, "Hey, where did those bullets go?"

"I don't know. We can't see."

DePouli was down low to the ground. When the guns came in, he shouted, "Holy shit. That was pretty fucking close."

On his second pass, Bartley emptied his guns. He lagged his turn, and Lipina cut inside, now ready to take the lead.

Self needed to know the effect of the bullets. He wanted to make a quick assault, uphill toward the bunkers, after the strafing runs. On Bartley's gun passes, the Viper had approached the hill over Self's right shoulder; he had turned around to watch a cloud of the Viper's 20 mm brass casings drop to earth. The rounds had exploded in front of the Rangers and uphill. Self smelled the same essence of pine from the shattered trees as Brown had.

Vance conferred with Self, then shouted down at Brown. Self wanted the pilots to make another run.

Brown replied, "They're cleared to come in again."

Lining up, "Rip" Lipina recalled that a thousand yards was as close as he'd ever strafed to friendly troops. When he rolled in, his cockpit's "pepper track"—the gaming dots pilots use to put down bullets—was touching the helicopter, and he was still trying to line up his shot when he rolled out. Things were moving too fast. If he had pulled the trigger on that run, his bullets would have hit the helo. He was feeling nervous. He came around for a second run.

"Clash 71 in, in thirty seconds," he radioed to Brown. He

popped a single flare with a thumb-activated switch on the stick. "Clash 71 in."

Brown satisfied himself that the Viper's nose was pointed in the right direction. He told him, "Clash 71, you are cleared hot."

Lipina was in the weeds at 2,000 feet over the peak to give the Rangers "good bullets." He was flying lower than his rules of engagement authorized, but he worked with the caveat to do what he needed to save lives. He emptied his guns.

As the jet screamed off to the west, the al-Qaeda and Taliban fighters on the peak rose from their hiding places and fired down on the Rangers, almost as if the strafing runs had not made a difference to them.

A half hour or longer went by, with Self waiting for an assessment of the runs. Then Brown heard from Masirah that the Predator was showing movement in the bunker. "They still see those guys," he said.

More time went by. Self checked back. "They still see 'em?"

"Yeah, they're there sitting behind the tree."

The 20 mm rounds had hit close to the target. What was happening up there? They could only guess at the resourcefulness—or the extraordinary luck—of the enemy that had enabled them to survive the runs. Maybe they had fled the peak, leaving behind only a rear-guard security element of two or three gunners, or maybe their installation included deep bunkers.

Vance asked Self about using bombs. Self replied, "No, we're not doing that."

This was a small but remarkable moment. In a sense, it defined the fight on the peak. Soldiers worked with age-old fundamentals—map reading, shooting weapons accurately, team tactics, endurance, channeling of aggression, and so on; these were elements that soldiers had carried onto battlefields since well before Homer. But in the twenty-first-century military, F-16 Vipers, Predators, AC-130 gunships, and other fantastic machines multiplied the soldier's power to an extreme only dreamed of before. On Takur Ghar, however, the close proximity between friendly and enemy fighters rendered these force multipliers useless. In a certain sense that Self appreciated, his QRF might as well have been fighting in Achilles' day. For instance, Vance and Brown were trained to a fine point to operate sophisticated computer/radios. On Takur Ghar, Vance was pulling a trigger. Self wasn't about to leverage two pieces of sophisticated communications equipment that early in the fight, when he needed trigger pullers. The fight from Self's perspective was simple, lethal, and harrowing. The enemy was in front of him up a hill looking down. It could have been a castle keep. It was daylight. The scale of the engagement was tiny by comparison to what was happening in the valley below. Takur Ghar had become a "paradoxical mix of simplicity and complexity."

Bartley was on the radio to Brown. "OK, what's next?" he asked him. Bartley was trained as a forward air controller, which meant he was good at hitting intended targets with bombs. He told Brown about his GBU-12s, and, leading Brown, he asked, "What can we do to help?"

Self had already said he did not want bombs. He had not worked with Brown, who would be calling them in. He knew nothing about Bartley. And Vance, whom he did trust, did not have a SATCOM radio. Self could not put the lives of his men in the hands of a combat controller he did not know, unless he had no other choice.

12

S ELF'S CHOICE WAS MADE FOR HIM WHEN THE mortars came in.

With an enemy force on the high ground in front of the QRF, the mortar rounds were coming in from their rear. And the mortar team, out of sight to the southeast, was bracketing their positions, using the downed Chinook as a stationary reference point. Each time a round went off in the tube with an audible popping sound, Self hugged the ground, waiting for its explosion.

The mortar rounds terrified Totten-Lancaster more than anything else that had happened or would happen that day. The fire was accurate, with the first round exploding only 10 feet from the helo's nose. Totten-Lancaster heard a *funk* and knew another mortar round was coming in. The second round was also 10 feet from the helo. The third was going to get them, he was sure. He buried his head in the snow and hoped it would not kill him.

Tabron was still humping ammo from the helo to Self's position across open ground. He listened for the echo of the mortar tube, waited, and prayed that this one would not hit him, before making a mad dash across the open snow. Tabron thought, *It's only a matter of time.*

Self yelled to Brown, asking him if the Vipers had anything to offer.

"Bombs," Brown replied.

"Well, let's try, and then we'll try an assault."

Brown felt electrified as he started to calculate. He linked with Bartley, and they talked over a bomb. The proximity distances were doomsday close. Bartley told him what he was seeing from the air, and Brown replied with a description of the terrain that Bartley should be seeing. They found a comfort zone of exchange, each investing his trust in the other. Brown wondered if Bartley knew, from the ground perspective, the power of his bombs. Brown was reading him the terrain to help him see what must have looked confusing from the air. He told Bartley to start his run on the reverse side of the peak. No matter how close, the bomb fragments would fly over the Rangers' heads, with the peak protecting them from the blast. Bartley agreed. If he dropped a bomb on the peak itself, the blast would probably kill the Rangers. Brown told him to hurry. The mortar rounds were exploding closer.

To Bartley, the bomb run was like throwing a dart down a gun barrel from across a room. He asked Brown again for the authority to come in danger close.

On the first run, a single bomb exploded down on the northern slope, without effect.

Brown told him, "Well, I need it a little closer to the tree. I really need that bunker taken out."

Bartley turned off his laser guidance system. In his head-up display, he lined up his cockpit-computed impact point and put the dot where he wanted the bomb to land. The Viper's computer tracked across the ground. Bartley held down his "pickle button" to give the computer his consent to release. The computer captured in an instant the bombing triangle of the slant range versus height above target versus bomb trail. Everything moved at 900 feet a second. The aircraft's sensors and the computer "read" the currents of winds and aimed the bomb with inertial-aided systems and a GPS.

Bartley knew it was safer to drive at a target from about 8 miles out, acquire the target in his pod, and consent to release, and then the computer would go to work. Once the bomb came off, Bartley would check away from the target to allow the targeting pod IR sensor to track the target and laser-paint the area while the bomb was in flight. But all that took time. It was much easier for him to go, *I want to aim at that spot, roll around, point at it, and drop my bomb*. He was shooting, more or less, with Kentucky windage.

Bartley told Brown that the target was in sight. He said, "I feel good about it."

"I see you, let's do it," Brown told him, and cleared him in hot.

The bomb exploded on the opposite side of the peak.

On his third run, about to trigger the bomb, Bartley's IR sensor picked up two small objects—pixel-sized—on his cockpit screen. These represented two enemy soldiers. He quickly slewed his targeting pod for the bomb to hit between the two pixels, about 10 feet apart on the ground. He threw the bomb in the last eight seconds time-of-flight away from the tree. The bomb went off exactly where he wanted it.

Brown came up on Bartley's radio. "Whoa, you almost got us with that one," he exclaimed. Then he added, unexpectedly, "Can you move it a little closer"—pause—"to the tree?"

Over his radio, Bartley expressed amazement. "No! I can't."

"OK, stop him," Self shouted at Brown. "They're getting a little too close."

Bartley and Lipina pulled off to rendezvous with a tanker. Fifteen minutes later they were in line to refuel. Fifteen minutes after that, their tanks were brimming and they were flying at full throttle about 20 miles back to Takur Ghar. Bartley received the instruction "Clash 71 RTB"—return to base. He asked the AWACS to repeat the instructions. He could not believe what he'd heard. He had bombs, and now he had gas. Why was he being told to go home?

Then he thought, *Oh, no! My last bomb, Slick 01 said, "You almost got us with that one."* Bartley was certain that he had injured or killed his own countrymen with his third bomb. With great trepidation, he obeyed orders and turned his Viper south toward the Arabian Sea and home to Kuwait. Over the next three and a half hours, alone with his thoughts, he pondered the unforgivable thing that he had done—killed the very men he had been trying to help. He remembered Brown's voice and the surprising ease with which they had coordinated the runs.

As he was checking out of the area of responsibility, he switched frequencies from the AWACS to that of an E-2 Hawkeye that controlled his flight between Afghanistan and Pakistan. He demanded, "Say your reason for RTB directive." Other fighters were inbound toward the Shah-i-Kot, he was told. Bartley had studied that night's master air attack plan. Other fighters were *not* due until later that evening.

He kept thinking, *I've killed some friendlies.* He was being sent home with a bomb under his wing (and four under Lipina's) because he'd killed the good guys.

On the peak, Self was not worried about Bartley's return. He was looking up in the air, following with his eyes the circular route over the mountain peak of the propeller-driven unmanned drone, the Predator. The sight of it gave him an inspired idea. He yelled back to Brown, "Find out if the Predator is armed."

Brown replied, "What are you talking about? It's just a Predator."

"Nope. Some of 'em are armed." The arming of Predators with Hellfire antitank missiles was kept a secret from anyone outside the CIA or JSOC arenas. As part of the QRF attached to a JSOC element, Self knew, but Brown, as a vanilla combat controller outside the black world, didn't. "Ask the question," Self told him.

Brown came back and said, "They got two Hellfires."

Self told DePouli crouched next to him, "We got a Predator on station. We're going to have them bomb the friggin' bunker."

"Cool."

From Self's perspective, the Predator was perfect. Its Hellfire missiles contained 14-pound warheads instead of the 250-pound warhead in Bartley's GBU-12s. The Hellfires were laser-guided. Self told Brown where to mark the target. Within minutes, the Predator fluttered into position. It fired, and the first missile hit on the opposite side of the peak, missing the bunker. Brown called the next and last Hellfire in closer. It hit the bunker, blasting what remained of the tree and partially scattering a barrier of logs that the enemy soldiers had set up for concealment and protection.

Self said, "We got to take out the positions."

DePouli replied, "Roger that."

No close air support was available now, with the Hellfires expended and the fast movers out of the area. The enemy soldiers continued to lob intermittent mortar rounds up from the south. Self ordered the helo's rear crew chief, Brian Wilson, to work with Gilliam behind the rocks to his right. Gilliam was going to lay down suppressing fire on the peak with his M-240 machine gun while DePouli, Vance, Self, and

Walker debouched across the open field under the bunkers.

Self needed to make one further preparation. He yelled at DePouli to accompany Ranger Specialist Anthony Miceli, the SAW gunner whose weapon was hit as he was leaving the helo, down about 150 feet to the rock outcropping on the eastern ledge. Self was worried about an attack from there; the mortars were being fired from that general direction. Miceli was over at the helo's nine o'clock covering the sector from nine to six o'clock. Bullets splattered around him—*from all over the place,* he thought as he ran. He reached the cover of the rock and set up his SAW. DePouli low-crawled the same distance over the snow. From the side of the rock, their view swept across the mountains out to the south and east.

Miceli was using Totten-Lancaster's SAW. His luck so far in the day was uncharacteristic. He was known among the Rangers as accident-prone. It was said about him that he would step on the only thumbtack on an entire football field. His misfortunes were both a running joke and a deep concern. The last Memorial Day he'd jumped out of a speeding boat for the joy of it, ruptured his spleen, and almost died; indeed, he had died on the operating table from an allergic reaction to histamine, but was resuscitated, brought back from the dead. None of his friends thought he would make it through this day.

While DePouli and Miceli were setting up security, Self huddled with Don Tabron, the air mission commander. Self was under constant pressure to assist the casualties, which meant to create conditions that would allow a helicopter to pick them up and take them to the forward surgical hospital at

Bagram. He could hear the moans of the wounded. The PJs and medics kept reminding him, "We have to get out of here. This is not right. When do we get out, team leader?"

Self replied, "Got it! Not now. It's not the time." He asked Tabron where he thought a helo could land for the wounded.

Tabron pointed down to the helo's six o'clock position, just to the west of DePouli and Miceli. He suggested that the medic and PJs could slide the casualties across the snow 150 feet; it would be easier than to move them up. Self understood intuitively that higher command—the "head shed"—would never approve of sending another helo as long as the enemy controlled the peak, but he needed to ask Masirah because of the insistence of the PJs and medics working with the casualties.

Originally, immediately after the crash, they had sheltered the wounded in the helo's cabin, but it continued to be targeted, especially from the front, and bullets were flying in the cockpit, down the companionway, and into the cabin. Everyone moved on their stomachs. Now, the casualties lay on litters in a small depression about 15 feet off the helo's ramp, with the fuselage providing some cover. The plan that the medics had worked out with Self was that they would move the wounded up if an assault succeeded on the peak. Otherwise, they would stay put. But if an attack should come from the south, across the open field of snow, then the casualties would be in peril.

Calvert, Razor 01's pilot, was in critical condition. The medic and the PJs worried that he might not live through the day. Calvert had thought in a lucid moment, *This is it*, and he had asked the PJs to tell his family he loved them. He was wearing an aviator's oxygen mask strapped on his face with bungee cords. Beside him on another litter the other pilot, Chuck Gant, was "packaged" and ready to be moved. Up in front of the helo outside the left door, Cory Lamereaux and Keary Miller gently had laid Dave Dube, the door gunner, on a bright red Skedco, a roll-up litter that looked like a snow sled. They paused for a breath in the thin air and released the Skedco's restraining straps. To their horror, the litter slid down the steep incline, with nothing to block it. The Skedco picked up speed. Dube was aimed at the saddle and the valley to the south. The litter slid down the length of the helo and veered at the last instant into Gant and Calvert's litters, which were braced against the incline.

Gant and Calvert tried to laugh, but it hurt. Calvert stared into a cloudless sky the color of lapis lazuli. He heard Gabe Brown issuing commands on the radio, and to give Gant and Dube warning of the bomb runs, he yelled, "Five-hundred-pounder coming in! One minute." Shrapnel and blasted rock had whistled and whined over their heads. Calvert had watched a bomb that he thought was heading straight at him. Watching it fall, he was thinking, *Man, I hope that pilot graduated first in his class*. The bomb made the shrieking sound of a small jet engine. The explosion rumbled him lightly on the litter. Even before the bombs, when mortars had come in around them, with hollow sucking sounds of the firing tubes, they had waited in terror for the rounds to explode. Calvert drifted in and out of consciousness, and Dube, in an effort to keep him awake, threw snowballs at him from his Skedco.

DePouli called Self on his MBITR. He had searched around the rock and found a recoilless rifle on the snow near two waist-high sleeping positions that contained blankets and other gear. He had also discovered the enemy soldiers' rustic mosque. He said, "There's a position down here. I'm going to clear it."

Self replied, "No, don't do that." Then he heard a couple of gunshots from that direction and thought that DePouli was shot. "What's happening?" he asked in his radio.

"We were just shooting," DePouli admitted, "to make sure." He and Miceli had shot into the dead body of an al-Qaeda fighter, and then rolled him over. Near him DePouli found a radio. He thought, *How the hell do these guys have a fuckin' MBITR? How'd they get hold of it?* Then found an American ballistic helmet, a ruck, and a water bottle with "Fifi" written on it.

He called Self. "I found an MBITR down here."

Self was confused. "Ah, OK, bring it up here."

A half hour earlier, Gilliam, the M-240 gunner to Self's right, had found a pair of binoculars on a dead enemy lying within arm's reach.

"Do you need them?" Gilliam had asked Self.

"Yeah," Self said.

Gilliam threw the binos to Self, who looked at them, thinking, *These aren't binoculars; these are NVGs.* That the enemy on the peak might use this type of sophisticated equipment worried him. He had no way of knowing that Turbo had dropped them after he was shot and was struggling off the peak.

DePouli came up the slope, leaving Miceli down below. He handed the radio to Self, who recognized a call sign that the radio's owner had laminated on the radio: MAKO 30. He thought, *Something here isn't right*.

Of course, Self had no idea about the SEALs. He knew only that someone had fallen off a helo, but no one had told him who. He'd thought the accident was in the valley near Mack's downed helo. He concluded that the enemy had stolen this gear and stashed it away. He also considered the possibility that an enemy fighter spoke English and had asked for a QRF through the captured radio to come to that position, to ambush them.

Self wanted to start the assault on the bunkers before he lost the advantage of the Predator's Hellfires. On his voice command, he and three Rangers—DePouli, Walker, and Vance, the Air Force TACP—stood up firing, and stepped from behind the cover of the rocks, sinking in snow up to their knees. As they trudged up the slippery gradient, they were laboring for breath in the thin air, occasionally dropping to a knee to rest briefly. In full view, they approached an enemy that was shooting from the side of the rock outcrop and hunkering down near the remnants of the tree. Self saw one of the enemy soldiers duck behind the shattered logs. He ordered Walker to clear it with his SAW.

Now halfway to the peak, Self could not see the enemy's defenses clearly except for a bunker shaped in an oval. The front wrapped behind the tree and around to the west and north. He worried that an enemy soldier was waiting for them to get closer to the peak. They were exposed. An enemy shooting down the slope from behind such good cover could kill them all in a single burst.

He shouted, "Bunker! Bunker! Bunker! Get down! Get back! Get back!"

The assault force of four turned and ran down the slope, taking cover behind the same rocks as before and feeling themselves lucky to get away with nobody wounded. Self decided to postpone another assault until the overdue Chalk 2 of the QRF came to reinforce him with more shooters.

V
"Dude, What the Fuck?"

1

CHALK 2, WHICH HAD LEFT BAGRAM ONLY MINUTES after Self and Chalk 1, was ordered into a holding pattern near Takur Ghar before being told to fly to Gardez and await further instructions. When he heard that, Arin Canon, the Chalk 2 leader, felt a sudden wave of anxiety. He said that learning that Self's helo was shot down made him feel like a mother whose child was ripped from her arms. He knew the numbers on board and that there were wounded. These were more than friends; the men with Self were like his relations. He found himself in turmoil and could only hope that his superiors knew what they were doing.

Waiting at Gardez, he asked, "What's happening to them?"

The ramp chief of the helo said, "Dude, I don't know. Go up front and talk to the pilots."

Canon was incensed. No one seemed to know. A helo with his fellow Rangers was shot down, and he was in a helo with its engines *shut* down on a hardscrabble airstrip in the middle of nowhere. He climbed over nine of his men sprawled on the helo's floor. Up front, he asked the pilot, "Who do you need to talk to? Someone doesn't know that they've only got ten guys in that Chalk and only seven are shooters. They need our ten."

The pilot said, "Yeah, it was a bad LZ. We're trying to get grid coordinates."

Canon walked back through the cabin to the ramp, where he met a SEAL lieutenant commander named Vic Hyder. A day earlier, Hyder had been sent down to Gardez to act as a liaison officer in preparation for taking over Slab's MAKO 30 team. Now he wanted to link up with them on the mountain. Canon told him, "I'm glad to have somebody with rank on their collar, sir." He told him what little he knew and said, "I can't get these yucks in the front of the plane to get this thing off the ground." He and Hyder walked through the cabin to the cockpit. Hyder asked the pilots, "What grid coordinates are you going into?" A pilot read them off his GPS. They were coordinates for the peak.

Canon was fuming. He thought, *Al-Qaeda must be sitting there saying, "You dumb infidels. How many times are you going to fly into the same death trap?"*

The pilot got on the radio. A minute later, he told Hyder and Canon, "We're good to go." Only after they were flying toward Takur Ghar did the pilot receive coordinates for an alternative LZ, an offset on the side of the mountain.

In flight, Canon was told, "When you come off the helo, Chalk 1 will be 300 meters at your eleven o'clock."

The ten in Canon's chalk, seated on the helo's floor, had a come-as-you-are appearance. No one looked quite prepared for what was to come. Sergeant Eric Stebner, one of the team leaders, had readied himself for a landing at an airfield in Khost, where it was warm during the day. Thinking that was where the QRF was needed, he'd worn desert boots, desert camouflage pants, and a T-shirt. Specialist Omar Vela, an assistant gunner, had chosen a light silky T-shirt and cold-weather boots; other men in the chalk wore fleece.

Over the noise of the engines, Canon shouted for his men to listen up. He commanded their attention; he was not a leader to be messed with. He "did the right thing when it was the right thing to do" and took "the hard right over the easy wrong regardless of what it leads you in." He told them, "It doesn't matter to me one way or another how I am perceived, because I can't change it. I do what I think is right in my heart, and if nobody else cares for it, that's not my problem." When he had walked into the recruiter's office in Osceola, Florida, in his senior year of high school, he said simply, "Take me!" He wanted to be a Ranger.

Canon now alerted the men to what they might face once they landed. He told them about the report he'd overheard on the ICS about the KIAs and wounded in Chalk 1. The men responded, as Canon hoped, with anger and determination.

They'd been "locked and cocked" for weeks now without ever playing a role. The QRF was "one of those things that sucks." "All right," he told them. "Get ready to go in." And when the cockpit gave him the two-minute call, he recited the Ranger Creed, which, with the men on their knees on the floor, sounded almost like a prayer: "Energetically will I meet the enemies of my country. I shall defeat them on the field of battle, for I am better trained and will fight with all my might. Surrender is not a Ranger word. I will never leave a fallen comrade to fall into the hands of the enemy and under no circumstances will I ever embarrass my country. . . . Readily will I display the intestinal fortitude required to fight on to the Ranger objective and complete the mission, though I be the lone survivor."

On the first pass across the north side of the mountain, the pilot was looking for a flat landing area large enough for the Chinook's wheels.

To MAKO 30, who watched them from the mountainside, the helo looked like it was lost.

Slab keyed his MBITR and said, "Razor flight, this is MAKO 30."

He told them how he had watched an RPG hit Razor 01 and, minutes later, heard machine-gun fire that he recognized as coming from a SAW, and he knew the helo had crashed. He talked the helo with the QRF toward him up the valley. Slab hoped for the possibility that he could get his wounded on the helo once it dropped off the QRF, but it was only a hope, what with the long, impossible distance to reach with his wounded between where he was directing the helo into and where he was watching from. To assist the helo, he told Randy to get out his orange panel, a blanket-sized cloth colored blaze orange for recognition from the air.

As Randy held it, Slab talked to the helo. "We're at your two o'clock, 200 feet above you. We've got an orange panel out. Can you see us?"

The helo's right door gunner saw them. "I got 'em."

"From our location, look left, eleven o'clock. There's open terrain area. That's your HLZ area. Land there!" There was no other place for them to go that Slab could see. He was afraid they might make the same disastrous mistake as Razor 01.

The helo whipped around. The LZ was located about a quarter mile as the crow flies from MAKO 30. Slab watched the helo hover over a flat patch to take an aft wheel while the helo's front wheels hung in the air. It was the best the pilot could do. The ramp and door crew chiefs called out the clearances on the sides and the height.

The ramp went down and the Rangers peeled off to the left and right, setting out a defensive perimeter in deep snow. It was bitterly cold despite the sun, which by now was 35 degrees or so off the horizon, peeking over the mountains to the east. The steepness of the terrain stunned the Rangers. It wasn't steep, it was precipitous, and it suggested to them that they could go nowhere off the LZ without mountain climbing gear.

Canon asked, "Is anybody shooting at us?"

"No, not yet," someone replied.

Hyder, the SEAL lieutenant commander, was getting his

bearings. He said, "Come on, let's go, let's go. We need to go now. Now." He was indicating that "go" meant go toward MAKO 30's position on the mountainside, not the top.

Canon wasn't having that. He said, "Look, you outrank me, sir, but these are my guys up there, and until we figure out where the hell we are, we are not going anywhere." He could hear gunfire above him, but the lateral direction was vague in his mind.

At that moment, Self's voice came up on Canon's radio.

Canon felt relieved to hear his voice and said, "Hey, we're on the ground but I don't see you. I can hear you making contact."

On the peak, Self noted the grid coordinates where he'd been told that Canon's Chalk 2 was supposed to land; Masirah had passed the map location to him through Brown's radio. Self had looked at the map. The location was to his southwest, which should have put the chalk across the mountain on the south side. He told Canon, "Well, good. I can continue to suppress 'em here and you can assault them from the back of the mountain and hit them from behind. And we'll be done. Let me give you a recognition signal so you can get a fix on where we are at."

Moments later, Walker shot a green star cluster out of the M-203.

"We don't see it," Canon reported to Self.

Something was wrong, and Self said, "Send me your grid."

Canon, with his Garmin GPS, marked a waypoint. He had programmed his starting point into the GPS from the coordinates he received from the helo's crew. He radioed Self his map coordinates and began plotting the terrain.

When he looked at the coordinates, Self realized why Canon had not seen the starburst. He was not where Self had thought; indeed, he was nearly 180 degrees off. He checked the new grid and told Canon, "Stop. We're south of you. You should come down the valley to our east and approach us to our rear, come up right on the ramp of the helicopter." The chalk had landed at the exact opposite compass direction of where Self had been told to expect them—to their northeast, not their southwest.

Self had just saved Canon and his men an impossible climb; now they faced a next-to-impossible climb.

"How long?" Self asked.

"Forty-five minutes," Canon guessed. He had no way of knowing the difficulty of the trek he was about to embark on; or the speed at which the chalk would be able to move.

By now, Hyder, the SEAL lieutenant commander, had a fix on MAKO 30 on roughly the same elevation "around a little draw," making their location sound in the neighborhood. Hyder told Canon, "Let's get my guys first, my wounded. We'll bring 'em down to the LZ on the valley floor and then we'll go up to the top for your guys."

Canon couldn't believe what he was hearing. "That's not such a good idea, sir."

Hyder pressed the point.

Canon wasn't listening. He always did what he thought was right in his heart, and if nobody else agreed, that was not his concern. His Ranger medic, Matt LaFrenz, offered his professional opinion. He had not examined Turbo's wounds, of course, but he did not think that the chalk needed to provide aid to the SEALs. They could see them coming down the mountain; they were still moving down. Chalk 2 had 2,000 feet to climb up. MAKO 30 had made it down 2,000 feet. LaFrenz said, "If they've climbed down 2,000 feet, they are fine."

Canon called Self to ask him his thoughts.

Self replied, "No way. Let him do whatever he needs to do. Or he can come up here. But you are here for us. The SEALs are fine. They are not getting shot at."

Canon told Hyder, "We're going to the top, and we'll come back down and get your guys later. That's how it's going to be."

Hyder said, "All right, thanks." And he walked off laterally over a finger of land heading to the east about 600 yards as the crow flies to link up with Slab and the SEAL team. He would have a grueling climb, up and down swales deep in snow. He wouldn't reach MAKO 30 for ninety minutes.

Self and the Rangers on the peak could have used Hyder as another shooter, but just as Self understood his own priority, he understood Hyder's priority, too. "Jointness," the Pentagon's concept of different services working together in a hoped-for new era of cooperation, went only so far. It had brought together on Takur Ghar the Air Force, Army, and Navy, and they had cooperated out of necessity and even by design. But true cooperation, they were finding, went only as far as unit loyalties, when the stakes were this high.

Canon radioed Self to request another star cluster to help

him with their location. With a mix of feelings, the men in the chalk watched the burst of bright light, like a fireworks display on the Fourth of July high in the sky over them. It represented an awesome 70-degree climb up a mountainside, and yet it was the first tangible proof of the existence of their friends. The two halves of this half of the platoon (the other half was at Kandahar, polishing their skills at Tarnak Farm) were like twins; they felt that they completed each other in ways that meant their existence. No matter how daunting the climb might be—and it would test Chalk 2's endurance beyond measure—each step would put them closer to being whole again as a tightly bound unit of men.

Watching the star cluster burst and extinguish itself high overhead, Vela, the assistant gunner, muttered, "Oh, shit." He took a first step and dropped into snow up to his knees. He thought, *Man, I'm from Texas, and we don't know about this shit*. He was dressed for the beach. He was humping an M-4, eight magazines, a barrel bag, and 550 rounds of 7.62 mm for the M-240 machine gun, or close to 100 pounds of dead weight.

"Come on," Stebner exhorted him, and he staggered uphill, huffing rarefied air that never allowed him a decent breath.

Jonas Polson was carrying 1,100 5.56 mm SAW rounds, front and back armor plates, four grenades, his SAW, and a CamelBak water pouch he had forgotten to fill. After only thirty seconds of climbing straight up, he was "sweating balls," and eating snow to hydrate himself. He kept thinking of the men on the peak. *The main thing, we got to go, we got to go.* For a while, Polson took Vela's ammo. He was a curious, even inspiring, soldier. At twenty, the youngest Ranger on the mountain, Polson had already lived a rebellious life that had included temporary solitary confinement in the county jail and "a hard route" through adolescence during which, for reasons he found difficult to explain even to himself, he "didn't care about anything or anybody except being the biggest, baddest guy who took the most drugs and got in the most fights." His bristling and often bewildering aggression disguised a sweet and intelligent disposition he did not want the world to know about. Tall and slim and powerful, he was also a natural Ranger whom nearly everyone in his platoon liked.

He was born in Sweden—his sisters' names were Anka and Elise, and his mother was a Lundgren. After their divorce, his American father raised the children as a single parent and tried to infuse Jonas especially with his own passion for Civil War history. On a family visit to Antietam and Gettysburg, he wanted Jonas to race across the open battlefields to give him the feel for the fighting there. On a different battlefield, father and son visited an ancient tree, still alive, that Matthew Brady had photographed during the Civil War. Jonas' father, a professional marriage therapist, said, "Jonas, this is the tree where men stood a hundred and fifty years ago." He carried the Brady photo in his hand.

Jonas, the son, told him, "That's great, Dad."

"What? You don't think that's fascinating?"

"Dad, we could take a picture of this now and five minutes

later, you know, we could say, we just stood there, and what fucking difference would it make?"

Up the side of Takur Ghar, Chalk 2 negotiated a good quarter of the 2,000-foot climb on all fours, crawling on snow and over slippery, sharp scree. They followed a military crest, on the finger's flank to conceal their profile from the enemy, and they did not traverse to reduce the pitch of the uphill climb. At some steeper junctures, the gunners threw their weapons up over them, praying they would not be staring down an enemy's barrel when they climbed up. They used the helping hands of those who reached down and would have used ropes if they had thought they might need them. The altitude starved their lungs of oxygen and dehydrated them, and the warmth generated by their exertions turned to chill the instant they stopped moving.

Canon told himself, *We are never going to make it.* He ordered the men to halt. "Ten minutes," he told them. "One by one, get your snivel gear off"—gloves, vests, caps, whatever each Ranger had chosen to wear for his personal comfort. Canon radioed Self and said, "We've got to ditch these back plates because there is no way we can make it to the top with them." The Kevlar armor plates weighed seven pounds each. They chafed and rubbed when the men crawled. Reluctantly, Self agreed with Canon to toss them.

Once the men had stripped down the weight they carried, one of the Rangers asked Canon, "What are we going to do with these?" Clearly, they could not leave the armor in one place for the enemy to scavenge.

"Scatter 'em," he replied, and the flat plates flew down the mountain as the "most expensive Frisbees," at somewhere around $2,000 a throw. Stebner and squad leader Staff Sergeant Harper Wilmoth held on to theirs for fear that the Army would make them pay for them later.

The climb was not easier, despite ditching equipment and reorganizing what they wore. The snow consisted of loose powder and changed in a single step from knee-deep to midthigh. They climbed around rock faces. Some slid downhill in the scree, forcing them to climb back up to a level with the rest of the chalk. Several of them threw up from altitude sickness. They felt dizzy. They could not catch a good breath. In some places, the mountain was steep enough for a tree to grow nearly parallel to the ground. The Ranger medic, Matt LaFrenz, pulled some of the Rangers over and across a tree trunk. This was not hiking; it was more like mountaineering, which forced each man to transcend mere physicality.

Willpower alone moved them up gradients of 45 to 70 degrees in 3-foot-deep snow. Secretly, as each man plowed on, concern over the fate of their buddies in Chalk 1 inspired them to rise above their own physical exhaustion. Who *were* the KIAs? they asked themselves. Vela and Stebner did not mention their fears to anyone. Vela told himself, *You are in your own world with that*. They worried about their friend Walker; Polson, who had always made light of Anthony Miceli's proclivity to hurt himself, was certain that he would be found among the dead when they reached the top. He reminded himself of a saying in the squad: "The only one who can kill Miceli is Miceli." Ranger Specialist Randy "Pork Chop" Pazder always said about him, "He can take a lickin' and keeps on tickin.'"

Canon was dreading injuries—or worse still, wounds caused by enemy fire—before they linked up, thus creating a *third* different isolated group on the mountain in need of extraction. With even one injured man, his chalk would no longer be able to negotiate this uphill climb; at best, they might be able to climb down to the dropoff LZ. His fear became real when, only a thousand feet from their starting point at the LZ, enemy soldiers to their south and east started to fire at them with small arms across open terrain. Canon believed that the shots were intended to slow down their progress or maybe turn them back. In his terms, it was not "effective fire." But the Rangers dropped to the ground each time the rounds came in. It was their first test under fire. Soon enough, though, they were almost used to sounds of bullets cracking over their heads. Canon thought, *Hey, wait. These bullets are going past us.*

But the small arms were a prelude to something worse. The chalk accorded mortars greater respect. The rounds, which Vela assessed aurally to be from a Russian 82 mm, flew in from down another ravine to their south and were "walking" in on them. The shells hit in the snow, which partly absorbed their shrapnel. After a short time, Canon, who was becoming quickly hardened, thought, *They aren't going to hit us with them, and even if they do, what can you do about it? So just keep walking.*

Vela, who knew about mortars from a casual study back in Savannah, calculated the minimum safe distance from a mortar of that caliber to be approximately 200 feet, and these rounds now were exploding at 40 feet. A round hit above them, another below them, a third directly to their right and on line. Vela thought, *Oh, shit. Now all they have to do is shift their line.* The chalk stopped, dropped, and waited, as if frozen in a tableau seen on the walls of military museums. Vela shouted, "What are we going to do, get mortared clinging on the side of a cliff? *Move!*"

About 800 feet below the peak, the chalk, climbing in a file behind Stebner at point, came across the mouth of a cave prepared by the Taliban and al-Qaeda. Canon thought, *You're kidding me. Can we just get to the top, please?* Polson trained his SAW on the cave entrance while the chalk climbed past, with Polson becoming the last person in line.

When Vela went past Polson, he told him, "This sucks."

"No shit," Polson replied, taking some of Vela's ammo to lighten his load.

Canon's radio crackled in his ear. It was Self, calling him from behind the large rock outcrop 150 feet below the peak. His anxiety was apparent in his voice. Canon's chalk had been climbing for nearly two hours but was nowhere in sight, and Self worried that they were lost. He told Canon, "I need to know exactly where you are at," and ordered Walker, beside him on the peak, to fire another star cluster. If Canon did not see the light in the sky, he was not even close, Self believed. He told Canon, "Move as fast as you can." He knew they were already moving as fast as they could move, but he said it anyway. He knew they were hurting physically, but no one was hurting as bad right now as the wounded.

Canon asked, "Where are you? What am I looking for?"

"A big outcropping, downslope from us."

"In the rocks, is that you?"

"Wave your arms."

Canon had sighted either Miceli or DePouli down by the rock outcrop with Self.

DePouli asked Miceli to get up on the rock to see if he could spot them.

"Where are you at?" Canon asked in his radio. "Ray, can you see us?"

"No," DePouli replied. Miceli couldn't see them either.

A few minutes later, Canon shouted, "We can see you!"

His point man, Eric Stebner, pulled out his compass to shoot an azimuth to give a heading for Miceli and DePouli to follow with their eyes for an idea where to find them.

"Can you see me now?" Canon asked in the radio.

Stebner looked back over his shoulder. Canon was throwing snow up in the air. Stebner went down on one knee and started laughing at the sight.

"Do you see me now?" asked Canon.

Miceli and DePouli were laughing, too. "Yeah, we see you," Miceli replied.

About thirty minutes later, after more than two and a half hours of an exhausting climb of 2,000 vertical feet humping heavy gear in thin air, Chalk 2 crested Takur Ghar.

Canon came around the rock outcrop, nervous now that

he had arrived at the fight, and asked DePouli, "Is this clear down here?"

"I don't know," DePouli told him. He thought it was clear. He and Miceli had manned positions down there for a couple of hours. However, what Canon was alluding to, DePouli supposed, was a grouping of trees a couple hundred feet downslope from the outcropping, near the rustic mosque. Canon knew what DePouli could not have known—that he had seen al-Qaeda fighters climbing in that direction who by now almost certainly were hiding in those trees, although possibly they had kept moving across the pass in the direction of the Pakistani border.

Miceli looked at the arriving Rangers, their faces rigid with expectation and eyes alight despite their exhaustion. By comparison, he felt almost relaxed, almost like a hardened veteran of many campaigns.

"I can't believe I'm seeing you," Vela told Miceli as he turned the corner of the rock.

"You're here! We wrote you off," Stebner joked.

Their attempts at humor notwithstanding, Miceli saw palpable relief in his friends' faces that the Miceli jinx was only superstition.

2

STEBNER GLANCED AT THE BODY OF THE DEAD enemy fighter while he paused to rummage through the sleeping positions that DePouli had cleared earlier. Stebner shot a couple of rounds into the blankets for good measure. Then he noticed an American Army rucksack. He told Canon, "That's weird." Packages of MREs were scattered in the hole. He thought, *Where did they get it from?* He also saw an American helmet with bullet holes front and back and a set of NVGs. "Fifi" was written on the helmet. A blue key chain was clipped to the ruck. He held it in the palm of his hand. It was a small blue unicorn. He put it in his pocket and stood up to walk around the rock.

"Where's the PL?" Canon asked DePouli, who pointed him to Self nearby.

"Boss, what do you want me to do?" Canon asked.

Self said, "We need to take the bunker. Now."

"Where do you want the guns at?"

"Gilliam will show you. Just get some ammo."

While his chalk went with Self up to the rocks beneath the bunkers, Canon made his way over to the casualty collection point at the rear of the helo for ammo. The sight of the dead shocked him. He was thinking, *Whoa.*

Totten-Lancaster, with a severed nerve from shrapnel, was sitting on the snow. It did not dawn on Canon that he might be wounded. Canon told him, "Get up! Get your shit! Get your gun!"

Totten-Lancaster said, "Sarge, I got a bit of a wound going on down here," meaning his leg. "I don't have a SAW."

"Where's your SAW at?" Canon demanded.

"Miceli's got it."

"Where's Miceli's SAW at?"

"It's shot."

"What are you guys doing up here, playing grab-ass?" He went over to Self, sheltering behind the rocks.

"All right, but why does Gilliam have the gun?" he asked Self. "I'm going to need an AG. Who?"

The 160th SOAR crew chief, Brian Wilson, was nearby. Canon asked him, "Do you know how to work a 240?"

"No," he replied.

"You can use an M-60, right?"

"Yeah."

"Close enough. Go start bringing ammo over here." Canon then turned to Gilliam. "Where are we going?" Gilliam pointed to the peak and the low rock outcropping. It looked a long way to Canon.

As nature would have it, and while Canon and Self worked out the details of the assault, Walker, behind the rocks to the right of Self, where he had sheltered since the first attempted assault, felt the cramps of a painful imperative that until now he had successfully ignored. With an occasional bullet from the peak snapping over his head, he rolled over on his side, pulled his pants down, and relieved himself in the snow before rolling back over to await the assault.

Vela was still wheezing from the climb when he reached the rocks where the assault force was getting ready. He and Pazder, with one of the two M-240s, positioned themselves on Gilliam's right, and laid out a plan for their supporting part of the assault. Vela pushed the body of an al-Qaeda fighter out of the way, thinking, *OK, he's dead.* On the way up, he'd looked around for his friend Marc Anderson and did not see him or Matt Commons. He'd seen Totten-Lancaster over by the helo. But he was wondering, *Where's Big A at?* He did not even consider that he might be dead.

Stebner already knew Anderson's fate. When the chalk had reached the top, he'd asked DePouli, who had told him, "He's dead. You stay alive. Settle it up. Make it even. Kick ass." Stebner thought indifferently about his own mortality, *If you get hit, you get hit. So throw that shit out of your mind and just do it.* But the loss of friends angered and confused him.

To reach the rocks from the southern outcrop, Polson had made a dash across the eastern edge of the saddle, over broken rocks in the snow, to reach Walker, in preparation for this, the second assault on the peak. As he ran, Polson's eyes were drawn over to the KIAs, their bodies scattered near the Chinook, 15 feet from the casualty collection point, where Cunningham was giving aid to Calvert, Dube, and Gant. Polson pulled up at the rocks, narrowly avoiding Walker's excrement. When Stebner ran over to join them, he headed straight for the pile.

Walker yelled, "Hey, watch out! I just took a crap right there."

Stebner daintily lay down prone, with Polson on his left, leaving a respectful space between them for the offending ordure. Unexpectedly, Sergeant Patrick George came bounding up to join them, too, and dove headfirst behind the rocks. Stebner warned him too late. His elbows slid through it.

Laughing, Polson chided him, "Awww, you got shit on you."

George was screaming, "Get it off me! Get it off!"

Polson said, "Naw, I don't want to touch it."

"Get it off me!" George stood up, clearly more worried about the crap on his sleeve than about the bullets flying past him from the peak.

For that moment, uproarious laughter muffled the sounds of pain, as if an asylum had been emptied on a mountaintop.

For Self, who was again in command of both chalks for the first time since leaving Bagram, the imperative for a second assault to take the higher ground came from the casualties. He was getting radio reports of enemy movement. Clearly, he thought, the enemy's main positions were below and possibly to their right. If there were to be one, an attack would leave the wounded out in the open and exposed to everything the enemy had to throw at them. The safest way to anticipate and defend against an attack, he thought, was to secure the highest ground, take over their enemy's positions on the peak, and move the casualties up to the western side of the mountain out of the way. The plan made perfect sense. Its success depended now on timing and luck.

Polson, waiting to begin the assault, struggled to keep his eyes off the dead laid out on the snow. He did not know who they were. He wanted to and he didn't want to know. He looked at George, finally asking him, "Who is it?"

"You really want to know?" George asked.

"Yeah."

"Brad's dead."

A sudden anger overcame Polson. He looked for Crose's body among the dead. Instead, he saw a corpse with reddish purple hair shining in the bright sunlight. Matt Commons was the only person in the platoon with natural burgundy-colored hair. Nobody needed to tell him that his friend was dead. Polson could hardly wait for the assault to begin.

Canon was behind the rocks farthest to the east, near the dropoff into the valley. A dead enemy soldier with an RPG lying at his side was wearing a blue ski parka with the goose down blowing out bullet holes. Canon thought, *Well, this guy can't stay here. We have to get in this position.* He pushed him with his boot down an incline and over the side. Canon noticed that he was wearing plastic shower shoes in the freezing cold. He had to respect that kind of toughness. He reported to Self that he was ready.

Self said, "OK, we're ready for you to initiate."

Canon asked, "Well, what's the signal?"

"Shoot," Self replied. "Start shootin'."

The first ten rounds in Canon's magazines were tracers. He stood up and yelled out, "On my mark!" Gilliam, with the machine gun, was looking up at him. "I don't know if I would be standing right there. I almost got shot there a while ago."

Canon told him, "Whatever! I don't plan on getting shot today. All right, here we go." He started shooting. The two machine guns fired alternately, first Gilliam's on the right with a one-second burst from the first squad's machine gun, then the second squad's machine gun for a one-second burst, back and forth across an interlocking field of fire.

On Canon's mark, Polson pushed off past the dead enemy with an RPG still in his frozen hands, his body riddled with holes. Half running and half walking with his SAW pointed at the peak, he sprayed the first bunker with bullets. Tracers from Vela and Pazder's machine guns ricocheted off the rocks to his left. Focusing on the front and left flank of the main assault, Polson and Stebner ran around the left side of the rock outcrop to flank whatever was behind the rock.

Stebner was moving up on Polson's right. Mere feet in front of bunker #1 by the rock, he saw a body lying facedown in the snow. A glance told him that the dead man was wearing American military boots with distinctive Vibram soles with yellow rubber logos. *Oh, well, they have our boots, too*, he was thinking. To him the redhaired dead man looked like a Chechen with a scraggly beard, but in fact Stebner was staring at the body of Neil Roberts. His attention was drawn away when, out of the corner of his eye, he saw an enemy fighter slip behind the rock outcrop. Stebner yelled to Polson, "Shit, somebody's behind that." He and Polson moved to the east behind bunker #1. A redheaded Chechen was backing up in an effort to move down the steep incline on the northern crest. Stebner shot him twice. Polson emptied a twenty-round burst in him. The dead enemy did "his chicken dance on the ground," his body twitching with the impact of the bullets. As he was firing, Polson's SAW went *kerchunk*. He told Stebner, "It's shit the bed on me." The operating rod had warped. They moved to their right.

They were throwing hand grenades on the other side of the rise. Polson threw three. Stebner threw one. George threw one. Polson checked his toss of another grenade at the DShK and an 82 mm mortar tube, fearing an explosion of the enemy's ammunition. He was staring at a pile of rocks where he thought an enemy might be crouching. Specialist Oscar Escano, Chalk 2's M-203 gunner, came up behind him and fired a round at the DShK. A grenade exploded against the enemy's ammo, causing a secondary explosion that was the equivalent of at least a quarter pound of C-4 explosive. Five feet away from the blast, Polson was blown off his feet. He looked at Escano, thinking, *Fucker, if you ever do anything like that again, let me know so I can get down.*

At the start of the assault, Canon took off to the right. He came across a one-man fighting position behind a fir tree with a sweeping, panoramic view of the entire valley. Canon yelled, "Has anybody cleared this hole back here?"

The Army medic, Matt LaFrenz, beside Canon, pointed his weapon at the position.

Canon said, "Let's frag it." He cooked off a grenade and counted, "One thousand, two thousand," hoping the grenade had a five-second fuse. He chucked the grenade and heard its explosion. He stood up, flipped his gun to auto fire, and let off a burst into the bunker. A bundle of RPG rounds exploded and blew him back off his feet. LaFrenz grabbed his body armor's drag handles and pulled him away, with Canon thinking this was the luckiest moment in his life.

The group who had assaulted the peak felt more relief than amazement that, it seemed, only one enemy soldier was left to defend the peak, and Stebner had killed him. Every other enemy fighter was either gone or had been blown apart by bombs and bullets. Even before the assault, Self had assumed that most of the enemy soldiers were dead or had fled. Shots had continued from the peak onto their positions through the morning hours, and it was now near 1130 local. And whether one Chechen or fifty had defended the peak from the assault, it was all the same to Self. With his assault force slogging up the open ground in high-altitude air, one enemy on the peak with an AK-47 could have killed them if he had not been trying to flee. Brown was surprised only that anyone on the peak was alive after the multiple fighter gun runs and the Hellfire attacks.

If not their numbers, what the enemy had built for an outpost on the peak amazed Polson and Stebner. It was an ideal fighting position *and* a command and control point for the entire area on and around Takur Ghar, with a cleverly concealed C2 tent in a crevice; a bunker network that extended well down the northern peak; a large kitchen area with a stove, gas lamps, containers of diesel oil, and a dead goat hanging from a tree; individual shelters with warm clothes and blankets; and the DShK aimed out at the flat valley area between Takur Ghar and the Whale. The clever concealment of the position impressed Polson. The peak looked like untouched natural terrain from just a few yards away, much less from the base of the mountain or from the air overhead.

Checking out the top, around the enemy's kitchen area behind the bunkers, Canon smelled the dead animals.

Polson moved over to the nine o'clock of the helo. He sat down, watching Stebner and a couple of other Rangers go across the peak and down at the helo's eight o'clock position. Polson looked to the south and saw no sign of enemy soldiers. Polson was thinking that their work for the day was just about done.

On the peak, Canon called Self. He said, "Boss, you need to come up here and look at this."

When he reached the top, Self saw what Canon was referring to. Self was *still* confused why Roberts would be there in the first place. He thought he might have killed an American in the assault. Canon pointed out Chapman's body buried under debris in bunker #1. On the north end of the bunker, Chapman's back was against the bunker wall. Self wondered if the al-Qaeda fighters had captured Chapman and Roberts, whom one of the Rangers recognized from a visit to their tent area a couple of times at Bagram. Canon searched their clothing for ID to confirm who they were.

Wasting no time, Self said, "Let's start moving the wounded up to the top of the mountain."

Canon walked down the incline to the helo. Totten-Lancaster told him, "Anderson, Crose, and Commons are KIA." Canon was visibly upset.

Self joined him a minute later. He told Canon, "Snap out of it. There's stuff we have to do here. Time to get back to the task at hand."

But Canon needed a moment to compose himself. He was thinking about this confrontation with death. He told himself, *You always know that people that work for you may die, and you do your best to make sure as many of them get home as possible. But it had never dawned on me that kids who worked for me, or I myself, might come home in a body bag. It's the invincibility of the team that's been shattered. Ten feet tall and bulletproof, and now you see two kids who work for you lying in the snow dead, and it's very surreal.*

As senior NCO, Canon was responsible for "these kids," as he called his Rangers. The three dead Rangers were closer to him, he said, "than his two blood brothers." He had spent hours with them, counseling them, listening to them talk about girl-friends, careers, their job performance. He *knew* them. Crose, Anderson, and Commons, their bodies lying out in the open by the Chinook, had trained under him. He had been their squad leader from the day they walked into the battalion.

He remembered Brad "Danger" Crose, Matt Commons, and Marc "Gentle Giant" Anderson as friends who did a lot of joking together. The biggest joke since deployment had been the day they were leaving Savannah's Hunter Army Air Field. It tore them up. Girlfriends, wives, mothers and fathers, children, pets, and friends came out to wave good-bye. The parting was sad, but it was also electric with anticipation. This was war, and the Rangers were lining up for their share of it. They felt proud and anxious, aggressive and tough, and hardly a man was not champing to leave.

Posters and flags, hugs and kisses, promises and vows, tiny mementos, lockets with photos exchanged at the last minute . . . And then they were gone. Fifteen minutes later, they were back again, wearing sheepish grins. The airplane that was to fly them to Afghanistan had weight problems. They went back home for the night. The next day, it began again—flags, banners, the works, though with slightly diminished brio.

"Are you really leaving this time?" a Ranger's girlfriend asked.

"I hope so, because I don't want to do this again," he told her.

But yet another mechanical problem kept them home.

Then on the third day, with a profound sense of relief, they waved good-bye, and they went. Once in the air, they laughed about how sick they were of saying good-bye.

Marc Anderson had not particularly minded the delays. His mom and dad had driven back to Florida after a first and last good-bye. Marc understood the complexities of troop deployments, and he knew how little things created frustrating delays. He was mature and even-natured, and as head of the weapons squad, he was arguably the most knowledgeable man in the platoon, the company, and perhaps the battalion. He seemed to know about everything, could comment on any-thing, was fatherly with good advice, and, like the teacher he had been before joining the Rangers, he loved to share with his buddies his knowledge of how things worked. He was a brute of a guy, 6 feet 3 inches and 240 pounds, named after Caesar's general Marc Antony. A few years back, he had scored 1,464 on his SATs and was recruited, for his talents as a track shot putter and a football player, by Brown, West Point, and Notre Dame. He'd gone to Case Western Reserve to study engineering and left after three years for Florida State, closer to home, where he graduated in 1995 with a 4.0 grade point average in mathematics education.

He taught at Ft. Myers Middle School for three years and loved his students. He even wrote one of them with the most potential into his last will and testament to receive $12,000 in case he died in battle. He had joined the military out of a sense of duty to his country that his father, Dave, a twenty-one-year Ranger veteran of Vietnam, had instilled in him. The Rangers assigned him to a weapons squad, responsible for a 25-pound

M-240 medium machine gun. He had an uncanny ability to put a first round on target at night with the 50-caliber machine gun, and before long, he was good enough to instruct the battalion. When other gunners needed help, Anderson found time. The math required to calculate target ranges was daunting to many of the younger Rangers. "If you couldn't figure something out, you went to Anderson," his platoon's first sergeant said of him. He took life as it came. Everyone in the platoon depended on him.

About a year before deployment to Afghanistan, Anderson's older brother, Stephen, was diagnosed with cancer. It weighed on Marc. At a last meeting, saying good-bye, Marc asked him, "Which one of us will be first?"

"Hey, guys—*enough!*" their mother, Judy, interrupted.

"I could get out of going," Marc told her, "but I won't because I'm a part of a team."

"No. Because it's your *job*," said Stephen, who would succumb to his cancer within the year.

Sergeant Brad Crose, now lying in a heap on the snow beside Anderson, had been an odd mixture of personality and emotions. He was as tough as any other Ranger, but he also loved to go Christmas shopping with his mom and in any season to bake cookies from her special chocolate chip recipe. Growing up in Orange Park, Florida, near Jacksonville, he did the things that adventurous young men do—skied, rode horseback, went sky diving, and biked 150 miles a year. Unlike other young men, he badgered his mom, Sheila, for new recipes, which he filed on 3-by-5 cards in a box. He baked her special cookies, she said, better than she did, and that last Thanksgiving before leaving for Afghanistan, Crose had prepared a home-style dinner for twenty-five Rangers at his friend Sergeant Eric Stebner's apartment off base. He'd baked three apple crumb pies, three batches of the chocolate chip cookies, a casserole, and enough homemade rolls to feed everybody. Stebner roasted a turkey. Staff Sergeant Joshua Walker brought a honey-baked ham. If this did not sound like a family, nothing did.

The first day that they were scheduled to leave Savannah for Afghanistan, Crose's mother and grandparents drove up to see him off. His mother was a devout Christian and member of the Assembly of God, and Brad was a church-going Presbyterian. She worried, and she asked if something happened to him, would he go to heaven? One way to ensure that passage came through prayer. In the privacy of his room, she had prayed with him, kneeling on the floor. Then his grandfather had prayed with him, and finally his grandmother. He was patient and wore a smile. A shy, quiet man of twenty-seven, he wanted nothing so much as to please. He told his mother when they were alone again, "Mother, if I die, I died doing what I believe in. It has to be done. I don't want you to be upset. Don't worry, Rangers don't die." He was certain of it. He told her, "Mom, I give you my word, I promise I'm coming back." She asked if he had written an "in case" letter that some Rangers left behind for parents, wives, and girlfriends. Brad said, "I'll be back."

Corporal Matt Commons, the last of the dead trio of

Rangers, was a fascinating and complex young man, from Boulder City, Arizona. He'd brought along a deep fascination with metaphysics and had asked about the meaning of death even as a child. For his high school senior project, he had researched good and evil, God and the devil. The subject upset his mother, who had raised Matt and his brother as a single parent since Matt was five. Now at twenty-one, he was buff, 5 feet 10 inches and 160 pounds of muscle, with a six-pack he was proud of. In Afghanistan, he dreamed of home and Brittany, the love of his life. As a Ranger, everybody liked him for using good cheer as an antidote to bad conditions. His friends joked that he was the first to volunteer, always the first one to accept challenges, and the guy who was never afraid.

Only one thing had seemed to bother him about the deployment to Afghanistan. He explained to his mother, "Mom, I've never gone hunting before. I never even killed a rabbit. I wonder what it's like to kill a human being." She said without an instant's hesitation, "Shoot first and think later. I want you to come home."

The other dead man, Sergeant Philip Svitak, wasn't a Ranger. He was handsome, with blond hair and golden eyes, a trim 5 feet 11 inches. At the 160th SOAR compound at Ft. Campbell, Kentucky, he'd often arrived at the mess hall for lunch wearing neon bicycling shorts and a gaudy Italian racing shirt, much to the amusement of his friends.

Svitak had not intended to make the military a career, but when his parents in Joplin, Missouri, did not have the money to send him to college, he decided to sign up to save what was needed. After one tour, once he was discharged, he worked as a FedEx deliveryman for a year, but he missed his "brothers" in SOAR. His wife, Laura, the mother of their two young boys, Ethan and Nolan, understood when Phil reenlisted as a SOAR door gunner. He was a crack shot with his mini gun, and he sharpened his skill playing paintball, which had become his latest passion. In a black "Terminator" T-shirt decorated with the drawing of a human skull, he had a knack for popping up behind his opponents, his paintball gun pointed at them. He told them in a drawl like John Wayne's, "Pilgrims, you want it the easy way or the hard way?"

Now, Canon took a long look at Anderson lying on his back with his shirt off from when the PJ, Jason Cunningham, had attempted to resuscitate him. Canon was thinking about what "a huge teddy bear, a bear of a man," Anderson was. *There he is lying in the snow, his DCU bottoms on, with his cold weather boots black, and that's just it. He's looking up at you. I'm like, "Dipshit, hey! It's cold! Get dressed!" It took an instant to realize that was not going to happen.*

3

EVEN 3 MILES AWAY FROM TAKUR GHAR, EYES WERE watching the approaches right up to the peak itself. James "Hots" Hotaling, an Air Force combat controller concealed on a ridge at 9,700 feet, peered through the lens of a Maksutov-Cassegrain, a specially designed telescope with the crispness and power to see and characterize individuals from 6 miles away. The day was bright and the air was clear over the southern pass that the military had designated as "Ginger." The enemy fighters could not move through wide terrain without Hotaling sighting them in his lens. With a sense of foreboding, he scanned the pass, which up to now had been empty. He knew that enemy soldiers used Ginger to escape east over the mountains toward Pakistan, and to reinforce and resupply their troops in the Shah-i-Kot. Indeed, it was a main "squirt" route. His job hiding in the trees was to spot the fighters and pound them with munitions from the air.

Beginning in small numbers, starting in the middle of the morning, Hotaling started to notice concentrations of the enemy moving up from the valley, and what worried him more than their presence was their direction. To his eyes, they looked like "cookie crumbs" or like "ants moving toward a honey pot." They were not fleeing the fighting in the valley. They were headed up toward the helicopter on the peak. He thought, *They are moving like they have the smell of blood.*

4

A T LEAST NINETY MINUTES EARLIER, AFTER SEAL
Lieutenant Commander Hyder finally linked up with
MAKO 30, completing an exhausting 90 minutes of
climbing laterally, up, down, and over fingers and wadis on the
eastern slope, Slab greeted him at first with relief, and then
with potent anger. "Why didn't you bring more dudes?" he
wanted to know. There weren't more dudes, Hyder told him.
The QRF had elected to head straight for the mountaintop.
Slab calmed down. He accepted the reality. He even agreed that
the Rangers had done the right thing by going up to the top.
Slab had no idea how bad their situation was on the peak.
MAKO 30 was about a thousand feet below, with high ground

all around, in a position that Slab judged to be bad. He thought, *We can't stay down here.*

He worried for Brett, but mostly for Turbo, who he felt would die if nothing was done for him soon. Turbo was exhausted, in pain, and nearly hypothermic with the cold. He was bordering on hypovolemic shock, brought on by a loss of at least a fifth of his blood. He was breathing in shallow gasps, his skin color was pale, and he was sweaty, with a rapid pulse. He needed replacement blood and fluids. Nothing else could reverse the downward spiral.

Slab tried to call for a medevac, but his MBITR radio allowed him to talk to aircraft flying overhead for only thirty seconds before they flew out of range. "You can get a 60 in here," he told them, referring to a Black Hawk rescue helo, which could drop a basket on a winch line. Slab wanted to send Turbo and Brett out, and he, Randy, and Kyle would go back to the fight.

Hyder and Slab conferred on what to do. Climbing over to where Hyder had landed was impossible with the wounded. They decided to follow a draw toward a potential LZ down to the south and look for opportunities along the way.

They moved out. With some steps, the weight of their bodies and the downward thrust of their legs drove them into the snow up to their thighs. The struggle for each step in the thin air was painful and exhausting. Randy helped Brett, who could walk and carry his heavy M-60 machine gun. But when he stopped his leg cramped; his pants were bright red from the blood he'd lost. Kyle took up the rear, while Slab and Hyder dragged Turbo on his back across the snow by pulling on his arms. After a short while, that became too painful for Turbo. They stopped and made a crutch out of a piece of wood, but that didn't work either. They put him on his stomach and he arched his back, and with his bad leg up in the air, they dragged him. Slab told him he looked like Frosty the Snowman. They stopped every 70 feet when Turbo couldn't take the pain anymore or Hyder and Slab needed a breather.

On one of these rest stops, Hyder climbed to a higher draw for a better view. A dark-haired man with a beard was running down the mountain about 300 feet away. Hyder observed him for five minutes. He was wearing pants and a long shirt in the style of the local Afghan Taliban and was moving fast enough for Hyder to assume he was running from the peak. The enemy soldier tripped, fell, and landed on his stomach. Hyder watched him rise onto his knees. The American brought up his sniper rifle, put the man's chest in the crosshairs of his scope, and fired. The man dropped on his side. Hyder shot him again in the chest.

When they started again, they came across a cliff about 10 feet high that they could not get around. Slab and Kyle used the slings off their guns to lower Turbo down. Slab jammed his hands in the rock and Turbo put his weight on Slab's shoulders, then jumped the last four feet, landing in terrible pain. Turbo lay in the snow, telling Slab, "Man, just leave me here."

Slab was enraged by the suggestion after what they already had gone through. He did not want Turbo to give up. He knew Turbo could be stubborn; as one of his commanders said, working with him was "like herding cats." He was a teammate who was valued. Slab knew he had to snap him out of it. He straddled him and slapped his face. "I'm *not* leaving you," he shouted at him.

Turbo mentioned the pain.

"You want some morphine?"

Turbo's eyes widened. But from the way Slab had asked him, Turbo didn't think he was going to get any, and it would admit weakness Turbo wasn't yet quite ready for. He said, "No." He could take it a while longer.

Slab said, "Good." He turned away.

Onward they moved, with a kind of grim determination born of hurt and cold and confusion about how the day would end. At the next stop, Turbo looked like he was going to die. His face was gray, and he was shivering uncontrollably. His wound left a continuous trail of blood in the snow. He was slipping in and out of consciousness and was on the verge of shock. Slab stopped, alarmed by his teammate's condition. Against his better judgment, he tried to start a fire to warm Turbo, whom Slab had tucked up against a tree. But then Slab thought, *Dude, this is wrong,* and even before it started to smoke, he put the fire out.

They moved out again, dragging Turbo over the next three hours for another 1,500 feet, until he could be moved no further.

Hyder took the Iridium satellite phone to higher ground to see who might answer. He tried calling the TOC at Bagram, but the phone was turned off. Hyder remembered the number of the SEAL base in Virginia Beach, Virginia, half a world away. He dialed and the communications room answered, surprised when he said, "This is Hyder, troops in contact, need you to go get the DCO."

The deputy commanding officer rushed to the phone, and Hyder gave him the grid coordinates for a little knoll that he said could serve as a landing zone. The next time he dialed the Bagram TOC, the phone was connected, and he asked for a medic to advise him how to treat the wounded men. A doctor told him there was little Hyder could do except to keep them warm. Slab, Kyle, and Randy set about stripping boughs from the neighboring pine trees to make beds for them to lie on. They wrapped them in down jackets. With rest and warmth, Turbo's color began to improve.

Now that they had reached their limit, Slab took a breath. He was sitting beside Kyle and said to him, "You know what, Kyle? You think anything else could go wrong?"

"I doubt it," Kyle said.

"What day is this?"

"March fourth," Kyle replied.

"My wedding anniversary."

5

ATTENDING TO THE CASUALTIES NEAR THE HELO ramp, Lamereaux noticed that Calvert was fading. In a weak voice, Calvert said, "Tell my wife and my kids I love 'em."

"What in the hell are you talking about?"

"Just make sure you tell 'em I love 'em."

"No, dude, *you're* going to tell them that."

"I don't think I'm going to make it."

He started to crash. Lamereaux reassessed the IV he had put in his arm and started going at a slow rate. He looked again. The IV had cautered off, and the plasma had stopped entering his veins.

"Hell, we got to get another IV going," Lamereaux said to Cunningham. "He's hypovolemic."

Stebner was standing nearby, waiting to move litters up to the incline to the crest. Just by the look of the slope, carrying a man on a stretcher for that distance was going to be grueling. The snow was melting in the sunlight. It was nearly noon. Stebner was told to start with Dave Dube, the door gunner with the wounded leg.

"Which one's Dube?" Stebner asked.

"He's the large guy that's there," Lamereaux replied, pointing.

Stebner walked up to him. "Are you Dube?"

"Yeah, I'm Dube, man. I'm sorry, I'm a little overweight. I'm going to be heavier to get up there."

"That's all right. We'll get you to the top of the hill."

Oscar Escano helped Stebner pull Dube's Skedco up the hill.

Someone yelled, "Hurry up, hurry up."

The remark annoyed Stebner, who wondered who they thought they were, and if they could do better, let them try. He soon found out what they were yelling about. In an instant he heard steady bursts of gunfire from the south. An enemy counterattack, as fierce as the initial attack on the helo, was starting from enemy soldiers who had moved up from where Hotaling had seen them. They were firing machine guns and RPGs from behind a ridge 300 feet to the six o'clock of the helo, placing the casualties in a direct line of fire across an open field of brilliant white snow. Strapped on the Skedco, Dube was trapped out in the open, halfway up the incline, and unable to move. Carrying him, Stebner and Escano dropped to their bellies in the snow.

On the peak with Self, Polson was the first to return fire with his SAW. The gun teams jumped over the rocks and aimed down the slope. Polson's SAW jammed again. He could see the enemy soldiers rise above the ridgeline. One of their gunners fixed on Polson and fired off a steady burst from an AK-47. Rocks kicked up around him, and he shouted, "Holy fuck, man! This is fucking bullshit!" He could not get his gun to fire.

RPGs flew up the slope. A few ricocheted off the snow and exploded up the hill. One flew straight at the peak, hit about 10 yards in front of the men fighting there, skipped off the snow, and went right past them, exploding a few feet to their rear. Self, who almost never cursed, shouted, "Jesus Christ!"

Self ordered Polson to move to an already cleared enemy bunker that overlooked the southeast. Brown was already working his radio to call in CAS. Rounds flew over his head and shredded the branches of an overhanging tree. PJ Keary Miller had been assisting Totten-Lancaster when the attack began. They were standing by the refueling boom, and for a moment Miller seemed dazed and confused. He was physically drained and out of breath. He and Totten-Lancaster hit the ground, then, under fire, they got up and moved as fast as possible to the crest. When they had reached safety, Miller sat on a rock and stared off into the distance, in shock.

From the bunker, Polson fixed his SAW, fired a burst, fixed his SAW again, fired another burst. Totten-Lancaster found a place to lie in the hole at his side, and Polson, ever the joker, stopped shooting to give Totten-Lancaster a look that said, *You sexy bitch.* He and Totten-Lancaster started laughing. Totten-Lancaster said he had to relieve himself. Airily, Polson advised him, "Shit away."

Brown had a picture of the terrain already in his head, and he was calling in close air support. Rounds were ricocheting off a rock in front of him, and he wondered why nothing was hitting him. The supersonic crack of the bullets that went past his ears amazed him. He ducked down. An RPG launcher flashed and a grenade flew in his direction, wobbling. He felt that he could have caught it in his hand.

The fire from below was fierce and directed, grazing, with flat trajectories up the slope. The rounds had a tendency to impact up the saddle, sometimes skittering. Self could gauge the effectiveness of their fire by their tracers. By the number of RPGs, machine guns, and AK-47s, he estimated that there were twenty-five enemy soldiers, and they were shooting at very close range. He yelled for the men in the open to spread out. Right now, yelling was the most he could do.

Stebner and Escano could run behind the cover of a nearby rock, but Dube could not move or be moved. Stebner and Escano were going to get killed if they didn't move behind cover. They jumped behind a rock and waited for a lull in the shooting. One came a few minutes later. Stebner ran out in the open. He pulled Dube uphill a few yards until the shooting started again, directed at him and Dube. He left him a second time and ran back to the rock. *Damn,* he thought, watching the bullets fly over Dube and kick up snow near his Skedco. *He's all alone.*

Staff Sergeant Harper Wilmoth was on the ridge watching Stebner, thinking he was seeing heroism that nothing ever could top. He had yelled at Stebner not to run out in the open like that. He was going to be killed. Watching from about 60 feet away, he said to himself, *OK, I'll just sit here and watch Stebner get killed.* He waited for a bullet to hit him.

Dube tried to get up from the Skedco. Stebner dashed out for him a third time as bullets bounced all around him.

Dube told him, "Just leave me here. You're going to get shot."

"No, man, I'm going to get you up to the top of the hill. You ready to go?" He started to pull the Skedco. The ridge was about 40 feet up the incline. He was dragging him just as a burst came in, and he bounded over to the same rock as before. He saw Vela dart past, and told him, "They don't like me. Every time I get up they shoot at me."

When the counterattack began, Vela, Canon, Pazder, DePouli, and Miceli started returning fire from the rock 150 feet to the southeast of the peak, where the chalks had linked up. They quickly were "winchestering," or running out of their ammo, down to fewer than 100 rounds of 7.62 mm. Vela was appointed to run up the saddle and across the snowfield to the helicopter to resupply, and then run back in the open. On the first effort, he reached the Chinook and was scavenging the interior. He filled a barrel bag with as much M-240 ammo as he could carry, strapped it on his back, and sprinted off the bird. The firing was intense over the tail, and Vela hit the ground beside Calvert and Gant's litters.

"Hey, man, good job," Calvert complimented him.

"I'm not staying," Vela told him. "I'm going to keep going." From below, Miceli was yelling at Vela to stay down.

Vela started running in the open and yelled back, "Why?"

"Because they're *shooting* at you!"

He didn't know they were shooting at *him*. "Damn," he shouted. He jumped behind the same rock as Stebner, just as an RPG flew straight at them and zipped over their heads, missing them by feet.

Stebner said, "What are you doing here, Vela?"

"I want to go down to the rock and get the ammo down there. Just start firing. I'm going to run." A second RPG wobbled overhead as he took off. Halfway down the slope, he tripped and fell. He looked around, quickly got back on his feet, and ran faster than he had ever run before. Miceli was screaming at him.

"What?" Vela asked.

"I was telling you to get the fuck down. You had tracers all over your ass."

Canon was sitting next to Pazder, acting as his assistant gunner, about 15 feet away from Miceli and DePouli. Earlier Pazder had found a firing position behind a rock shelf; he rested his M-240's muzzle on the lip. The enemy could not see his muzzle flash. He had cover and an "awesome" field of fire. He was aiming at a tree with a crooked branch that served him as a perfect targeting window. He watched as one of the enemy popped up, shot, and went down, again and again.

Polson was sitting on the eastern ridge, overlooking the saddle to his front and the sloping ground to his right. He was waiting with his erratic SAW watching the same crooked branch, which he laid in his sights. He was waiting to fire when an RPG rocketed over his head. He saw a slight movement near the branch, so he pulled the trigger and lit up the tree, which was about 250 feet away. He heard Pazder's machine gun open up at the same instant.

Canon had exhorted Pazder, "Next time that guy puts his head up, if you don't blow it off, I'm going to fire you."

A second RPG came from behind the tree. Polson did not see the shooter this time, and he assumed the enemy soldiers were putting the weapon on the branch and pulling the trigger, hoping for an effective shot without aiming. Pazder hit the tree with a burst. Suddenly, the RPG gunner, with an odd disregard for his own life, stood up in clear view. Polson aimed a burst of 5.56 mm.

"Oh, I got him," said Pazder.

This episode, along with the behavior of the enemy, gave Canon pause. Previously he had wanted to dismiss the al-Qaeda and Taliban as "Third World monkeys," but he now recalled that they had been locked in combat with Soviets, had traveled to Chechnya and fought the Russians, and now they were fighting the Americans at 10,000 feet dressed in pajama bottoms and 99-cent plastic shoes. He thought, *The minute you don't respect your adversary is the minute you are going to die.*

6

BEFORE THE COUNTERATTACK STARTED, LAMEREAUX had been inserting a new IV in Calvert's arm. The sounds of the enemy gunfire shocked him. He thought, *One minute you're safe from this threat in the front, and the next you're getting it from the rear.* Lamereaux and Cunningham picked up their weapons. Joined by the air mission commander, Tabron, they started to fire down the saddle to protect the casualties any way they could.

Lamereaux yelled, "Hell, we've got to move these patients. We have to get them behind cover." But he, Cunningham, and Tabron could not lift the litters. They called for help and then picked up their rifles and began shooting, lying on the snow.

The shape of the saddle over which they fired offered an awkward shot. They sat up and were shooting down over their boot tops.

With the bullets flying over them from two directions, Calvert and Gant decided to play dead. "Maybe they won't shoot at us," Calvert said. He turned his face away from the enemy gunfire, but after an instant of anxiety too great to endure, he turned back. He saw the enemy pop up and shoot. He could hear their voices—taunting them, he guessed, though he spoke not a word of Arabic or Pushto. The enemy fighters were less than 100 feet away, and he looked for Lamereaux and Cunningham.

The enemy soldiers were firing RPGs with time fuses set to explode in the air. Lamereaux heard the first RPG before he saw it—coming straight at him. It spluttered over his head and exploded over the helo's tail. Lamereaux told Cunningham, "Man, those things aren't anything. I'm not worried." But mortars were now coming in around them, too.

The medics had to make a decision. "What the hell," Lamereaux said. "We'll sit here and shoot it out. I'm not going to leave these guys."

Cunningham said he wasn't going anywhere, either. He told Lamereaux, "Let's sit here until this is over with."

Cunningham and Lamereaux shot it out for forty minutes. Oddly enough, Lamereaux did not feel himself to be in danger. He did not feel like he could be shot. As he fired down the saddle he talked to the wounded. He'd started firing with eight magazines in reserve. Now, he was shooting out of his seventh magazine.

Suddenly, two bullets hit a foot in front of him. Their impact chipped snow in his face. He thought, *Oh, this is really going to suck!*

The enemy had targeted him and Cunningham. Lamereaux turned over and crawled up the hill 4 feet from where he was sitting, hoping that this would take him out of the enemy's sights. He turned over and started shooting again. At that instant, he and Cunningham were both shot in a burst of enemy gunfire.

"You all right?" Lamereaux shouted at Cunningham.

"You all right?" Cunningham asked him. They both groaned in pain.

Lamereaux was hit in the belly. Two rounds had found a space below his body armor. To describe the impact, he used the same sledgehammer analogy as the others who'd been hit. He turned over on his side and curled into a fetal position. A third bullet hit him in the buttocks. So intense was the pain of the stomach wound, he did not notice the third shot. He and Cunningham were out in the open, in fetal positions, moaning. Cunningham had been shot once through the small of his back to the right of his spine through his pelvis; the bullet had shattered his liver. He told Lamereaux, "I think I'm OK."

Lamereaux was not as certain about himself. He understood the prognosis of abdominal wounds. The other men whom he had treated that day would live; he felt certain of that.

He had controlled even Calvert's bleeding. Neither Calvert nor Gant had internal injuries. But as a medic, he knew that there was nothing to be done about internal injuries in the field. He thought, *I can't understand it. It's very unlucky. I am going to die. There is just no . . . I'm shot in the belly.* His specialized knowledge gave him reason to fear. *I am not getting to an OR anytime soon. I am going to die.* He was mentally preparing himself. *How unfair to my wife and my children.* He said a couple of prayers, and then he concentrated on the facts.

He wasn't bleeding out; at least, he did not think so. The pain was paralyzing. In one or two minutes, some feeling returned to his legs and he could move them again. *I have to gain the nerve to reach my hand down there to see how bad it is,* he told himself. *If my hand comes back and it's bad, I have a chance of dying.*

He needed several minutes to build up the resolve. He slid his hand below his body armor and turned over on his knees. Any second, he thought, he could be shot again. He pulled his knees higher under himself. The thought of seeing his own blood spilling out on the snow terrified him. The ground was wet. He did not know if he was feeling melting snow or blood or what. He looked between his arms. Only a small spot of blood stained the snow. He thought, *That's awesome. That's great.* The warm wetness was urine, not blood. The rounds had torn off the top of his bladder. He thought, *Well, maybe I've skated it.*

Cunningham also was trying to diagnose his injury, probing and feeling and assessing the flow of blood on the snow. He was not bleeding that he could see. Indeed, he saw nothing to cause him serious concern. He and Lamereaux were more worried about the counterattack, with bullets flying around them and over them from two directions.

Matt LaFrenz, who had come in with the second chalk, was up on the peak by the bunkers with Self, trying to find a good firing position, when he heard over the radio, "Medic has been hit!" He ran with his aid bag down the slope at the front of the helo. The bullets were flying past him and impacted on the snow. He was thinking, *I am not Sergeant York*. A graduate of Vanderbilt University in premed who had grown up in the San Francisco Bay area the son of hippie parents, he was better trained, if not equipped, than all but a few medics in the entire Army. He brought prodigious medical skills to bear on Cunningham, who he believed was bleeding internally. Cunningham was lucid. He told LaFrenz he hurt bad. He was surprised and even angry, and he told him, "This is bullshit. Cannot believe they shot me."

LaFrenz thought he had controlled Cunningham's bleeding and hooked him up to a bag of Hespan, the same volume expander that Lamereaux had used earlier on Calvert. LaFrenz believed that Cunningham would not bleed out if he was kept still. It was imperative that he not be moved, and yet he was lying in the line of the enemy's fire. He had to be moved. Cunningham was still talking. He asked LaFrenz about his wound, curious about where he was hurt and what it looked like.

Polson and Stebner rushed Dube up to the peak to safety.

They ran back down the slope to the helo for Cunningham. Polson told Stebner that he did not have a weapon that worked, and Stebner pointed to a pile of guns by the helo. Polson grabbed what turned out to be Chapman's M-4, with a bullet hole in its pistol grip. He slung the weapon over his shoulder and grabbed a handle on Cunningham's litter.

Stebner looked down at the wounded young Air Force PJ. "Are you ready to go?" he asked Cunningham. "You're priority now. We need to get you up there."

Cunningham said, "Go over there, there's a little cooler, grab my blood."

Stebner placed the cooler on the litter between Cunningham's legs and started moving him.

Stebner's nose was bleeding from the altitude, and he was winded and exhausted. He staggered with his end of the litter.

Polson, Vela, and the crew chief, Brian Wilson, rushed down to help him. Halfway up the icy slope, under fire, the frame of the litter snapped. Cunningham fell off and hit the ground hard. His pelvis crunched, and the sound horrified Polson. He apologized and put Cunningham back on the litter.

Moving the five litter casualties took more than an hour. It was now early afternoon, around 1300. The enemy ceased firing. Stebner, Vela, Polson, and Wilson stayed out in the open carrying litters up the slope. Seeing them exposed, the enemy fighters opened fire again. Watching from the peak, Self was amazed that his Rangers and Wilson were not killed.

Lamereaux told LaFrenz, "Tell me what you see. I'm ready for it."

LaFrenz replied, "You got a couple holes down there, but I don't see any blood."

"That's great. Give me dressing, and go talk to Jason."

LaFrenz reported the medical details of the casualties to Self, who relayed the information to Masirah. LaFrenz made it clear that Lamereaux and Cunningham were in category highest—urgent surgical. Self requested a medevac. LaFrenz did not think that Masirah grasped the urgency of the moment, and he took the radio. He stated the realities of their medical needs. He said in plain language that Cunningham and maybe Lamereaux would die if they were not flown out to a forward surgical team immediately.

"Roger, understand," came the reply.

The wounded helo pilots, Calvert and Gant, knew what Masirah was really saying.

LaFrenz turned and told the wounded, "We know they're coming."

The pilots said, "They'll come, but not until nightfall."

Masirah told Self, "We have a seventy-man reinforcement that we are going to push in there for you."

"We don't need it," Self replied. "We don't have room for them. It's not going to help us. We just need to get out what we got. What's the possibility of a medevac in here?"

"We're trying to work that out."

All afternoon the answer would be the same, no matter how Self and LaFrenz phrased their demand. Each time, they were told, "Yeah, we're working to get the package ready for you. Just continue to fight."

This incensed DePouli, who understood the rational point that Masirah did not want another helo shot up, but his emotional response, hearing the cries of the wounded, overwhelmed him. On the radio, he asked Masirah, "Why? If we don't get them out of here, more guys are going to die."

"It's not nighttime," came the reply. "It's a hot LZ. We don't feel safe."

Canon heard Masirah ask, "Is the LZ cold?" He shouted, "Just bring somebody in here!"

The calls went back and forth. The urgency of their calls created even more confusion. Canon thought, *Cunningham and Lamereaux might not see it off the mountain without medevac now.* But in the end, the SOAR pilots were right. Nobody was going to leave the peak until after night fell.

7

FROM THE MOMENT THE COUNTERATTACK BEGAN,
the Air Force TACP, Kevin Vance, and the CCT, Gabe
Brown, began to call on air support. Vance worked the
SATCOM radio from a position on the peak near Self. Brown
was working a line-of-sight radio close enough to speak with
the other two in a normal voice. Together, they plotted the
coordinates and ranges of enemy soldiers whom they could see
down the slope. Orbiting F-18s from the Navy and Air Force
F-16s came over. Hearing the screams of the engines, some
enemy fighters stayed down; others picked up and ran down
the valley to the south.

The first 500-pound bomb that they called in was errant.

Self was standing near the low outcrop on the peak looking down the slope when the bomb flew over the helicopter and landed 150 feet down the saddle. The explosion knocked off his helmet. Shrapnel whistled by. It had hit so near the Rangers by the rustic mosque that Self thought they must be dead.

When that bomb landed, Miceli was sitting under a rock ledge. The F-18 came in as a blur across his vision. The blast felt like the jet had landed on him with an enormous *bam!* that blew him backward. His chinstrap held his helmet on. His head hit the side of the rock. Nearby, Canon, who was thrown back, watched the ridge nearly disappear.

"What the hell was that?" he shouted to DePouli.

"Dude, what the fuck?" DePouli said.

Canon dialed up Self on the radio. "Hey, sir, what's the deal with that?"

"Yeah, sorry, I'll get back to you."

Canon keyed his radio. He had last seen Walker under a tall tree even closer to the blast. He yelled to DePouli, "Jesus Christ, Josh is dead!" He got no reply. "Ahhh, he's dead," he told DePouli and Miceli. A moment later, Walker answered that he was all right. DePouli felt so relieved, he laughed. He switched channels back to Self to ask him to please give them a heads-up the next time ordnance was coming in.

The second bomb hit on target over the ridge. All enemy fighters stopped shooting. That bomb effectively ended the counterattack. The Rangers stood up and screamed for joy, Canon said, "like the Tennessee Titans had just scored a touchdown." It was a moment like none other the entire day. Exhaustion and terror turned to exhilaration. With no assurance that the enemy was done with them, stopping the counterattack seemed like their piece of victory, and it tasted fine—tens of the enemy were killed and probably would not be reinforced, and now that their wounded were moved up the slope and under cover, they had only one direction to guard.

Their shouting wasn't over when a third bomb flew in over a parallel ridge to the east and landed on a front slope not as close as the previous bomb but still close enough to send powerful shock waves over the saddle. From higher ground, Self watched with utter fascination as a ragged hunk of steel the size of a Volkswagen Beetle somersaulted through the air up the saddle, past the helo and the smaller rocks, directly at him, and flew past him a hundred feet over his shoulder down the mountainside into the valley below. Self thought if its trajectory had been slightly lower and to the right, the flying steel hulk would have scythed the Rangers along its path.

On the peak, Stebner was smoked. He could hardly catch his breath from the exertion of lifting the wounded, his nose was bleeding, and the altitude was starting to give him a severe headache. The effects of fighting at that elevation had reduced everyone's stamina by half. Stebner felt like he was about to collapse. He would fall, get up, take two steps, and fall again in the snow. He needed water and rest. Self told him to get out of there; he was "done for."

Stebner walked down the slope to the helo to make certain

of something important. He stopped near where the KIAs were lined up side by side in the snow. Out in the frozen air lay the three dead Rangers and Svitak, the door gunner. Stebner saw his friend Brad Crose. He stood over him for a moment, then bent down on one knee, reached down, and closed his friend's eyes.

VI

"I Haven't Stopped Bleeding Yet..."

1

THE LONG DAY WAS WEARING DOWN. IT WAS
around 1700, and blue shadows were closing over the
valley. Canon ordered the Rangers from both chalks
to pull back to the peak along the ridge running east to west
behind the bunker and overlooking the Shah-i-Kot.

Self was thinking about the counterattack. *There is a
tendency to become extremely relaxed in combat, because there
are very sporadic, intense bouts of gunfire, followed by lulls of
nothingness where everything seems completely peaceful and
calm. Al-Qaeda guys, if they had experienced combat before,
would have a tendency to become comfortable. They were not
even looking down at us. They were not going to get up until they*

heard bullets cracking over their heads. The same happened to us a couple of times. We'd eliminated the threat, we thought, and then bang! It started again. It was not yet time to relax.

The men uneasily had accepted that they were not leaving the mountain until after nightfall. They had been on Takur Ghar now for more than twelve hours. They had survived an ambush, climbed a mountain, assaulted a peak, and repulsed a counterattack, but killers still were present around them. These now were the wind and cold and the clock. Lamereaux, Calvert, and most urgently Cunningham waited for dark to fall, too.

Every twenty minutes, Self reminded Masirah—and everyone else on the net—of the urgent need for medevac. After a while, Masirah stopped responding to each call. He had to remind them and would not let the issue go. He was afraid that Masirah was avoiding a decision.

Far from avoidance, commanders at Bagram, especially General Trebon, whose decision it was to make, struggled with an impossible choice, the hardest any person could ever make. He had to take seriously reports that more enemy fighters were entering the southern draw and, worse still, were trying to reach the peak from the north. Of all things, Trebon did not want another helo shot down. He wanted to rescue Cunningham and the other wounded Americans, but he did not want to make an already bad situation worse.

Everyone on the peak understood that. But they did not like it. For one, Self was adamant about the medevac. He told commanders that the LZ was cold. Sure, a counterattack had surprised them earlier, and there was sporadic gunfire coming from the south, but the LZ was cold *enough*. And with close air support overhead, a medevac could swoop in and fly out safely. Self reported his conversation with Tabron about an LZ. A Chinook had room to put down on an angle a few yards from the casualties, and the enemy would only be able to see the helo's rotor blades. He said, "We'll put a couple of guys on the back and the helo will be gone."

With the lowering of the sun, the temperatures were dropping, freezing the melted snow. The sweat and blood that soaked the men's clothing and boots now was starting to harden to ice. A stiff wind blew up from the valley. Self notified Masirah that all his men, not just the wounded, risked hypothermia; now that the shooting had stopped and the men were inactive, their muscles were starting to cramp. They were dizzy and throwing up. The wounded were bleeding out and in terrible pain. Self hoped he did not need to remind his commanders that an HH-60 helo, called a Jayhawk, like a Black Hawk modified for combat search and rescue, was flying in the area. He had seen it. And this helo could land and take out their casualties in seconds. Maybe the HH-60 was not designed to perform at 10,240 feet, but Self had seen one flying over the valley, only 2,000 feet below.

Professional was not a word that Self would have used at that moment to describe the standoff between him and his commanders. He was proud of his men for accepting the inevitable. After the first hour, they no longer complained; the men understood that if a third helo was shot down, everyone on the peak was doomed. Self had made his points. After the medic LaFrenz briefed Masirah on the wounded, Self was told, "We're going to give you the order and brief the plan for the extraction with all players at this time," and they gave Self a time: after dark.

Self asked himself, *Why are they waiting?* Why, if it was the creed to never leave anybody behind—why, if the SEALs went back for Roberts and the QRF went for the SEALs—why wasn't anybody coming for *them*? Self knew he risked insubordination, but he had gone past such distinctions. He called Masirah a final time to say, "Look, you *got* to understand. I may lose three guys up here if you do not get them out now."

"We understand the nature of your casualties. It's going to happen on the timeline."

2

CANON ORDERED STEBNER AND PAZDER, TABRON, Polson, and Vela to move down the slope to "zero out" the helo, removing everything that the enemy might conceivably use against the Americans once they were gone, knowing how quickly and thoroughly the enemy scavenged everything they left behind. He'd already requested permission from Masirah to blow up the helicopter and was told not to bother. A bomb, once they were off the peak, would destroy the $30 million bird. The men at the helo gathered up gas masks, ammunition, and other gear that was scattered around the helo on the snow. They scrounged for food and filled their pockets with smashed Snickers bars, MRE packets, and PowerBars, anything with nutrition to give to the wounded. They cut down the padding on the helo's walls with pocketknives and Polson's TOPS Condor Alert, with its 9½-inch blade.

Lugging what they found up the slope, they covered the wounded with the insulation and layered them with a foot's thickness of jackets, pine boughs, ponchos, and their own clothing to keep them warm. Cunningham, wearing only a sweatshirt, lay in a sleeping bag augmented with the helo linings. Makeshift shelters protected the wounded from the gusting wind. Helping to warm him, Polson looked at Cunningham. He had a feeling that he might not make it. LaFrenz and Keary Miller were standing over him, telling him, "Don't quit." But Polson knew the look on his face wasn't good.

All that Harper Wilmoth needed to hear was the sound of LaFrenz's voice to read Cunningham's condition. He could not wait for nightfall. Wilmoth heard Cunningham talking to LaFrenz: "I haven't stopped bleeding yet." There was nothing LaFrenz could do except what he had already done—infuse him with the last of the whole blood from the cooler. Earlier, Lamereaux had used the other blood on Calvert, and despite his wounds, he offered medical advice for LaFrenz to use on Cunningham. He was almost calm, knowing he would live. He lay beside Cunningham, sharing warmth. He had asked Tabron to retrieve his aid bag with the narcotics. He talked with Cunningham, trying to keep him alert, and Cunningham answered him, though his pain was great. As a last resort, LaFrenz pushed Curlex, a kind of bandage, deep into Cunningham's entrance wound to stop the bleeding.

Cunningham had discussed internal wounds with his mentor, Dr. Burlingame, at the 274th Forward Surgical Team at Bagram. He was fully aware that whether he lived or died depended on how soon he reached a surgical table.

3

NEAR THE DShK EMPLACEMENT, STEBNER LAY down behind a rock and sandbag wall, shaking with cold, his teeth chattering. He took off a boot to check his feet, and his toes were blue with the beginning of frostbite.

Wilmoth came by. "How're you doing?"

"I'm cold," Stebner replied, hardly able to get the words out.

Wilmoth went away and came back carrying a black fleece jacket. "Here, Stebner," he told him, throwing him the jacket. "Someone wants you to have this."

"Who?"

"Don't worry who, just put it on."

Stebner slipped his right hand through the sleeve, and it came out covered in blood. But he was grateful, and kept it on. He lay down on an evasion map of the valley that was about the same size as a picnic blanket, and he waited for nightfall.

With a pure, even reckless sense of duty, Totten-Lancaster separated himself from the other casualties, as if he did not think he belonged among them. He hobbled to the north side of the crest in the enemy's cooking area to be with Gilliam on his M-240 gun.

Gilliam said, "You know we're going to get home."

Totten-Lancaster said irritably, "I know that. You don't have to tell me."

Canon saw him standing on one leg like a flamingo knee-deep in freezing water. He was shivering and pale. In his usual abrupt manner, Canon asked him, "Totten, what in hell are you doing?"

"I'm his AG, sergeant," he replied, using shorthand for assistant gunner.

"What about your leg?"

"Ummm . . ." He had not been able to feel it for some time.

"How long have you been standing there?"

"A while, sergeant."

Canon was furious with him. "Bullshit." He sat Totten-Lancaster down and wrapped his own poncho around his legs for warmth.

Polson was keeping busy staying warm. He had no idea what was going to happen. He half expected to remain on the mountain the whole night. The last he had heard, no more helos were coming to the mountain. Canon asked him to help Wilmoth with the bodies of Chapman and Roberts, who lay untouched where they had fallen. No one had dared to move them. Knowing that eventually they had to be shifted out of sight of the wounded, Wilmoth tied ropes to their legs, and from behind cover he and Polson pulled them to make sure they weren't booby-trapped.

Canon was curious about his friend Marc Anderson. He knew he was dead, of course. He had spoken to him last at Gardez, when he slapped him on the ass and told him to load up, telling him, "I'll see you in a little while." Cunningham would be able to tell him about his friend's last moments, since he was the medic who had treated him in the helo. Canon asked LaFrenz, "Can I talk to him?"

"Yeah, you should be able to," he replied.

Canon walked over to Cunningham's litter. He thought, *He doesn't look good. He is in the middle of dying. That's not right.* He shouted, "Matt, get over here!"

LaFrenz ran over. "He's crashing," he said.

He and Miller struggled to save the other PJ. They incised his windpipe for a tracheotomy; they could probe his entrance wound with bare fingers, pushing down more Curlex, and feel around exposed nerve endings, muscle, fat, skin, and vessels to reach for the perforated section of liver. But they knew that a liver cannot be clamped off like an artery. With the minutes running down to seconds, with no more blood and empty IVs, without expertise, LaFrenz and Miller watched him slip away. They injected him with morphine. Against all their instincts to do anything rather than nothing, they watched him die. The time was approximately 1800.

His passing focused the emotions on the tragedy of the whole day. Cunningham's death deeply touched the men on the mountain, whether Army or Air Force, SOAR or Ranger or Special Tactics, whether or not they even knew his name or what he looked like. They were all one in this harrowing play. Cunningham had treated anyone who was wounded without regard to their service. His death was felt even more profoundly than the violent, instantaneous deaths of the other men. Cunningham's passing was a loss that did not need to be, in their eyes. It symbolized their sacrifices like none other because it was slow and painful and because Cunningham was someone who helped others in need. Miller thought, *He was not supposed to die.* A PJ like Cunningham, his team leader, Miller was in a dazed state of grief and shock. He wandered over to Gabe Brown by his radio. He spoke quietly to him, shaking his head sadly, and broke down in tears. He fell to his knees and hugged Brown around his legs, his grief pouring out in waves.

4

AS THEY WAITED FOR DARKNESS, THE COLD, misery, and sadness numbed their bodies and dulled their emotions. All they could concentrate on was the cold. Miceli, who had come up earlier from below, talked with Polson and Josh Walker about the cold. They wrapped themselves in their survival maps, like homeless vagrants, against the wind. For a further shred of warmth, they sat "nut-to-butt," spooning, and they munched MRE snacks and shivered.

The body of a dead enemy soldier lay near them. Pointing to him, Miceli said, "Pull his jacket off. He doesn't need that shit anymore." His brains were spilled on the jacket and no one wanted to wear it. A 38 mm Chinese grenade launcher was beside him. The Rangers looked at him and cursed him. They were trying to talk about anything that would help them forget the cold. Polson was railing at the cold, the wet, the day, his dead friends, even his boots. His feet were wet and freezing. They shared stories about themselves that day, and one subject led to another as they tried to stay warm and help the time to pass quickly. The topic turned, as it often does even in the most unlikely settings, to girls and sex.

Canon told Polson to join Escano, Specialist Christopher M. Cunningham, himself, Stebner, and Pat George, who were sitting in each other's laps in a line, lying on their sides, half looking one way and half the other way, with guns pointed. They talked about whether they'd killed anybody that day. There were inevitable challenges to claims of derring-do. "If you shot him, where's he at?"

"Over there, if you want to go see him."

"Naw, it's too cold to move, man."

They talked about home, how they would tell their families.

"Are you going to tell anybody about this?" Polson asked.

"Naw, I don't want to," Stebner said.

Interrupting their reveries, bombs dropped from B-52s and B-1s exploded around the peak from 800 yards out. "Hots" Hotaling on a distant southern ridge was working his kill cycle with a real vengeance, calling in targets around the peak. Hotaling, who had watched the enemy come up the valley before the counterattack, was ticked off. He'd lost his friends Chapman and Cunningham. As al-Qaeda exposed their positions on the mountain, he ordered destruction from the air.

Self, with Vance and Brown operating the radios, worked out a plan with Masirah to evacuate them off the peak. In his discussions, long and detailed schemes involved A-10 Warthogs that would be flown up from Kuwait to provide close air support, AC-130 gunships, and two Marine Corps AH-1 Cobra helicopters to protect five extraction Chinooks of the 160th SOAR. Self and Brown plotted the helo's approach headings, the landing heading, and the departure heading. Self was specific and insistent that the tail of the Chinook point toward the casualties to minimize the time and effort of loading them aboard. General Trebon, who was directing the rescue from Bagram, gave a team of SEALs the task of loading the casualties. The SEALs would switch out with the Rangers, setting up security, while the Rangers flew home to Bagram. Before the Chinook arrived for the wounded, a Predator would shine its IR spotlight on the landing zone, marking the grid for the helo. Self ordered DePouli to put out an IR strobe near the casualties. The Chinook was to use the strobe as a beacon, and in the final minute, the Predator would "burn" the LZ. The same aircraft and crew that had dropped off Canon's chalk on the mountainside was the lead aircraft for the extraction.

5

T HE CLATTER OF ROTORS SOUNDED SWEET. IT WAS 1930.

The helo flared and put down with its rotors spinning and its ramp *opposite* the casualties. The SEALs ran off and disappeared in the darkness. Exhausted Rangers carried the litters over ground that was hard and icy. Miceli's lungs felt like they would burst.

Calvert had cut the straps on his litter; he did not want to be tied down if they were attacked, not like Dube. Carrying him to the Chinook, under the rotor wash in the dark, Rangers dropped him twice. Accepting their apologies, he told them, "Just grab my feet and drag me." Traversing the slope, they reached the ramp. Bundles of CSAR equipment blocked the cabin. They carried the wounded around the gear and the machine gun to the other side.

Loading took twenty minutes. The exhausted Rangers tried to stay alert. Their anxiety—so close to the end and yet, remembering the shock of the counterattack, so far—drew from them the needed reserves. In those minutes while the helo was on the peak, anxiety was felt around the U.S. military globe. At MacDill Air Force Base in Tampa at Special Operations Command's operations headquarters, General Tommy Franks, the commander of CENTCOM, sat in a swivel chair watching on a plasma screen Predator images of the loading. He turned to the officer at his elbow and asked, "What's taking them so long?"

The first helo lifted off into the night with DePouli's squad, minus DePouli, and with Sergeant Walker in charge. A second Chinook landed for the dead soon after, this time with its ramp facing the KIA collection point. Four Rangers carried each KIA in a grueling effort to treat their dead with dignity. They walked a few feet, put the body down, rested, and then picked it up again, until they reached the ramp. Polson thought about Marc Anderson as he carried him. He recalled in their training at Ft. Bragg and on other bases that Anderson was usually the one who was "killed." During those exercises, Polson and Miceli would drag him on a Skedco cursing him for his size and weight, and Anderson had laughed, saying, "Someday you might have to carry me for real."

The ramp could not be lowered because of the height of

the ridge and the snow, and the men lifted the bodies nearly at shoulder level over the ramp. They pulled them forward in the cabin to make room. When they had loaded everybody, Wilmoth walked down the interior of the helo counting his men. He could not find Pat George. He panicked and ran to the back of the helo: "Hey, is George back here?" Somebody told him, "He's up there." He turned and saw him by the companionway and started walking back. His dead friends were sprawled on the floor in the dark, and Wilmoth avoided stepping on them. By accident, his foot touched an arm, and the body reached up and grabbed his leg. He shouted, "One of 'em's alive!" and jumped back, by his measure, 5 feet, with a panicked scream. He aimed his light on the "corpse." He had stepped on Tabron, who sat in the dark between two of the dead, his knees up to his chest and his hood over his head. Wilmoth settled down, thinking about the dead. *They were our friends, and I'd rather take them out with us than not.*

After liftoff, Gabe Brown was sitting beside the corpse of Jason Cunningham. He stared at him. *What are you doing lying there? Get up!* It took him a second to realize. He focused his mind with an effort, preparing himself to operate again as a CCT. Mentally he was ready. He was thinking, *Step one, where am I? What are my surroundings?* He was getting ready to go back to work.

6

A N HOUR AFTER THEY LANDED AT GARDEZ, nobody seemed to be in charge of getting them back to Bagram. Miceli and Walker, who had been waiting for a ride, walked over to a Chinook that was spinning up. It belonged to the British Royal Marines. Miceli asked the crew chief, "Hey, you guys going to Bagram?"

"Yeah."

"Can we come?"

"Yeah."

They loaded on and the Royal Marines stared at them, as if to say, *What the fuck have you been through?* The Brits gave them chocolate bars, and with their stomachs full, in the warmth of the cabin, they went to sleep. Sometime later, they felt the helo bank hard, and they woke up. They were not landing at Bagram after all. It was Kandahar. Miceli thought, *Who cares where it is? It's* not *on Takur Ghar.*

MAKO 30 HAD WAITED FOR NEARLY SIX HOURS for extraction since reaching the knoll where Turbo could go no farther. Hyder had passed their grid coordinates on the Iridium cell phone. Slab planned for a helo to hover and lower a basket for Brett and Turbo, and the rest would walk to an LZ where a helo could actually put down. The ravine they occupied was narrow and deep and had served to hide them well. But it was not an acceptable LZ. Slab commented that he could not have thrown a ball without hitting a cliff wall. He set out a strobe when they heard gunships. He wanted to identify himself so the gunships would not mistake them for the enemy. He could hear helos over the southern and eastern ends of the valley. He told Kyle to put his gun's laser on high power and shine it straight up at the sky.

From two miles out, a helo saw the laser and realized that since the enemy didn't have lasers they should check it out. Then they saw the strobe. The Chinook, piloted by Friel, who had brought MAKO 30 to Roberts' rescue, hovered straight over MAKO 30. A SEAL in the helo stood on the ramp and waved. The Chinook made a dog-track circle and flew down a ravine with steep cliffs on either side.

Friel brought the helo to a hover over the SEALs, with rock walls on three sides. He was flying down in the dead of night with only the moon and NVGs to see by. A few feet separated the twin helo rotors from one wall. With the pressure altitude at 8,900 mean sea level, Friel prayed that he had not fudged on the performance levels and could actually maneuver the helo in to pick up the team. He could not set the helo down or the rotors would disintegrate. He dropped down bit by bit. His crew chiefs called out clearances. A rock rise at the chasm's bottom gave Friel enough height to put a single wheel down. He maintained a stable hover, full power, while the rear crew chief lowered the ramp. SEALs jumped off to set up security while MAKO 30 carried their wounded toward the helo.

That the Chinook could fly in such a narrow space amazed Slab, who helped to carry Turbo toward the helo, but the blast of the rotor wash with the engines at full power pushed them backward. Turbo could not reach the ramp, and the helo could not lower power. He crawled on hands and knees under the rotor blast, which pelted him with loose rocks and debris. The ramp crew chief stepped forward and grabbed him. Brett went aboard next, followed by the rest of MAKO 30, and finally, with the security team of SEALs back on board, the helo flew straight up and away.

After they had transferred Brett and Turbo to a medevac aircraft at Gardez, Slab, Kyle, and Randy flew back to Bagram. Turbo and Brett were flown that night directly to Karshi Khanabad, called K-2, in Uzbekistan for medical treatment, and soon after to Landstuhl, Germany, for further care. Brett recovered fully. Turbo lost his leg below the knee.

When Slab, Kyle, and Randy landed at Bagram, no vehicles on the flight line were waiting to pick them up, and they walked back to camp. Slab was limping from a deep bruise on his leg. He walked in the TOC. His nose was swollen, and he silently stood in the door with his gear. His commander gave him a hug and said, "Good job." Slab's mind was in neutral. His job was done.

8

WHEN D. J. TURNER LANDED GRIM-32 AT K-2 IN the unfamiliar light of day, he'd had nearly two hours to reflect on what he had left behind on Takur Ghar, and he examined his actions and those of his sister gunship's crew from several perspectives. His crew, as senior evaluators, held the highest and second highest positions of achievement and certification in the Air Force's Special Operations Command. He knew enough to know that he and his crew were damned if they had stayed and damned if they hadn't. They had disobeyed a direct order in time of war from a superior officer, but they left before they had wanted to, with men on the ground unprotected and in danger.

After they landed, the crew could not sleep or eat. For Turner the experience had been "gut-turning," and he dwelled on the choices he had made. He what-if'd himself, and as proud as he was of his crew, questions would remain. Turner was called before an Air Force colonel, the deputy commander of his group, who laid into him for disobeying an order. He tried to put Turner in his shoes, saying, "Hey, were you willing to drive the staff car up to Mrs. Smith's house like I'd have to do and explain to her why her husband was dead and why he wasn't coming home, because you disobeyed my order? I can understand, but flying in daylight is *not* what we are trained to do." On his way back to his tent, Turner thought, *Sometimes there is no right answer*.

9

THE RANGERS GOT BACK TO BAGRAM IN THE DARK. As they walked a half mile to their tented compound to rest and decompress, looking around at familiar sights, the thought passed through Polson's mind, *Nobody here has a fucking clue what just happened and what we went through.* He felt different, changed. He and his squad smoked cigarettes outside the tent and talked into the night. Their battalion commander came in, looked at them, did not say a word, and then left. Miceli lay down on his bunk, staring at the canvas ceiling. The emotion of the day started to sink in. He had lost three good friends whose cots were empty next to him.

DePouli did not know what anything meant. He thought,

Everybody did their job. And as far as he was concerned, that defined them. The thought dawned on him that the fight on Takur Ghar would stay with the Rangers for years, and even become part of their legend. At the cost of friends' lives, they had entered a new era. He was exhausted. He could think about it no longer. He wanted to sleep. He took off his boots and went for a hot shower.

Thirty minutes after getting back, Gabe Brown was dialing the United States. He thought, *I was lucky. You stick a bunch of guys in a metal tube and shoot at it for twenty seconds and see who comes out. I would not mess with fate. I would not change a thing. I believe in fate, but I'm not a lucky-charm guy.* The phone rang. His wife, Gloria, answered. Trying to convey a lightness he did not feel, Brown told her, "Hey, we had some extra-ordinary circumstances here. I did good."

When he hung up, he went over to his cot and threw down his gear. He said to nobody in particular, "I wouldn't wish that on anybody." It sucked. People had died. He thought, *I don't know why I'm here. But if there was ever a moment when I did everything right, that was it. I did good. I did all right.*

Captain Self dealt with the removal of the bodies from the helo. Then he hobbled back to the QRF's compound. The shrapnel wound had swollen his right thigh and stiffened his leg. He decided not to mention the wound for fear that he would be flown out of the country against his will and would be separated from his men. He limped through the gate. As he approached his tent, a Ranger he had never seen before walked up to him. He was a new arrival. He'd noticed Self's worn, haggard look, and assuming that he knew his way around, he asked, "Hey, sir, where's the pisser?"

Self thought, *Welcome home.*

Dr. Brian Burlingame, of the 274th Forward Surgical Team, waited for word of his friend Cunningham. He already knew about his wounds from listening to the radio net. He had worried about him through the day. The doctors and nurses in the 274th waited and prayed. When the extraction helos arrived, Burlingame ran from the 274th's med tent. A medic had died, but he did not have a name. He did not know which one. A Ranger who looked sort of like Cunningham came off the helo, and Burlingame thought, *Thank God it was just a rumor. He's OK.* He immediately realized his mistake.

He worked until every casualty was cared for. When he did not see Cunningham, he began to worry again. He was waiting and looking, waiting for Rangers to come in, refusing to believe the rumors. After he finished his duties in the OR, someone, and he could not remember his name, told him that Cunningham had died. He was thinking, *He was like the little brother you have when you go to the ball game or to the park that tags along.* Within minutes everyone in the 274th knew Cunningham was gone.

In Burlingame's official capacity, he pronounced the KIAs officially dead. Later that night, he went down the line of bodies lying on the ground in zipped rubber bags. With a clipboard in his hand, he logged their names, confirmed identities, pronounced them dead, and then filled out their paperwork for Mortuary Affairs.

He processed one body at a time, seven in total. He had a glimmer of hope that the rumors were wrong. He kneeled by each body and looked at the faces. He came to the last bag, thinking, *Hey, Jason's not here! They made a mistake. He's not dead.*

He unzipped the bag. He looked down and he broke into tears.

10

H ALF A WORLD AWAY, THE MUFFLED BOOMS OF artillery training at Ft. Bragg, North Carolina, sounded in the distance. Valerie Chapman walked out her driveway to the mailbox. Her neighbor saw her and came over to say good morning. He was ex-military; everybody in the neighborhood seemed to have something to do with the service, past or present. The neighbor knew and loved Chappy. And Val was like a daughter. He glanced at her and commented, "You look so somber."

She felt somber, and she was embarrassed and guilty for her feeling. If she were to put a name to it, she thought she knew that something bad had happened to John. She was not superstitious, and she tried to banish the thought. It kept returning, twisting and turning the most innocuous events into shadowy proof that her fear was founded.

The visit of her mother-in-law, Terry Giaccone, who was about to arrive on Val's doorstep from Connecticut for the weekend, was a sign. She had visited Fayetteville twice before, and Val wondered if this time she had an ulterior motive. At work, someone remarked that she looked different. Val was a home nurse, and she visited a patient. She drove home after picking up the girls from school and prepared for her mother-in-law's arrival, picking up the house, doing what daughters-in-law do when their husband's mother is about to come to stay.

She had called John's squadron at the JSOC compound at Ft. Bragg in the morning. She rarely did that. She was calling to ask if they could give her a new address to send packages to. She was given an APO address, and before hanging up she asked, "Hey, by the way, have you heard from any of the guys? Are they doing OK? Are they safe?"

"Yeah, everybody's cool," she was told.

In the evening, she caught the briefings on TV, whatever was being said about Operation Anaconda and a mention of special operations troops being in a fight. She was up late with the girls, and they were about to call it a day—the girls had to get up early for school, and Val had her job. The latest news she heard from Afghanistan, a number of special operations troops had died. She said to Terry, "Oh, my gosh. I wonder if they're any of the guys I know?"

She assumed that the military already had notified the next of kin, not thinking about time zones far away. Terry went to bed, and the girls were sleepy. Usually this was the hour when John took over, reading to them, tucking them in, and turning out the lights. She turned off the TV, and she was walking down the hall. She heard a knock on the door—it was around 9:30. She thought, *Who the hell's at my door at this time of night?*

She looked out the window. She thought, *Well, of course.*

VII
"Phwoww"

1

FIVE DAYS AFTER THE BATTLE, SLAB HAD JUST finished breakfast—it was just after 0830—and was hanging out in his tent in the forecourt of the mud fort at Gardez when a call came in. A roving Predator was spying on a convoy of SUVs. It was moving swiftly along dirt roads from the Shah-i-Kot toward the Pakistani border. This in itself was plenty to set off Task Force 11's alarms; these few days after Anaconda would have created enough breathing space for a high-value target to escape Afghanistan. The risk of a convoy traveling in daylight signified a certain urgency, and besides, the Predator was identifying a security force rolling with the SUVs, which was typical of the way that bin Laden and his top lieutenants traveled the backcountry. As always, the problem was intercepting them; as the crow flies, the border was no more than 5 miles away, but the biggest imponderable was always whether they could reach them in time.

Slab ran for a truck to take him, Randy, and Kyle to the flight line. This was their mission, after the detour of the fight on Takur Ghar, with the loss and pain of that day, and Slab was ready to rumble, if for no other reason than, as he told it, "to get his head back in the game." He was mindful that Task Force 11 had spun up many times before in anticipation, and each time they had returned to Bagram with empty hands, in some instances not even sighting what they'd hoped to destroy.

Three Chinooks of the 160th SOAR were waiting with their rotors spinning, along with two MH-60 Black Hawks, to carry a QRF of Rangers as a blocking and security force. They were told the code name for the mission was Wolverine.

After taking off, the Predator vectored them in, and from a distance they could see, without being seen, what the convoy consisted of—two SUVs and one accompanying pickup truck. The helos sheered off and flew away to orbit out of sight when the convoy suddenly halted at a grouping of huts by the roadside. The SEALs aboard the helos preferred to catch them in the open and on the road, and they waited while the al-Qaeda fighters entered the houses, possibly for food or tea. They were not long, and soon the hunt was on.

The helos came up on the convoy from behind, flying down on the vehicles at full speed no more than 50 feet overhead. The first Chinook's mini gunners in the side doors and the ramp gunner with an M-60 opened up, and the strafing stopped the vehicles in a line. There was a white Toyota 4Runner and a red one, plus a white Toyota pickup truck crowded with nineteen men bristling with RPGs, AK-47s, and hand grenades. As the helos turned to come back around, the al-Qaeda fighters scrambled out of the vehicles and ran for cover, some toward a dry creek bed with a low bank for protection.

They were fleeing along terrain that would not be to their advantage if the helos returned. Indeed, it would have made a perfect ambush on a road that doglegged over a dry creek. They ran into the creek below a gentle rise on one side sloping downward into low ground. Dressed in traditional Arab garb, long shirts and pants, they huddled against the bank, aiming their weapons at a rise about 50 feet away.

Unseen by the enemy, the three Chinooks touched down in two defilades to let off their shooters.

When he ran off the Chinook's ramp, Slab was carrying his SR-25 high-powered sniper rifle. He went up the incline to just under its crest and got down on his belly, crawling the final yards. When he looked over and down, what he saw nearly made his heart leap. About 150 feet in front of him sat the two SUVs. The other Chinooks had landed to his left, and their teams ran up another rise, looking down on the creek bed and the pickup truck. Lying beside Slab were Kyle and Randy and "mobility guys" with heavy machine guns. Slab leveled his rifle's sights on one al-Qaeda fighter who had waited too long to leave his vehicle. He killed him with a single shot.

Now, other enemy fighters began bailing out and dashing away, while still others struggled just to get out and raise their weapons. One was shot in the driver's seat and fell to the ground.

Next to Slab on his belly, Kyle could express his view no better than by saying, "Phwoww."

Slab shot two more fighters scrambling out of the two cars. Another one was loading an RPG in the back of the 4Runner. The driver of the lead 4Runner fell out of his door.

In less than five minutes, all nineteen were dead.

Slab ran down the hill. For the most part, he was looking at the bodies of ginger-haired Chechens, some Uzbeks, and a few Arab Afghans, certainly all al-Qaeda fighters. One man was wearing a woman's burka and jewelry, and one carried hand grenades on straps under his arms. Searching their SUVs and the truck, the SEALs later found a Ranger's flash suppressor, grenades from a manufacturing lot that was traced back to the Rangers on Takur Ghar, and a white Garmin GPS with *Gordon* stenciled on it that one of helo crewmen on Takur Ghar had lost, *Gordon* being a reference to the name of an earlier task force.

When the time came, they piled back aboard the Chinooks and headed for Gardez. They could not help but characterize Wolverine as some kind of "payback" for what had happened, but it wasn't that, no matter what they said.

Some months later, after Slab had returned to America, he was sitting in the warm air of the Florida Gulf, outside a steak house named Ruth's Chris, sipping a Crown and Coke with ice. As he was telling this story about Wolverine in a quiet voice, several SUVs drove up to let out passengers, who included numbers of men Slab's age, sleek civilians who behaved and looked like they were Masters of the Universe. A swagger and studied indifference suggested a self-assurance born of success, which was clearly their measure of combat and their victory; they knew how to order filet mignon and single malts and fire up Cohibas with the polish of practice. Their brush with shooting war had occurred not far away, at the Cineplex. Of course, their gaze went right past Slab on the bench in a muted buttondown shirt and khakis. A companion said to him, "You know, they'd like to be you, these men, to do what you do. They compensate by eating steaks and talking sports and making money."

Slab stared back with a look of complete incomprehension, as if to say, *Why would anyone want to be me?*

AFTERWORD

OPERATION ANACONDA WOUND UP WITH NUMBER-less al-Qaeda and Taliban killed or captured. For now and in the immediate future, the enemy would be deprived of their ultimate redoubt in the Shah-i-Kot. With 3,250 bombs dropped during the operation, amounting to a bare minimum of three and quite possibly five bombs per enemy dead, the valley was empty and abandoned and the villages there were turned to rubble and dust.

American forces suffered eight dead, seven on Takur Ghar.

Cory Lamereaux recovered fully from his wounds, as did Brett, Totten-Lancaster, Dube, and Gant. Rushed to an operating table, Calvert refused to allow surgeons at Bagram and later at Landstuhl to amputate his hand. He insisted on a second and third opinion despite warnings that infection could cost his arm. At Walter Reed Army Medical Center, he underwent repeated surgeries and rehabilitations, and two years and four months after Takur Ghar he was reinstated to his former pilot status on full active duty with the 160th SOAR, good as new. Madden, because of his back injuries, had to give up his position as crew chief but remains active with the 160th SOAR. Turbo lost his leg below the knee but amazed his SEAL teammates by adapting to a prosthesis in a matter of months. Despite this recovery, he did not feel confident that he could remain on the teams as a full member, and he retired from the service in late 2004.

The commander of the conventional ground forces from the 101st Airborne Division and the 10th Mountain Division said later, "We went in with 1,411 soldiers and killed hundreds of al-Qaeda. We proved to them they have no safe harbor anywhere. They can't hide. We came in right on top of them. Of the 1,411 soldiers brought in, we brought out 1,411. That's my task force. We fought for eleven days at 9,000 feet, had no cold-weather injuries, and one case of altitude sickness. We own Shah-i-Kot to this day. We haven't seen a single pocket of al-Qaeda or Taliban of that size since. We moved throughout the country, touched every cache, every ratline, have not seen a single grouping of al-Qaeda that could do or plan anything since. If some people see that as a failure, I don't understand what the definition of failure is. I can't even guess."

General Hagenbeck said after the battle was over, "The

coalition won one of the most lopsided victories in the history of warfare. We killed several hundred hard-core, midlevel al-Qaeda, Taliban," and other fighters. "Unfortunately, eight U.S. and three Afghan soldiers lost their lives, but their sacrifice does not change the fact that this was a historic victory."

A week after Takur Ghar, the commander of JSOC, General Dell Dailey, chartered then Lieutenant Colonel Andrew Milani, a bright and independent-thinking Army helo pilot, to research and write a report that would "capture a factual, historical chronology of the events of 3–4 March 2002 at Takur Ghar Mountain, Afghanistan." His charter included a mandate "to develop and provide a level of certainty, where possible, to the sequence of actions, and actions, of our deceased personnel" and was meant, in summary form, to be read by the families of those who died, for a better under-standing of what happened that day. No matter what else inspired the report, it was a generous, thoughtful initiative. Milani began on March 20, 2002, traveling to Bagram and Kandahar among other places, where he spoke with partici-pants and commanders; he scaled Takur Ghar with Slab and Randy and studied forensic evidence provided by the Armed Forces Institute of Pathology, Washington, D.C., and inter-viewed "most, but not all of the participants in this battle." The resulting document was a full compilation of "participant statements, operational graphics, Joint Operations Command logs, video streams, photographs, forensic reports and a physical exploitation of what remained on Takur Ghar after the battle."

Milani concluded his report with this summary: "This is a story of courage and sacrifice. It is a story of how seven great Americans died fighting for their country—and for each other. It is a Joint Service story. The Departments of the Army, Navy and the Air Force all lost members in this one battle." For the men who fought on Takur Ghar, the day was a victory. They had prevailed in the harshest test of those who have chosen to take up arms, elevating them to a higher realm of experience and on a plane with those who have struggled and died in tests of courage in other small, forgotten places.

Yet, regardless of the virtues of the men, Milani said, "The mission was obviously not a success because MAKO 30 never got in. They became the focus instead of the mission. Takur Ghar played no part in the success of Anaconda. It was an unwanted distraction. Al-Qaeda soldiers—probably no more than 20 or 25 of them—died on or around the peak. The loss of seven Americans was not a fair trade. For something positive, it served as a honey pot. It was not the intent of planners but the enemy did come out and piled on, looking for a fight, and destruction was brought down on them."

Perhaps out of a desire for the battle to mean more than a mere distraction from the main event of Anaconda, Milani sifted through the evidence in 2003 while he was assigned to the Army War College, Carlisle Barracks, Pennsylvania, and ended up with a paper that he titled "Pitfalls of Technology: A Case Study of the Battle of Takur Ghar."

He took to task the trust that commanders and their troops too often place in technologies, particularly the newer ones introduced during Operation Enduring Freedom in Afghanistan. Milani wrote, "As long as adversaries continue to be thinking, reacting entities, and as long as the elimination of fog and friction remains an elusive goal, chance will inevitably affect the outcome of conflict. Although technology can reduce fog and friction, it cannot eliminate them, nor can it eliminate chance. As Clausewitz [the nineteenth-century German military genius] suggests, ' . . . the general unreliability of all information presents a specific problem in war: all action takes place, so to speak, in a kind of twilight, which, like fog or moonlight, often tends to make things seem grotesque and larger than they really are.' When the course of a campaign takes a wrong turn, only the grit and determination of personnel and commanders can enable commanders to navigate cascading. And this is why it is imperative that U.S. forces not forget such ancient methods of warfighting as map-reading (GPS failure), basic rifle marksmanship, and fire and maneuver (to generate combat power)."

Milani later related, "Technology has certainly done much to reduce fog and friction, but as on Takur Ghar, it can concomitantly create a different dimension. The potential for technological over-reliance and the rule of the law of un-intended (and undiscovered) consequences characterizes this different dimension. Recognizing that this dimension exists is the first step toward dealing with the real world. U.S. military capabilities already outpace potential adversaries and allies alike, and have created an imbalance unheralded in history. Time is on the Americans' side. As the U.S. military looks to 'skip a technological generation,' it should remember that it has not fully vetted the current generation of technology. Prudence suggests that a more careful, methodical approach to developing this leap-ahead generation would represent a low-risk strategy. . . . The U.S. military needs to learn an overarching lesson from Takur Ghar and leaven its zeal for rapid technological advancement with a more deliberate analysis and evaluation of new systems. Force developers should not make the soldiers discover technologies' inherent flaws in the old-fashioned way, through the death of their comrades.

". . . This process has humans at its heart. Humans are a learning entity. It will be humans who direct and conduct fighting. The Achilles' heel will not so much be technology, but the expectations and predispositions humans take with them into battle about technology and about themselves. The history of warfare possesses innumerable examples of counter-measures against every weapon system ever developed. The fog and friction of war will continue to be ubiquitous. One must understand that fog, friction, and chance dictate limitations. To survive on future battlefields, U.S. military commanders should understand war for what it is—a complex and un-predictable endeavor that requires warriors, educated and prepared to encounter uncertainty. Such warriors must under-stand not only the capabilities of the latest technologies, but also their limitations."

EXECUTIVE SUMMARY

Written by Lieutenant Colonel Andrew Milani, and released through the Department of Defense, May 24, 2002.

In the early morning hours of March 4, 2002, on a mountaintop called **Takur Ghar** in southeastern Afghanistan, al Qaeda soldiers fired on an MH-47E helicopter carrying a Special Operations Forces (SOF) reconnaissance element. This fire resulted in a Navy SEAL, ABH1 Neil Roberts, falling out of the helicopter, and began a chain of events culminating in one of the most intense small-unit firefights of the war against terrorism; the death of all the al Qaeda terrorists defending the mountaintop; and, sadly, resulting also in the death of seven U.S. servicemen. Despite these losses, the U.S. forces involved in this fight again distinguished themselves by conspicuous bravery. Their countless acts of heroism demonstrated the best of America's Special Operations Forces (SOF) as Army, Navy and Air Force special operators fought side by side to save one of their own, and each other, and in the process secured the mountaintop and inflicted serious loss on the al Qaeda.

U.S. SOF had been monitoring for well over a month a large-scale pocket of forces in the Shah-e-Kot valley, southeast of Gardez, Afghanistan. In February, the headquarters for U.S. ground forces in Afghanistan, TF MOUNTAIN, commanded by MG Hagenback, conceived a classic military "hammer and anvil" maneuver—code-named Operation ANACONDA—to clear out this threat. U.S. and Afghan forces in Gardez would push from the west in an effort to clear an area of reported high concentrations of al Qaeda in the western part of the Shah-e-Kot valley. ANACONDA planners believed this maneuver would cause the enemy to flee east into the blocking positions of awaiting American soldiers from the 10th Mountain and 101st Airborne Divisions located in the eastern sector of the valley. Augmenting the conventional forces would be small reconnaissance teams. These teams were drawn from U.S. and Coalition SOF—they included U.S. Navy SEALs, U.S. Army Special Forces, and U.S. Air Force special tactics operators. The plan was to position these reconnaissance ("recce") teams at strategic locations where they would establish observation posts (OPs) to provide information on enemy movements and direct air strikes against observed enemy forces. This was done in several locations resulting directly in effective airstrikes on observed al Qaeda positions and the death of hundreds of al Qaeda in the Shah-e-Kot area. ABH1 Neil Roberts served in one of these reconnaissance teams.

In war, however, things rarely go exactly as planned—the enemy has a "vote." Operation ANACONDA proved to be no exception. Rather than flee, these disciplined and well trained al Qaeda soldiers stood and fought, and at times were reinforced—all along a series of draws and trails at the southern end of the valley near Marzak, dubbed the "ratline." The enemy halted the Afghan forces pushing east toward "the Whale"—a distinctive terrain feature southeast of Gardez—and the Afghan forces then withdrew back to Gardez. Because of a brief period of bad weather and the unexpectedly heavy enemy resistance, only a portion of the TF MOUNTAIN troops inserted into their intended positions on D-Day. Some of those that did insert, fought under intense mortar and small arms fire. SOF, well hidden in their observation posts, used direct fire weapons, and coordinated close air support bombing onto enemy fighting positions. This provided some relief for the TF MOUNTAIN forces, especially in the south at HLZ Ginger east of Marzak. MG Hagenbeck repositioned his soldiers to the northern end of the Shah-e-Kot valley and attacked the al Qaeda from this direction. As the battle became more fluid, TF MOUNTAIN recognized the need to put U.S. "eyes" on the southern tip of the valley and the "ratline." They needed additional observation posts near HLZ Ginger to provide surveillance and to call in U.S. air power on the numerous concentrations of enemy forces. A 10,000-foot, snow-capped mountain, named **Takur Ghar**, appeared to U.S. planners as a perfect location for an observation post. It dominated the southern approaches to the valley and offered excellent visibility into Marzak, two kilometers to the west. The mountaintop also provided an unobstructed view of the "Whale" on the other side of the valley. **Takur Ghar** was a perfect site for an observation post, and unfortunately, the enemy thought so too. The enemy had installed a well-concealed, fortified force, which included a heavy machine gun perfectly positioned to shoot down coalition aircraft flying in the valley below.

On 2 March, 2002, U.S. forces began planning to insert forces into two observation posts the following night. Two MH-47Es from 2nd Battalion, 160th Special Operations Aviation Regiment (Airborne) would insert two teams; one MH-47E—Razor 04, would emplace a team to the north while the other MH-47E—Razor 03, would deploy a team of U.S. SEALs and an Air Force combat controller (CCT) on **Takur Ghar**. Late the next evening, the two helicopters took off from their base north of "the box," as the ANACONDA operational area became known to U.S. soldiers.

At approximately 0300 local time, Razor 03, carrying ABH1 Roberts' team, approached its HLZ in a small saddle atop **Takur Ghar**. Originally planned to go in earlier to an off-set HLZ, maintenance problems with one of the helicopters and a nearby B-52 strike in support of TF MOUNTAIN delayed the insert. As Razor 03 approached, both the pilots and the men in the back observed fresh tracks in the snow, goatskins, and other signs of recent human activity. Immediately, the pilots and team discussed a mission abort, but it was too late. An RPG struck the side of the aircraft, wounding one crewman, while machinegun bullets ripped through the fuselage, cutting hydraulic and oil lines. Fluid spewed about the ramp area of the helicopter. The pilot struggled to get the Chinook off the landing zone and away from the enemy fire. Neil Roberts stood closest to the ramp, poised to exit onto the landing zone. Roberts and an aircrew member were knocked off balance by the explosions and the sudden burst of power applied by the pilot. As Neil and the crewman reached to steady each other, both slipped on the oil-soaked ramp and fell out of the helicopter. As the pilots fought to regain control of the helicopter, other crewmembers pulled the tethered crewmember back into the aircraft. Un-tethered, Neil fell approximately 5–10 feet onto the snowy mountaintop below. The crew managed to keep the aircraft aloft until it became apparent it could fly no more. The pilots executed a controlled crash landing some seven kilometers north of where Petty Officer Roberts fell off the helicopter. He was now alone and in the midst of an enemy force.

Nobody knows exactly what transpired over the next few minutes on that mountaintop. There were no surveillance aircraft over the mountaintop at the time Roberts fell from the helicopter. Based on forensic evidence subsequently gathered from the scene, we believe Roberts survived the short fall from the helicopter, likely activated his signaling device, and engaged the enemy with his squad automatic weapon (SAW). He was mortally injured by gunfire as they closed in on him.

Meanwhile, following Razor 03's controlled crash landing, the SEALs did a quick head count that confirmed what they already knew—Petty Officer Roberts was missing. TSgt John Chapman, the team's Air Force combat controller, immediately contacted a nearby AC-130 for protection. A short time later, Razor 04, after inserting its "recce" team, arrived on the scene and picked up the downed crewmen and SEALs, taking them to Gardez. The SEALs and pilots of Razor 04 quickly formulated a plan to go back in and rescue Roberts, despite the fact that they knew a force of heavily armed al Qaeda manned positions on **Takur Ghar**. An AC-130 gunship moved to **Takur Ghar** and reported seeing what they believed to be Roberts, surrounded by four to six other individuals.

Knowing how the al Qaeda brutally treated prisoners, Roberts' teammates and commanders knew that time was running out on Neil Roberts. Razor 04, with its cargo of five SEALs and TSgt Chapman, departed Gardez and returned to Roberts' last known location on the mountaintop. There were no known nearby, suitable landing zones—other than where Roberts had fallen. Inserting the rescue team at the base of the mountain was not an option—they would lose valuable time making the 2 to 3 hour climb up the mountain. Their only real chance of success was to reinsert in the same proximity of where Razor 03 had taken intense enemy fire.

At about 0500 local time, Razor 04 approached the HLZ

atop of **Takur Ghar**. Despite enemy fire cutting through the MH-47E, all six members of what had been a "recce" element were safely inserted, and the helicopter, although damaged, returned to base. Once on the ground near Roberts' last known location, and using the waning darkness for cover, the team assessed the situation and moved quickly to the high ground. The most prominent features on the hilltop were a large rock and tree. As they approached the tree, TSgt Chapman saw two enemy personnel in a fortified position under the tree. TSgt Chapman and a nearby SEAL opened fire, killing both enemy personnel. The Americans immediately began taking fire from another bunker position some 20 meters away. A burst of gunfire hit Chapman, mortally wounding him. The SEALs returned fire and threw hand grenades into the enemy bunker position to their immediate front. As the firefight continued, two of the SEALs were wounded by enemy gunfire and grenade fragmentation. Finding themselves in a deadly crossfire with 2 of their teammates seriously wounded and one killed and clearly outnumbered, the SEALs decided to disengage. They shot two more al Qaeda as they moved off the mountain peak to the Northeast—with one of the wounded SEALs taking "point." As they moved partly down the side of the mountain for protection, a SEAL contacted the overhead AC-130—GRIM 32—and requested fire support. GRIM 32 responded with covering fire as the SEALs withdrew.

Back at the US staging base, the Ranger quick reaction force (QRF)—a designated unit on standby for just such situations, was put on alert and directed to move forward to a safe landing zone at Gardez. This was to position them closer to the fight, within 15 minutes response time. The 23-man QRF loaded on two waiting MH-47Es: Razor 01 and Razor 02. Razor 01 carried 10 Rangers, an enlisted tactical air controller (ETAC), a combat controller (CCT) and a Pararescueman (PJ). Razor 02 carried 10 Rangers. Taking off from their base, the QRF had little knowledge about what was actually happening on **Takur Ghar** due to very limited communications. As the QRF flew toward Gardez, the embattled SEALs, withdrawing from **Takur Ghar**, requested their immediate assistance. Headquarters approved the request and directed the QRF to proceed quickly to the problem area and insert their team at an "offset" HLZ—not the same landing zone where Razors 03 and 04 had taken fire. Due to intermittently functioning aircraft communications equipment, the Rangers and helicopter crews never received the "offset" instructions which also hampered attempts to provide tactical situational awareness to the QRF commander aboard Razor 01. Communications problems too plagued headquarters' attempts to determine the true condition of the SEAL team and their exact location. As a consequence, the Rangers went forward believing that the SEALs were still located on top of **Takur Ghar**, proceeding to the same location where both Razors 03 and 04 had taken enemy fire.

At about 0545 local, Razor 01 and 02 flew toward the **Takur Ghar** landing zone. At this point, the QRF was unaware that a squad of al Qaeda fighters, who by this time had already killed two Americans, were poised and expecting their arrival.

The sun was just beginning to crest the mountains to the east when Razor 01 approached from the south. On final approach, an RPG round exploded on the right side of the helicopter, while small arms fire peppered it from three directions. The pilots attempted to abort the landing, but the aircraft had taken too much damage. The right side mini-gunner, SGT Phil Svitak, opened fire but was hit by an AK-47 round and died almost immediately. The helicopter dropped ten feet and landed hard on the snow-covered slope of the landing zone. Both pilots were seriously wounded as they crash landed their crippled aircraft. The helicopter nose was pointing up the hill toward the main enemy bunkers—where TSgt Chapman had been killed. The impact of the crash knocked everyone to the helicopter floor. The Rangers, CCT and the eight-man Chinook crew struggled under intense fire to get up and out of the helicopter fuselage. The rear door gunner and a Ranger opened fire out the back of the aircraft, killing an al Qaeda soldier. SGT Brad Crose and CPL Matt Commons survived the initial landing but were struck and killed by enemy fire as they exited the rear of the aircraft. Another Ranger, SPC Marc Anderson, was hit while still inside the aircraft, dying instantly.

Despite the intense small arms fire, the PJ, Senior Airman Jason Cunningham, and another medic remained inside the helicopter and began treating the wounded. At the same time, the surviving Rangers quickly assembled at the helicopter ramp to assess the situation and fix the enemy locations. Using their M-4s, the Rangers killed two more al Qaeda, including an RPG gunner. Using natural rock outcroppings as cover, they began maneuvering to better positions. The Ranger platoon leader formulated a plan to assault the bunkers on top of the hill—but after an initial attempt to do so, he quickly realized he would need a larger force. Instead, the Air Force combat controller worked to get close air support on station. Within minutes, U.S. aircraft began to bomb and strafe the enemy positions, dropping 500lb bombs within 50 meters of the SOF positions. By 7 am local time, the Rangers were no longer in danger of being overrun. They consolidated their position and established a casualty collection point to the rear of the helicopter. After the shootdown of Razor 01, Razor 02 was directed to move to a safe area and await further instructions. Later, Razor 02 inserted the other half of the QRF with its force of 10 Rangers and an additional Navy SEAL at an "offset" landing zone, down the mountain some 800 meters east and over 2,000 feet below the mountaintop. The Navy SEAL linked up with the SEAL "recce" element, which was by now some 1000 meters from the mountaintop. The Rangers' movement up the hill was a physically demanding 2-hour effort under heavy mortar fire and in thin mountain air. They climbed the 45–70 degree slope, most of it covered in three feet of snow, weighted down by their weapons, body armor and equipment.

By 1030 am local time, the men were completely exhausted, but still had to defeat the enemy controlling the top of the hill—a mere 50 meters from their position. With the arrival of the ten men of Razor 02, the Rangers prepared to assault the enemy bunkers. As the Air Force CCT called in a last airstrike on the enemy bunkers and with two machine guns providing suppression fire, seven Rangers stormed the hill as quickly as they could in the knee-deep snow—shooting and throwing grenades. Within minutes, the Rangers took the hill, killing multiple al Qaeda. The Rangers began to consolidate their position on the top of the mountain, which the platoon leader deemed more defendable—and safer for their wounded. The Rangers, Army crewmembers, and Air Force personnel began moving the wounded up the steep slope; it took four to six men to move one casualty—it was a difficult and slow process.

As the soldiers moved the wounded, additional al Qaeda began firing from a small ridgeline some 400 meters to the rear of the downed helicopter's position. The wounded at the casualty collection point were completely exposed to the enemy fire, as were the PJ and medic tending to them. While the Rangers maneuvered to return fire, enemy fire struck the Army medic and PJ at the casualty collection point as they worked on their patients. Rangers and helicopter crewmen alike risked their lives, exposing themselves to enemy fire, to pull the wounded to the relative safety of nearby rocks. Once again, the combat controller called in close air support, and a few well-placed bombs and Ranger machinegun fire eventually silenced the enemy fire. Unfortunately, this attack claimed another life. The stricken PJ, Senior Airman Jason Cunningham, eventually succumbed to his wounds. Throughout the ensuing hours, the Americans continued to take sporadic sniper and mortar fire.

The Rangers consolidated their position, moved their dead

and wounded to the top of the hill, and waited for a night extraction. The enemy air defense and ground situation in the vicinity of **Takur Ghar** did not lend itself to another daylight rescue attempt using helicopters. Throughout the day, observation posts on adjoining hilltops, manned by Australian and American SOF, called in fire on al Qaeda forces attempting to reinforce the mountaintop.

At about 2015 local time, four helicopters from the 160th SOAR extracted both the Rangers on **Takur Ghar** and the SEALs down the mountainside. Two hours later, the survivors and their fallen comrades were back at their base. A team of experienced medical staff of the 274th Forward Surgical Team, operating out of the Bagram airport tower, awaited the eleven wounded personnel. Their quick and professional medical treatment likely saved the hand of a wounded pilot. By morning, all the wounded were headed to hospitals in Germany and elsewhere. Operation ANACONDA would continue for another 19 days. These same units continued to play a decisive role in defeating the al Qaeda in the largest Coalition ground combat operation thus far in the war against terrorism.

DEDICATION

Spc. Marc A. Anderson, 30, Company A, 1st Battalion, 75th Ranger Regiment, Brandon, Florida; Bronze Star with V Device, Purple Heart

Tech. Sgt. John A. Chapman, 36, 24th Special Tactics Squadron, Waco, Texas; Air Force Cross, Purple Heart

Cpl. Matthew A. Commons, 21, Company A, 1st Battalion, 75th Ranger Regiment, Boulder City, Nevada; Bronze Star with V Device, Purple Heart

Sgt. Bradley S. Crose, 27, Company A, 1st Battalion, 75th Ranger Regiment, Orange Park, Florida; Bronze Star with V Device, Purple Heart

Senior Airman Jason D. Cunningham, 26, 38th Rescue Squadron, Camarillo, California; Air Force Cross, Purple Heart

Petty Officer 1st Class Neil C. Roberts, 32, Naval Special Warfare Development Group, Woodland, California; Silver Star, Purple Heart

Sgt. Philip J. Svitak, 31, Company A, 2nd Battalion, 160th Special Operations Aviation Regiment, Neosho, Missouri; Bronze Star with V Device, Purple Heart

Sic itur ad astra

These men went into battle with the comfort of knowing that should they die, their children, of whom there are eight, would have their college educations paid for, when the time came. The Special Operations Warriors Foundation was set up more than twenty years ago to provide this support, based on need, to the children of Special Operations personnel who are killed in operational missions or training accidents. Today, more than five hundred children are eligible, with nearly one hundred of them receiving assistance between 2003 and 2010; the Foundation's estimated financial need through 2010 is $34 million. The author is contributing a portion of the proceeds of this book to the foundation, which can be reached for tax-deductible contributions at: **SPECIAL OPERATIONS WARRIORS FOUNDATION**, P.O. Box 14385, Tampa, FL 33690.

ACKNOWLEDGMENTS

This book began on the naive assumption that military leaders who dictate these affairs would want to have this story told. Soon after the events, the Department of Defense issued an eleven-page executive summary of Takur Ghar and conducted a background briefing for the media in which little that wasn't already known was brought to light. A briefing officer politely declined to respond to questions on the grounds of revealing "tactics, techniques, and procedures," which seemed to cover anything that anyone wanted to know about that day. The Special Operations Command (USSOCOM) and CENTCOM seemed to imply through this and other gestures that the story of Takur Ghar might be told, but without their support—

and without their support, good luck telling the story.

This is not meant as a criticism. Reasonable men—whether in business or government, science or the arts—act out of their own self-interest, as we all know, and in this instance, USSOCOM believed that information in a book about Takur Ghar might give an advantage to enemies who might actually read the book, and thus endanger American troops.

My belief in the story fueled a dogged and necessary persistence.

I had no institution—a newspaper, magazine, or network—to front for me. I knew nobody in the civilian or uniformed military establishments, past or present; I had never set foot inside the Pentagon. Long ago, I served in the Marine Corps, but so had a lot of other people. Therefore, I would like to thank first those individuals who helped to make my persistence worthwhile: **Gordon England**, then Secretary of the Navy, sent me to his military assistant, **Admiral John Morgan**, who set me up with **Vice Admiral Eric T. Olson**, a taciturn SEAL who was pleasant but hardly encouraging.

These men believed in the value of telling the story of Takur Ghar. Olson explained that I had stumbled into the wall of JSOC, a group based at Ft. Bragg that doesn't officially exist and therefore can't tell stories. The men who fought on Takur Ghar—except for the Rangers and the 160th SOAR, in other words, MAKO 30—were off-limits. I wasn't convinced, with a story like this to tell, that JSOC would bar the door. But first, I needed a coalition of the willing, which led me to Iraq on assignment for *Time* magazine and there, while living in the Republican Palace, I met the American Proconsul, **Jay Garner** (Army lieutenant general, retired), a generous man and true, a friend. Jay encouraged me to pursue the story and put in a word where it counted. At the ruins of Babylon, **Larry DiRita**, later to become the Pentagon's Deputy Secretary of Defense for Public Affairs, became a convert. My desire to tell this story was being heard at last. Through Admiral Morgan, I met **Tom Katana**, a whirlwind of energy, efficiency, and enthusiasm, and the former commander of SEAL Team 8, who showed me how to navigate the system; without Tom important doors would have stayed closed. Among others, he introduced me to the founding father of Air Force Special Tactics, **John Carney**, who runs the Special Operations Warriors Foundation. John lobbied the CO of the U.S. Special Operations Command in Tampa. Tom also put me in touch with another friend, **Ed Rowe**, a former Ranger and a policy analyst in the Pentagon, and through his efforts, **Thomas O'Connell**, the Assistant Secretary of Defense for Special Operations and Low Intensity Conflict, who helped with access. Finally, **General Bryan D. Brown**, CO of USSOCOM, was persuaded to go along. And while the wall did not crumble, at least crumbs came over to my side, which I gathered up like a famished squirrel. Men, thank you.

Finally, the soldiers, sailors, and airmen who had fought on and over Takur Ghar began to appear. The stories they told were gripping. I readily accepted the help of Air Force **Captain Denise Boyd** of AFSOC at Hurlburt Field, Florida; the can-do

Kelly Tyler, the PAO at the 160th SOAR and a paradigm of
military public affairs efficiency; and **Carol Darby**, the PAO at
USASOCOM, who organized the Rangers. Thanks also to
Lieutenant Commander Steve Mavica of USSOCOM at
Tampa; each time I would ping him on the phone, I could hear
his voice flatten in despair of further demands. He never
lost his cool. I also wish to thank **the CO of TF Blue**, who will
remain anonymous, a Navy SEAL, gentleman, and guide; and
Army **Colonel Andrew Milani**, an astute, caring leader, warrior
and pilot, and the CO of the 160th SOAR, who believed that if
the story of Takur Ghar was going to be told, it should be told
with accuracy and a wider scope of knowledge.

JSOC politely declined official cooperation; their
professional modus operandi excludes media, unless it
includes it, which makes for an Alice in Wonderland
experience for a writer. SOCOM prevailed on JSOC to let me
speak for as long as I wished with Slab in an unprecedented
meeting. I wish I had the confidence to believe that as an
institution JSOC and SOCOM were only protecting security
and "tactics, techniques, and procedures" by their reluctance to
let their Tier 1 operators describe past events in which they
took part. I am certain that their concerns are sincere, but in a
new world of terrorism in which special operations shoulder
an increasing share of the fighting, Special Operations still
answers to the American public. As the past has witnessed,
secrecy can seem designed to protect leaders from public
scrutiny and even accountability. Because they are better,
special operations fighters deserve better guidance, starting

with commanders with modern intellectual flexibility that can bridge the military and civilian worlds. The American military has tales to tell of the exploits of those who serve in uniform. They and not their commanders create the dramas, heroes, histories, and legends; in a media-saturated society, the military leadership must find a middle way to inform the public of the greatness of these men and women.

On the publishing side, I wish to express my considerable gratitude to **John Flicker**, my editor at Bantam, for his forbearance of delays, his generosity of spirit, his enthusiasm, and friendship. I have never known such editorial stewardship. A young man, he approaches the craft of editing from a perspective rarely found; more than liking writers and writing, he infuses books with his enthusiasm and belief in what they can be. My agent, **Michael Carlisle**, a principal of Inkwell Management, led me to Flicker and other important opportunities, as well.

Personally, I want to tip my hat to **Mr. and Mrs. Brewster Barlow Perkins** and **Mr. and Mrs. David Auchincloss** for hospitalities, friendship, and advice; to **Douglas Combs** for his counsel and direction; and finally, to my wife, **Charlie**, whom I adore, for what I would like to interpret as grace—and not mere indifference—for her restraint in *not* asking the most mortifying question of any writer bogged down in the middle of a project: "How's the book goin', honey?"

SOURCES

INTERVIEWS

Army Captain Nathan Self, Silver Star, Bronze Star with V Device, Bronze Star, Purple Heart; Staff Sgt. Raymond M. DePouli, Silver Star; Spec. Aaron Totten-Lancaster, Silver Star, Purple Heart; Spec. Anthony Miceli, Bronze Star with V Device; Staff Sgt. Joshua Walker, Silver Star; Staff Sgt. Arin Canon, Silver Star; Sgt. Eric Stebner, Silver Star; Staff Sgt. Harper Wilmoth, Silver Star; Spec. Jonas O. Polson, Bronze Star with V Device; Spec. Randy J. Pazder, Bronze Star with V Device; Spec. Omar J. Vela, Bronze Star with V Device, Sgt. Matt LaFrenz, Silver Star—all from Company A, 1st Battalion, 75th Ranger Regiment. Major (Dr.) Brian Burlingame, CO, 274th Surgical Team; Staff Sgt. Kevin D. Vance, Bronze Star with V Device, Purple Heart, interview augmented by his seven-page sworn statement on March

29, 2002, before Erin Bree Wirtanen, at Bagram; Staff Sgt. Gabriel Brown, Silver Star; Tech Sgt. Keary Miller, Silver Star; Tech Sgt. James Hotaling, Bronze Star with V Device; Lt. Col. Burt Bartley, 18th Fighter Squadron, Silver Star; Captain Andrew Lipina, Distinguished Flying Cross; Carol Darby, PAO, USASOCOM; CWO4 Alan Mack, 160th SOAR, Distinguished Flying Cross; Sgt. Dan Madden, 160th SOAR, Distinguished Flying Cross, Purple Heart; Col. Andrew Milani, CO, 160th SOAR; CWO4 Jason Friel, 160th SOAR, Distinguished Flying Cross; CWO4 Greg Calvert, 160th SOAR, Distinguished Flying Cross, Purple Heart; Cory Lamereaux, 160th SOAR, Silver Star; CWO5 Don Tabron, 160th SOAR, Silver Star; CO TF Blue, U.S. Navy SEALs; SEAL Master Chief Petty Officer "Slab," Navy Cross; Kyle, Turbo, Randy, Vic Hyder, and Brett, Silver Stars; Vice Admiral Eric T. Olson, U.S. Navy SEALs and Deputy CO USCOCOM; "Brian" and "Rick," U.S. Navy, SEAL Team 8; Capt. Donald Lee Sayre, CO, SEAL Team 8; Maj. D.J. Turner, Distinguished Flying Cross; Capt. Ian Marr, Distinguished Flying Cross; Major Dwight Davis. I used interviews conducted by Special Operations Command, Col. Milani, and two USSOCOM historians, Maj. Dave Christ, USMC, and Master Sgt. Eric Nunes, for SEAL Lt. Cmdr. Vic Hyder; Col. Frank Anders; Sheila Maghuhn (Crose's mother); Kelly Tyler, PAO, 160th SOAR; Dave and Judy Anderson (Marc's mother and father); Pat Marek (mother of Matt Commons); Pat and Jeanne Miceli; Jackie and Red Cunningham (mother and father of Jason); Terry Giaccone (mother of Chapman); Valerie Chapman (wife of John); Mike West, AF CCT and friend of Chapman; Roseann Svitak (mother of Philip); Marie Thompson (Gabe Brown's mother); Gloria Brown (wife of Gabe); Tammy Klein (sister of Chapman); Kenny Longfritz (24th STS's "first shirt"); Lori McQueeney (sister of Chapman); David Klein (Chapman's brother-in-law); David Rabel; Brian Torpor; Dave Allen.

BOOKS

The Hunt for Bin Laden, Robin Moore, Random House, 2003. Nobody can fault Mr. Moore's timing of his account of Operation Enduring Freedom, including a thumbnail report of Takur Ghar, though I would look elsewhere for a comprehensible view of the fighting of U.S. Army Special Forces Task Force Dagger.

Strategy: The Logic of War and Peace, Edward N. Luttwak, Harvard University Press, 1990. Describes the dynamics of reversal at work in the crucible of conflict. Invaluable, brilliant, original.

Maneuver Warfare Handbook, William S. Lind, Westview Press, 1985.

Al-Qaeda's Great Escape, Philip Smucker, Brassey's Inc., 2004. A highly readable, detailed, and often amusing account of the hunt for bin Laden from the fall of Jalalabad onward, leading up to and including a lively account of Operation Anaconda by a sharp-eyed journalist for *Time* magazine and the *Christian Science Monitor*. Smucker's views of Tora Bora and Anaconda are based on his own observations and interviews in Afghanistan at the time. A worthwhile read.

No Room for Error, Colonel John T. Carney and Benjamin F. Schemmer, Ballantine Books, 2002. Carney, who is the father of AF Special Tactics, and Schemmer present an overview of SOF missions from Desert One to Operation Enduring Freedom, showing the growing pains of America's efforts to raise special operations forces.

U.S. Special Forces, Alan M. Landau, Frieda W. Landau, et al. MBI Publishing Co., 1999. A thorough rundown of SOF forces, their equipment, histories, training, etc.

U.S. Special Operations Forces, Benjamin Schemmer and John T. Carney, Hugh Lauter Levin Associates, a bulging compilation of information about SOF from the Special Operations Warriors Foundation.

The Anatomy of Error: Ancient Military Disasters and Their Lessons for Modern Strategists, Barry S. Strauss and Josiah Ober, New York, 1990. Another important work on, basically, the "fog and friction" of war.

In the Name of Osama Bin Laden, Roland Jacquard, Duke University Press, 2002.

Chechnya, Carlotta Gall and Thomas de Waal, New York University Press, 1998. Gall, a great reporter, tells the tragic story of the meat grinder of Chechnya and helps readers to infer the motivation and character of Chechens who fought at Takur Ghar.

Al-Qaeda: Casting a Shadow of Terror, Ahmed I, Yale University Press, 2000.

ARTICLES

"Report on Takur Ghar Mountain, 3–4 March 2002," Lt. Col. Andrew N. Milani, Joint After Actions Reports Service Office, Ft. Bragg, classified secret (unpublished). Cited hereafter as **JAARSO**, this lengthy and exhaustive report of Takur Ghar, consisting of forensic reports, individual statements, call signs, key players, photos, and enemy interrogation reports. JSOC chartered Milani "to capture a factual, historical chronology of the events of 3–4 March 2002 at Takur Ghar Mountain, Afghanistan. This charter included a mandate ... to develop and provide a level of certainty, where possible, to the sequence of actions, and actions, of our deceased personnel." Milani began research on 20 March 2002, traveling to Bagram and Kandahar among other places, where he spoke with participants and C2; he scaled Takur Ghar with the team leader of MAKO 30. Milani studied forensic evidence provided by the Armed Forces Institute of Pathology, Washington, D.C., and interviewed "most, but not all of the participants in this battle." The resulting document is a full compilation of "participant statements, operational graphics, Joint Operations Command logs, video streams, photographs, forensic reports and a physical exploitation of what remained on Takur Ghar after the battle." Milani concluded: "This is a story of courage and sacrifice. It is a story of how seven great Americans died fighting for their country—and for each other. It is a Joint Service story. The Departments of the Army, Navy and the Air Force all lost members in this one battle." I made liberal use of this material. Milani's timeline was invaluable in reconstructing the battle, and while I diverged to collapse time for narrative purposes, the horse remained before the buggy.

"Pitfalls of Technology: A Case Study of the Battle of Takur Ghar," by Col. Andrew N. Milani (Dr. Stephen D. Biddle, Project Advisor), U.S. Army War College, Carlisle Barracks, Pennsylvania. A fascinating and original thesis paper that uses examples from Takur Ghar to explain "fog of war" created by the modern technological instruments that were designed to cut through that very fog. Hereafter cited as **PITFALLS**.

"Executive Summary of the Battle of Takur Ghar," Milani and Crist, DOD, May 24, 2002.

"High Altitude Warfare: The Kargil Conflict and the Future," Marcus P. Acosta, June 2003, Thesis, U.S. Navy Naval Postgraduate School.

"Anaconda a Success: Enemy Killed Unknown, Say Officials," Armed Forces Press Service News Articles, March 15, 2002.

"Operation Anaconda Is Winding Down," Linda Z. Kozaryn, American Forces Press Service, March 12, 2002. The bombing campaign over the Shah-i-Kot in support of Anaconda.

"All Necessary Means—Employing CIA Operatives in a Warfighting Role Alongside Special Operations Forces," U.S. Army Col. Kathryn Stone, USA War College, Carlisle, April 7, 2003. A general discussion vehicle for those legal issues associated with the employment of the CIA with SOF.

"Afghanistan—Operation Anaconda," Richard Cooper, Military Visions, March 29, 2003. A very good, brief history of Anaconda.

"Interview of SSgt Kevin Vance, 25 March 2002—Bagram, Afghanistan," certified on March 29, 2002, before Erin Bree Wirtanen, military notary. A 33-page transcript of an interview with Vance which offered a wealth of details about the day at Takur Ghar.

"U.S. Policy on Chechnya," Steven Pifer, Dep. Assistant Sec. for European and Eurasian Affairs, Statement Before the Commission on Security and Cooperation in Europe, Washington, DC, May 9, 2002.

"A Full Report on Operation Anaconda—America's First Battle of the 21st Century. A Complete After Action Interview with COL [Frank] Weircinski," Austin Bay, FreeRepublic.com, June 27, 2002.

"Army Analyst Blames Afghan Battle Failings on Bad Command Set-Up," Elaine M. Grossman, *Inside the Pentagon*, July 29, 2004. Article details thesis of Maj. Mark Davis, writing for a master's degree at the School of Advanced Air and Space Studies, in which he blames Afghan battle failings on a faulty command setup. "Ambiguous command structures established on an ad hoc basis and approved by U.S. Central Command created conditions that inadvertently excluded the Air Force from the planning of Anaconda," Davis wrote in "Operation Anaconda: Command and Confusion in Joint Warfare."

According to Grossman (*Inside the Pentagon*, Oct. 3, 2002; and Nov. 21, 2002), a superb reporter who is acknowledged widely for her trenchant military analyses, "A plan to use Afghan troops as the vanguard force fell apart in the opening days of the campaign when they encountered heavy resistance and lost three soldiers. In the days that followed, a fierce battle against al-Qaeda fighters hidden in the steep mountainous terrain of southeastern Afghanistan resulted in eight U.S. losses and dozens more wounded. The battle's Army commander—initially convinced he could wrap up the fight in just a few days using ground forces with little external support—was forced to issue an emergency appeal for air and naval fires and logistical assistance."

METHOD

This work of nonfiction describes the events of March 3–4, 2002, on Takur Ghar Mountain, Paktia province, Afghanistan, between 2330 and 1930 hours local. *Roberts Ridge* is a true story that represents an accurate and detailed accounting of facts from firsthand witnesses and other research, some originating in the U.S. Special Operations Command (USSOCOM) and classified secret. The participants trusted me with the treasures of their memories. They responded to my queries with candor and often with emotion in seventy-one hours of taped interviews and half as many hours again of background discussions. They told what they saw and heard and felt; secondhand testimony was for the most part discarded. Loved ones and friends shared, in sometimes tearful detail, memories of the men who perished on Takur Ghar. A complex, layered re-creation of the drama, remembered by the men who were there, would not have worked without the use of dialogue, which I based on the only source available to me, participants' "best memory." Differences related to word choices, not to meanings or emotions; conflicting best memories were dropped or resolved. I italicized witnesses' thoughts, given to me as direct quotes that in the event were not spoken.

NOTES

PROLOGUE

Overall, this section derives from a variety of sources, including interviews with Slab, Smucker's "Al-Qaeda's Great Escape," contemporary published press accounts in *Time, Newsweek, New York Times*; Austin Bay's interview with Col. Frank Weircinski; CENTCOM CINC briefing on Takur Ghar by Tommy Franks, May 24, 2002. The Afghans' abandonment of the valley in the first ten minutes of the operation was originally ascribed to a fierce opposition, when the expectation was that the enemy in the valley would flee; instead, friendly Afghans, under General Zia Lodin, fled the field mainly due to a series of mishaps, including fratricide from a C-130U Spooky gunship, GRIM-31, that fired on the friendly Afghanis and their 5th SOG mentors, killing two and wounding fourteen. Air Force Special

Operations Command at Hurlburt Field chose not to respond to inquiries about the incident, while acknowledging the incident itself. As Milani put it in **PITFALLS**, "Heavy and sustained enemy resistance, coupled with an AC-130 friendly fire incident, halted the advance of Afghan military forces and caused a withdrawal to Gardez." **"The highest mountain . . . amounts of ordnance"**: In **PITFALLS**, Milani wrote, "A 10,000-foot, snow-capped mountain, named Takur Ghar, appeared as the perfect location for such an observation post. That mountain dominated the southern approaches to the valley and offered excellent visibility into Marzak, two kilometers to its west. It also provided an unobstructed view of the 'Whale,' on the other side of the valley. . . . Takur Ghar was a perfect site for an observation post but unfortunately, the enemy thought so too."

1: "SLICKER'N SNOT"

Sections 1 & 2 Mack, Slab, Madden, **JAARSO, PITFALLS; "Over all the hours . . . helos could not"**: At the time of Takur Ghar, the U.S. military services owned 24 MH-47Es, bought from the manufacturer, Boeing Helicopters, at a cost of nearly $40 million a copy, and since that time, three E models have been taken out of service. The MH-47E comes equipped with a midair refueling boom, larger long-range fuel tanks, and among other specifications, the most advanced avionics system of its kind ever installed in a U.S. Army helicopter that includes forward-looking infrared (FLIR) and multimode radar for nap-of-the-earth and low-level flight operations in conditions of extremely poor visibility and adverse weather. Special Operations uses MH-47E helicopters for overt and covert infiltrations, exfiltrations, air assault, resupply, and sling operations over a wide range of environmental conditions. They are used for shipboard operations, platform operations, urban operations, water operations, parachute operations, forward aerial refueling point (FARP) operations, mass casualty, and combat search and rescue operations. With the use of special mission equipment and night vision devices, the aircrews can operate in hostile mission environments over all types of terrain at low altitudes during periods of low visibility and low ambient lighting conditions with pinpoint navigation accuracy. " 'I can't look at your LZ' . . . in less than an hour": The dimensions of the Shah-i-Kot battlespace were so tight—approximately 9 miles by 9 miles—that the air overhead was crowded with aircraft and every move required "deconflicting" of the space, which caused inevitable delays, required aircraft to move off station even when they were covering troops in contact, and the need to line up to deliver ordnance on targets. Thus being the choreography of Operation Anaconda, any interruption or disruption of the scenario, like Takur Ghar, had multiple adverse consequences, like ripples on a pond. "His first option was to push . . . 2,000 feet higher than the valley": Slab, Mack, JAARSO, TF Blue commander. I have given a shorthand of this complicated back-and-forth discussion concerning the decision to go. Complicated and important, with conflicting memories, everything that followed stemmed from this one decision. Slab did not want to go, and his commanders wanted him to. "In no time . . . you are clear in": The central question why NAIL-22 failed to see the obvious signs of human presence on the peak of Takur Ghar remains a mystery, even to those who were involved, and no investigation that I am aware of was undertaken to determine an answer. The enemy had camouflaged their outpost on the peak in the most low-tech of manners (to defeat the most high-tech of detection systems). Snow-covered trees made the bunkers unrecognizable from the air, and tarps covered other signs, like a cooking area, a heavy machine-gun emplacement, etc. When I requested an interview with the crew of NAIL-22 to find out what they saw and did not see that night, and why, I was informed in an e-mail from AFSOC, "[The wing] said they don't have records demonstrating who flew that particular flight, so are unable to assist you." No one knowledgeable about those events will rule out that by mistake NAIL-22 had "swept" the wrong LZ. The dynamics of that night created confusion that men in aircraft and on the ground tried and failed to reconcile. In **PITFALLS**, Milani writes, I believe somewhat with tongue in cheek, "This fact that the team was relying more on the AC-130's optics than on its ability to provide immediate and accurate fire support is consistent with the high regard with which the special operations community have held AC-130 optics." These optics consist of a suite of television and infrared sensors, and radar. Milani writes, "These sensors enable the gunship to identify friendly ground forces and enemy targets visually or electronically during the day or night and in virtually any weather conditions." **"The original timeline . . . or, frankly, wanted to do"**: SEAL Team 6, referred to throughout, changed to its present official name, "Naval Special Warfare Development Group" or just "Dev Group," and is also known as "Dam Neck" for its home base location near Virginia Beach, Virginia. In addition to Team 6, its lesser known names, MOB 6 or MARESFAC, are also, like SEAL Team 6, not in current official use. I chose to use Team 6, despite its datedness, because it is better known to the general public and is not such a mouthful as Naval Special Warfare Development Group. As for Task Force 11, during Operation Enduring Freedom, military public affairs officers warned journalists not to refer to this task force in print on pain of having press credentials pulled, such was its secret nature. As for JSOC, this is a CINC every bit as independent as every other CINC—CENTCOM, for instance or USSOCOM. Commanded by U.S. Army General Dell Dailey, a Army helo pilot, from behind imposing walls in a special compound at Pope AFB, on the grounds of Ft. Bragg, NC, JSOC controls operations for DELTA, the SEALs' Dev Group, the AF's 24th STS, and components of the 160th SOAR. It is small in manpower, decidedly secret by its nature, and rich in resources. During Takur Ghar, JSOC set up a staging base on Masirah Island, off Oman, near the Straits of Hormuz, at least a thousand miles from eastern Afghanistan. At the request of SOCOM and to ensure their safety, I chose not to use the full names of the surviving men of MAKO 30 but refer to them by their nicknames. Given the nature of their work, these men feel that knowledge of their names and the publication of their photos could well threaten the lives of them and their families. **"By now low on fuel ... up in the air"**: A source in the Pentagon, when asked how these operations' names and call sign names are created, scratched his head and then made a concerted effort to find an answer; there is no single source, nor is there, as I had suspected, a creative wordmeister hidden in a basement office who generates these words. A computer does. The names and words are also drawn from call sign books and something called "communication electronic generating instructions," and as for Just Cause and Operation Enduring Freedom and Iraqi Freedom, Desert Storm and Desert Shield and such, these are the work of the CINCs and the Pentagon's public affairs mills. **"Slab may not have ... success"**: Comes from a reading of Luttwak's *Strategy,* in which he concentrates on the dynamics of reversal—if you want peace, prepare for war; a buildup of offensive weapons can be purely defensive; the worst road may be the best route to battle, etc. Luttwak shows that strategy is made of such seemingly self-contradictory propositions. One in play at Takur Ghar was the paradox of Slab's trust in the success of the AC-130s' abilities without questioning the limits of those abilities. **"Despite the clearance ... We're going"**: CO of TF Blue, **JAARSO, PITFALLS**, Mack. In **PITFALLS**, Milani writes, "The MAKO 30 team leader became concerned that he would not have sufficient darkness to walk from his insertion point to his observation post. He radioed his parent headquarters, Task Force BLUE (instead of the DELTA commander running the Advance Force Operation from Gardez), seeking a twenty-four hour delay.... Although neither approving nor denying the request, TF BLUE reminded the team leader of the observation post's significance to the overall Anaconda operation." The ground rules for my interview with the CO of TF BLUE included anonymity. The CO of the Advance Force Operation (AFO), the group of the special operations teams setting up observation posts in the Kush mountains to the east of the valley and on the Whale to the west, including MAKO 30, was a DELTA Lt. Colonel named Pete Blaber who that night was in the mountains in a radio-equipped Toyota. In his absence, Slab contacted the CO of TF Blue, who had no direct responsibility for the AFO; Blaber was soon taken out of the C2 loop and C2 then was assumed by JSOC at Masirah Island and by JSOC's on-the-ground commander at Bagram, AF General Greg Trebon; I do not pretend to know how Masirah and Trebon split the C2 responsibilities, except to say that Trebon was command and Masirah was control. Trebon alone was responsible for the decision to wait until after dark to extract the QRF from the peak. It was not a unanimous decision, by the way, but it was an unenviable choice, and his alone to make. Trebon retired as the CO of the Pacific Special Operations Command in Hawaii in early 2005; he declined my request for an interview, stating in an e-mail, "In response to your phone call and in consideration of another phone call I received this morning from a respected friend and team-mate may I offer the following: The Operation in question was and remains appropriately classified at the secret level. Our Nation, and the families who lost their loved ones, should be exceptionally proud of how all of the men involved performed that day. It is my long standing view however, that any accurate account of the events (by me or others) would require a fairly detailed description of the Tactics, Techniques, Procedures and C2 methods used which, if further revealed at the unclassified level, would only serve to enlighten and advantage our terrorist adversaries in our current and future efforts and, as a direct result, would avoidably increase risks to our people and their future missions." (See Acknowledgments.) **"Snowy summit . . . these ruts in the snow too?"**: Mack, Madden, Slab, **PITFALLS**. Moonrise that night was at 1802Zulu at 114-degree azimuth 09-degrees elevation, at 72% illumination. In **PITFALLS**, Milani writes, "The helicopter crew passed the coordinates of the new landing zone to the AC-130U, NAIL-22, and asked them to look it over. NAIL-22 overflew both MAKO 21 and 30's landing zones. Its fire control officer and navigator, using onboard sensors, scanned both areas. It then reported both locations secure." **"Weapons hold . . . only if fired upon"**; The three levels of weapons status for the 160th SOAR's gunners are weapons hold, weapons tight, and weapons free. Hold is the most restricted status, in which the gunner can only fire if the helo is being fired on or if there is hostile intent; for the entire time that Mack and his crew had flown in Afghanistan, they had operated on the basis of weapons tight, requiring the identification of a target. The consequence of the friendly fire incident involving the AC-130 was every pilot flying the operation, including Mack, was hyperaware of the presence of friendly Afghans without knowing where they might appear, and thus the change from the usual weapons tight to the more restrictive weapons hold that night. **"Mack looked up through . . . Glare blinded him"**: Mack, Slab, Madden, Luttwak; although he does not mention hollow-charge RPGs specifically, Luttwak discusses the "fundamental innovation" of RPG-like weapons when he writes, "Instead of depending on kinetic energy to penetrate armor by brute force, which requires high-velocity guns of great weight and cost, hollow-charge warheads function by projecting a high-speed stream of vaporized metal. . . . Any means at all of conveying charge to target will do, whether by rockets light enough to be hand-launched as in the original bazooka and the German Panzerschrek, or cheap low-velocity recoilless guns, or even by hand in the form of satchel charges simply thrown at tanks."

3 Madden, Slab, Tyler, Mack, who gave me a tour at Ft. Campbell of an MH-47E, stem to stern, which helped with an understanding of the dimensions and forces involved when Roberts fell off the helo, and time in a MH-47E simulator, simulating the angle at which Razor 03 went off the peak of Takur Ghar.

4 Mack, Slab, Madden, **JAARSO; "He envisioned him . . . his despair"**: Madden alone saw Roberts on the ground as the helo went over the crest and into the valley, and he swears by his observation.

He is haunted by the memory; he says he sees him without being able to help him nearly every night in his dreams.

5 This entire section was sourced from clippings from the *Sacramento Bee* newspaper, Internet searches, and reminiscences in interviews with a former high school teacher, Slab, and three active-duty SEALs from SEAL Team 8 in Virginia Beach who knew and worked with Roberts and whom I afforded anonymity; the Roberts family members, including his wife Patricia, have spoken to no one in the media about Neil since his death, for reasons of their own choosing. **"He earned his Trident . . . watchful manner":** the reference to the Budweiser escutcheon derives to the similar superficial appearance between the SEALs' Trident symbol and the beer company's and often is referred to as "the Budweiser."

6 Mack, Katana. The description does not approach the measure of what Mack achieved. In the middle of a moonlit night against a veritable two-dimensional moonscape, he had jockeyed a mechanical beast 3,500 feet, two-thirds of a mile, at a 35-degree nose-down angle with intermittent controls in an amazing display of piloting skill and sheer sang-froid that had saved the lives of every soul aboard Razor 03.

7 Madden. Madden later complained to Mack about the crash landing and Mack told him, "Hey, it was your fault."
"*My* fault?" Madden replied.
"If you hadn't pumped the fluid, you could have died in one big smoking hole." Mack was telling Madden, in other words, that he'd saved their lives. If the two bullets that struck Madden's crew helmet had hit two inches lower, they would all be dead no matter what the quality of Mack's flying skills.

8 JAARSO, PITFALLS, Slab, Mack; **"He thought, That's my mountain . . . ass up there,"** NODs are night observation devices, the same as NVGs.

9 Mack, Slab, Madden, **JAARSO**. As Razor 03 sat on the valley floor, confusion reached a very high level. Orders were being issued to the men at the crash site even as the nets lit up with questions aimed at providing commanders in the rear with "situational awareness," to give them a picture of events: Where had Roberts fallen off the aircraft? Where had Razor 03 landed in relation to where Roberts fell? Where was the helo shot up, on the valley or the mountain peak or the original offset LZ? Were enemy troops closing on the downed helicopter now? Who if anyone was picking up the downed team and the helo's crew? Rank was thrown around, voices were raised, tempers flared. Ignorance of the situation created different layers of confusion and, of importance to the men at the crash site, wasted valuable time when they could have been returning to Roberts. Slab had no problem with going back to Gardez, before returning for Roberts. But while he was still at the crash site, he wanted first to determine whether another, better option was open to him. Always warning him was the thought *Solve one problem first, then go on to the next*, and he was afraid that he might otherwise create cascading problems. As he was in charge of everybody while the helo was on the ground, he had to ensure the safety of the helo crews *before* returning for Roberts.

10 Marr, Mack, Calvert, **JAARSO**.

2: "WE ARE NOT GOING TO LEAVE HIM"

1 Turner, Marr, C-130 Hercules Headquarters (web).

2 Davis, Milani in **PITFALLS**: "As each command and control node learned of the incident, increasingly frantic calls cluttered the radio net with requests for information. GRIM-32 reported seeing an IR strobe light on Takur Ghar, surrounded by eight to ten personnel. This report quickly became confused with the situation on the ground at Razor 03's location, where the same number of personnel gathered around *that* IR strobe light. . . . Within ten minutes of its sighting, the IR strobe-light on Takur Ghar disappeared." As for the agreement to go back from Gardez, rumors at the time circulated that Slab argued with Friel, even threatening him with a gun if he did not go back. Slab denies any of this happened. Friel was set to go back from the start, answering him with a simple, "OK."

3 Slab, **JAARSO. "No one commander . . . a fuzzy Predator feed,"** Davis writes in his analysis of Operation Anaconda, "The DOD failed to establish proper command structures and relationships needed for integration among the services." Grossman writes in "Inside the Pentagon," "The top commander [Hagenbeck]—attempting to adapt to a new brand of warfare in which special operations forces, supported by air power, would take the lead role in the Afghan war— created an ad hoc command system that was destined to become dysfunctional, Davis argues. '[General Tommy] Franks designated himself as the unified commander for Afghanistan and established numerous subordinate [joint task forces] and functional commands. By mixing options rather than simply choosing one approach, he continued a long and problematic tradition' in which an overly complex command chair can lead to chaos in battle." Hagenbeck told Grossman that "in the case of the 'black' special operations forces [in Anaconda] 'they had a distinct, different authority to report to, which went back through [another] general officer, and directly to Gen. Franks.' " Federation of American Scientists, Intelligence Resource Program, RQ-1 Predator MAE UAV; Sierra Pacific Inc Web site, "Library/thermal IR/How IR Imagers work, at www.x20.org; **PIT-FALLS,** "The fidelity of video feeds from the RQ-1A/B Predator is nowhere near that of cable television. Nighttime Predator surveillance imagery comes from a forward-looking infrared (FLIR) turret mounted on the undercarriage of the unmanned aerial vehicle (UAV). FLIR images, by their nature, are distorted before a satellite link digitally processes them. The FLIR translates the thermal energy transmitted by infrared wavelength into data that is processed into a visible light spectrum video display. Visible light depends on a light source, e.g., the sun reflecting off an object. Objects above 0 degrees Kelvin emit thermal infrared energy, so thermal imagers can passively see all such objects regardless of ambient light. But they are seeing the differential emissions of heat from those objects, not reflected light. The images captured during the battle at Takur Ghar were fed through a Ku-band satellite link to produce a continuous, secure signal video. This secure-link process further degrades the image. The Predator orbiting Takur Ghar was at 17,000 feet Mean Sea Level (MSL)—more than a mile above the 10,200' mountaintop. Although the FLIR was at its highest magnification level for most of the battle, the images left much to be desired. Consequently, one can describe the video taken of the battle at Takur Ghar as nearing only 20/200 visual acuity. Regardless, even with improved acuity, it would have been difficult to ascertain exactly what was transpiring below."

4 JAARSO, Self. This section derives from the best interpretation of the Predator feeds, later confirmed by identifying where Roberts' body was found on the peak, as explained in **JAARSO** (see Sources—Articles); the human image on the feeds, later thought to be Roberts' according to where his body lay; after he died, his body lay cooling (his infrared signature faded) and remained where it was, unmoved, until the Rangers found him. However, no one really knows Roberts' exact movements. Most observers of the feeds at SOCOM now believe that Roberts was caught and killed quickly, if he did not die of his wounds, and his "execution" was a "security round." **"Watching the Predator feeds . . . control of Takur Ghar."** The Predator did not come on station over Takur Ghar, according to **PITFALLS**, until 90 minutes after Roberts fell; the IR videos that were being watched came from GRIM-32, which shared similar optical qualities with the Predator. To reduce the possibility of confusion in the readers' minds, I have characterized the videos as coming from Predator.

5 Terry Giaccone, Tammy Klein, Kenny Longfritz, Lori McQueeney,

David Klein, David Rabel, Brian Torpor, Dave Allen, Mike West, Valerie Chapman.

3: "HE'S IN A HURT LOCKER"

1 Turner, Davis, Marr, Slab. The debate over preassault fires has equally strong arguments on both sides, I feel; it is hard to make judgments, because both sides were doing exactly what they thought was right and, indeed, needed to do in the circumstances. There are so many judgment calls in an action like Roberts Ridge, taking place in real time, that to criticize, in my judgment, months or years afterward, seems facile.

2 Smucker, Roland Jacquard, Carlotta Gall and Thomas de Waal, Steven Pifer, Deputy Assistant Secretary for European and Eurasian Affairs: Statement Before the Commission on Security and Cooperation in Europe, Washington, D.C., May 9, 2002; Council on Foreign Relations: Chechnya-based Terrorists, 2004. TF Blue CO, **JAARSO**, Milani.

3 Slab. The information in the footnote derives from **PITFALLS**. Slab was utterly convinced that he had not left Chapman on the mountain alive. As he and his teammate Kyle were the last to see Chapman, it is hard to disagree with them on the basis of what Milani later discovered. No one knows what happened. The scenarios are just that. Interestingly, Slab told Milani that he found Chapman's body 12 feet from bunker #1, according to Milani, but he told me and pointed out on photos where Chapman's body was lying when he left him, on the very lip of bunker #1, making it feasible for him to have been blown by one of the Hellfire missiles into the bunker where he was found. The Predator feeds offer nothing to close this matter. However, as Chapman carried an M-4 with a flash suppressor, it is

unlikely that he would have been seen on the feeds firing from the bunker.

4 Slab.

5 Turner, Marr, Davis. In most of his actions that day, Turner could not win for losing.

6 Slab.

4: "TALK TO ME, BUDDY"

1 Self, Brown.

2 & 3 Calvert. Calvert cannot explain how the radios in Razor 01 failed; he calls the failure a mystery. But a suspicion lingers that jamming of enemy radio signals in the valley was interrupting some transmissions and unintentionally blanking out Razor 01's radios altogether. Problems with both SATCOM and line-of-sight radios bedeviled the Razor helos all day long, leading them into ultimately fatal consequences. SATCOM radio communication is notoriously fragile and unreliable with heavy use on the nets and over some long distances; line-of-sight communication is what it says and has only limited applicability, certainly not the strength to stretch from Takur Ghar to Bagram or Masirah Island.

4 Calvert.

5 Lamereaux.

6 DePouli, Totten-Lancaster.

7 Self, Totten-Lancaster, Miceli, DePouli, Vance, Walker, Brown.

8 Lamereaux, Burlingame, Jackie and Red Cunningham, Miller.

9 Tabron, Self, DePouli.

10 Gabe Brown, Gloria Brown, Marie Thompson.

11 Bartley, Lipina.

12 Self, Totten-Lancaster, Brown, DePouli, Tabron, Lamereaux.

5: "DUDE, WHAT THE FUCK?"

1 JAARSO, Canon, Stebner, Vela, Slab, Self, Polson, Miceli, DePouli. When Milani retraced the steps of Chalk 2, climbing up the side of Takur Ghar weeks after the fight was over, the steepness of the climb surprised and impressed him. This was no "walk in the sun," and its success was a tribute to the discipline and conditioning of the Rangers of that chalk.

2 Stebner, Canon, DePouli, Self, Vela, Polson, Walker, Sheila Maghuhn, Dave and Judy Anderson, Roseann Svitak, Pat and Greg Marek.

3 Hotaling.

4 Slab, JAARSO.

5 Calvert, Lamereaux, Stebner, Totten-Lancaster, Miller, Polson, Self, Wilmoth, Vela, Calvert, Pazder.

6 Calvert, Lamereaux, Self, DePouli, Canon.

7 Brown, JAARSO, Vance (from interview March 25, 2002, Bagram, before Capt. Erin Bree Wirtanen), DePouli, Canon, Walker, Totten-Lancaster, Acosta. **"On the peak, Stebner was smoked"**: While observing that Anaconda (and thus Takur Ghar) was the "highest battlefield" in U.S. history, Acosta concludes, "Revolutions in technology drive tactical change. Yet certain regions of the world remain largely unaffected by the full reach of advances in military technology. Thin air, cold weather, and mountainous terrain combine to create a uniquely inhospitable battlefield at high altitude. . . . The emergence of precision warfare has yet to dominate combat in the timeless environs of the world's highest mountains." Acosta also notes, quoting a finding of the U.S. Army Research Institute of Environmental Medicine (February 1994), "Medical Problems in High Mountain Environments," "High altitude is generally defined as those areas 8,000 to 14,000 feet above sea level where a reduction in human performance is common." The altitude at which the men fought on Takur Ghar (10,240 feet) thus created "a unique and unforgiving battlefield, in which the altitude can prove as deadly as the enemy. . . . Reduced oxygen causes a wide range of physiological effects and illnesses. The atmosphere inflicts casualties and degrades soldiers' abilities to carry out and sustain military operations." Acosta goes on to detail how "rapid ascent to elevations beyond 8,000 feet above sea level generally causes Acute Mountain Sickness. Headaches and nausea are the most common symptoms. . . . High altitude pulmonary edema and cerebral edema are more severe syndromes that occur when soldiers rapidly ascend beyond 8,000 feet above sea level. High altitude pulmonary edema, fluid accumulation in the lungs, is the most common cause of death among altitude illnesses."

6: "I HAVEN'T STOPPED BLEEDING YET"

1 Self, **JAARSO**, CO TF Blue.

2 Canon, Polson, Wilmoth.

3 Stebner, Wilmoth, Totten-Lancaster, Miller, Brown.

4 Canon, Polson, Miceli, Walker, Self, Brown, Tabron.

5 **JAARSO**, Miceli, Calvert, Milani, Wilmoth, Brown.

6 Miceli, Walker.

7 Slab, **JAARSO**, CO TF Blue.

8 Turner.

9 Polson, DePouli, Brown, Self, Burlingame.

10 Valerie Chapman.

7: "PHWOWW!"

1 Slab, CO TF BLUE.

AFTERWORD

Milani, **PITFALLS**.

Bay-Weircinski, Milani, Kozaryn. **"General Hagenbeck . . . historic victory"**: Grossman, "Inside the Pentagon."

INDEX